Sex and Gender in the 2016 Presidential Election

**Recent Titles in
Gender Matters in U.S. Politics**

Sex Scandals, Gender, and Power in
Contemporary American Politics
Hinda Mandell

The Right Women: Republican Party Activists,
Candidates, and Legislators
Malliga Och and Shauna L. Shames, Editors

Sex and Gender in the 2016 Presidential Election

Caroline Heldman, Meredith Conroy, and
Alissa R. Ackerman

Gender Matters in U.S. Politics
Juliet A. Williams, Series Editor

BLOOMSBURY ACADEMIC
NEW YORK • LONDON • OXFORD • NEW DELHI • SYDNEY

BLOOMSBURY ACADEMIC
Bloomsbury Publishing Inc
1385 Broadway, New York, NY 10018, USA
50 Bedford Square, London, WC1B 3DP, UK
29 Earlsfort Terrace, Dublin 2, Ireland

BLOOMSBURY, BLOOMSBURY ACADEMIC and the Diana logo
are trademarks of Bloomsbury Publishing Plc

First published in the United States of America by ABC-CLIO 2018
Paperback edition published by Bloomsbury Academic 2024

Cover design by Silverander Communications
Cover photos: Democratic presidential candidate Bernie Sanders in Washington, DC, May 20, 2015.
(AP Photo/Jacquelyn Martin); Democratic presidential nominee Hillary Clinton in Hempstead,
New York, September 26, 2016. (AP Photo/Julio Cortez); Republican presidential candidate
Donald Trump in Clear Lake, Iowa, January 9, 2016. (AP Photo/Patrick Semansky)

Library of Congress Cataloging-in-Publication Data
Names: Heldman, Caroline, 1972- author. | Conroy, Meredith, author. |
Ackerman, Alissa, author.
Title: Sex and Gender in the 2016 Presidential Election / Caroline Heldman, Meredith
Conroy, and Alissa R. Ackerman.
Description: Santa Barbara, California : Praeger, an Imprint of ABC-CLIO,
LLC, [2018] | Includes bibliographical references and index.
Identifiers: LCCN 2018015126 (print) | LCCN 2018030594 (ebook) |
ISBN 9781440859427 (eBook) | ISBN 9781440859410 (hardcopy : alk. paper)
Subjects: LCSH: Women presidential candidates—United States—Case studies. |
Presidents—United States—Election—2016 | Clinton, Hillary Rodham.
Classification: LCC E911 (ebook) | LCC E911 .H45 2018 (print) |
DDC 324.973/090512—dc23
LC record available at https://lccn.loc.gov/2018015126

ISBN: HB: 978-1-4408-5941-0
PB: 979-8-7651-2856-5
ePDF: 978-1-4408-5942-7
eBook: 979-8-2161-4380-2

Series: Gender Matters in U.S. Politics

To find out more about our authors and books visit www.bloomsbury.com
and sign up for our newsletters.

Contents

Series Foreword   vii

Introduction: Sex and Gender in the 2016 Presidential Election   1

1   Labyrinths and Glass Ceilings: Barriers to Women's Political
    Leadership   13

2   "The Emperor Has No Balls": Masculinity and the
    Presidency   31

3   "A Different Hill Than Men Have to Climb": Women
    Who Have Run for the Presidency   49

4   "I Don't Vote with My Vagina": Hillary Clinton's
    Primary Elections   73

5   "Such a Nasty Woman": The 2016 General Election   103

6   #CrookedHillary: An Analysis of Social Media
    Discourse during the 2016 Election with Eric Vorst   131

7   Conclusion: "Within Spitting Distance"—Barriers
    to a Female Presidency   153

Notes   167
Index   205

Series Foreword

From the nearly century-long campaign for women's suffrage, to ongoing contestation over reproductive rights, to 2012 presidential candidate Mitt Romney's meme-worthy claim of having "binders full of women," politics has been a central staging ground in the United States for debates about gender. The 2016 presidential campaign was no exception. For the first time in the nation's history, a woman received a major party nomination to head the ticket as candidate for president. As it happens, the Republican Party nominee also served as a lightning rod for discussions of gender issues, particularly in the days following revelations of his vulgar boasting about the sexual assault of women. The eventual outcome of the 2016 presidential election took many experts by surprise, revealing that many observers had badly misjudged how women would cast their votes. In the end, the 2016 campaign season confirmed not just the ongoing centrality of gender in U.S. politics but also the fact that we still have a long way to go in understanding *how* gender matters—to each of us as individuals and as members of a shared polity.

The *Gender Matters in U.S. Politics* series pushes the boundaries of existing research on gender and politics. Traditionally, political scientists have engaged the subject of gender primarily by looking at differences in the way men and women behave—as voters, candidates, leaders, policy makers, activists, and citizens. Today, there is growing recognition—within the field of political science and beyond—of the critical need to think more broadly and more deeply about gender. Across the social sciences, researchers now recognize that gender is not only an individual attribute but a "socially constructed stratification system" that plays a central role in determining an individual's place in the social order.[1] At the same time, scholars are bringing a more intersectional perspective to the study of gender in recognition of the influence of race, sexuality, and other axes of social difference on gender identity and gender politics.[2] These new ways of conceptualizing gender have far-reaching implications for political scientists with interests in topics ranging from electoral behavior to social movement mobilization to media and politics.

The books in this series address a wide array of topics—from conservative women pundits to political cartoons—to demonstrate the far-reaching, and sometimes quite unexpected, ways that gender is mobilized in contemporary political discourse. Some authors bring new insight to the study of gender in familiar settings, such as grassroots political campaigning. Others take a closer look at gender politics in less well-studied contexts, such as media coverage of political sex scandals—thereby reminding us that that politics doesn't stay neatly within the boundaries of official institutions. And while some books in this series highlight the persistence of gender inequalities, others draw attention to the distinctive ways women's political roles have changed in the wake of second-wave political activism and legal reforms as well as technological advances that have given new forms of voice and visibility to historically marginalized groups.

Finally, while the terms "women and politics" and "gender and politics" have in the past sometimes been used synonymously, the authors in this series emphasize that gender affects the lives of women *and* men. The books presented in this series are intended to inform, engage, and inspire readers to think in new ways about issues of deep importance to all of us. In making clearly written, empirically grounded, and thoughtfully argued research available to interested audiences, this series aims to spark conversation and produce new understanding.

—Juliet A. Williams
Department of Gender Studies, UCLA

INTRODUCTION

Sex and Gender in the 2016 Presidential Election

Several months before Hillary Rodham Clinton announced her candidacy to be the 2016 Democratic presidential nominee, political commentators speculated about whether or not she would run for president "like a woman"—a peculiar question since she had no alternative. The presence of a woman in the race means that sex and gender played a role in shaping public opinion and votes. The purpose of this book is to analyze how sex and gender influenced the 2016 election. The first half of the book presents decades of research on female candidates in the U.S. context, while the second half of the book applies this knowledge to help readers better understand the 2016 election. Many factors determine the outcome of presidential elections, from voter perceptions of the state of the economy to scandals and candidate personalities.[1] We conclude that candidate sex (male/female) and gender (masculinity/femininity) were also influential factors that shaped election dynamics, public discourse, public opinion, and vote choice in the 2016 presidential content. Our study uses original data, analysis of secondary data, and case study analysis to document how sex and gender influenced this contest.

This election provides an excellent case study for dissecting sex and gender in presidential politics in some ways, but it is unusual in other ways that limit the findings. The 2016 contest is ideal for analyzing the role of sex and gender in presidential politics because it is the first election in which a woman won a major party nomination and ran in the general election. Twelve women have previously made serious bids for this office, but Clinton's primary win and general bid furnish the first data points for studying actual female presidential primary and general candidates. The 2016 election is also ideal to study because it pitted a female candidate with

34 years of previous public service experience against a candidate with no public service experience. (For context, the average president brings 22 years of previous public service to the office, with Woodrow Wilson on the low end with two years of service and a doctorate in political science and Harry S. Truman at the high end with 62 years of service.[2]) Had the imbalance run the other way, or had Trump had military experience that Clinton lacked, it would be easy to chalk up the findings of this book to basic competitive variables. The sharp contrast between Clinton and Trump on this variable makes it easier to untangle the influence of sex and gender because if both candidates were male, public discourse would logically give the more seasoned candidate an edge. The third reason the 2016 election is ideal for analysis is that Trump's hypermasculinity played such a central role in the electoral contest that the question is not *whether* sex and gender mattered but *how* they manifested and mattered.

One factor that limits the findings of this book is Trump's exceptionalism. He was unique as a presidential contender in many key ways, but Clinton was not. Aside from her gender, Clinton was not an exceptional candidate. When it comes to basic empirical measures, she looked remarkably similar to past candidates in terms of likeability, the "cool" factor, policy positions, perceived scandals, and ambition. If Clinton were a white man running with the same years of experience, credentials, and personal traits, she would have been seen as a rather typical presidential candidate— a knowledgeable, somewhat boring policy maven. Trump, on the other hand, was an exceptional candidate in many ways, including his zero years of previous public service, his braggadocio, his hypermasculinity on the campaign trail, the volume and size of his scandals, and his frequent, impetuous use of Twitter to communicate directly with his supporters. His unique candidacy may limit the applicability of our findings to future elections since he enlarged the role of both sex and gender in the 2016 contest relative to what a more typical Republican contender would have done.

We use the terms "sex" and "gender" throughout this book to mean two distinct concepts. We define sex as the categories "male" and "female," which are generally thought to be based in biology.[3] We define gender as the cultural roles that are ascribed to men and women and that are simplified into the categories "masculine" and "feminine." Gender roles are not fixed in biology, as evidenced by the fact that what is considered "masculine" and "feminine" vary widely by culture and dramatically shift over time. Feminist theorist Judith Butler describes gender as a performance that creates gender through internalized, routine actions, the parameters of which are determined by societal ideas of gender roles.[4] In other words, gender is socially constructed, not natural, although sex and gender are linked as one and the same in the minds of many people.

It is important to study the influence of sex and gender in the 2016 election for many reasons, the first being to better understand why the United States has yet to achieve gender representation in our highest office. Decades of scholarship confirm biases against female political candidates that come in many different forms. These biases are especially pernicious for the presidency. We address our primary question from a democratic approach, the idea that campaigns should be free from identity-based bias so that they better represent the identities and interests of the people. The United States has never had a female president, a remarkable fact in a 240-year-old democratic republic where citizens elect leaders to represent them and where women constitute 51 percent of the population.[5] In 2016, Clinton came closer than any of the other 11 women who have made serious bids for the presidency. She garnered 66 million votes—3 million more than her competitor, Trump—but ultimately lost in the Electoral College 306 to 232.[6] Decades of previous research indicate that female candidates in general, and female presidential candidates in particular, face barriers to winning elections that their male counterparts do not face. Identity-based barriers in elections limit representative democracy, and documenting these barriers is the first step in addressing them. It is important to understand what barriers persist for a woman winning the White House so that we can achieve equitable representation, a cornerstone of democracy.

Clinton has been a household name since her husband's successful presidential runs in 1992 and 1996. She has been subject to enormous criticism from the moment she was thrust into the public spotlight, and it is easy to dismiss what happened in the 2016 race as simply being about her personally or about her campaign strategies. But doing so disregards the gendered nature of the American pastime of Hillary hating that started when Bill Clinton ran on a "buy one, get one free" slogan with the assumption that Democratic voters were sufficiently progressive on gender relations that his wife's influence would be a selling point. For some voters, the two-for-one idea boosted the ticket, but as Karrin Vasby Anderson and Kristina Horn Sheeler point out, "Republicans recognized Clinton's 'buy one, get one free' statement as a golden opportunity to paint Rodham Clinton as a radical feminist and play on cultural fear about powerful women."[7] The framing of Hillary Clinton as a Lady Macbeth–type character has been a staple of American political life since that time, and it cannot be extricated from sexism.

In the 2016 contest, we find that sex mattered because Clinton was held to different standards than her male competitors in terms of negative framing, consideration of scandals, and evaluations of fitness for the office. Gender also shaped the contours of the election because Trump frequently injected unapologetic sexism into the contest. He made masculinity one of the pillars of his campaign, in terms of both his hypermasculine persona and his criticisms of Clinton in ways meant to demean her as feminine and weak (e.g., saying she lacked the "strength" and "stamina" to be president). Trump's hypermasculinity positioned him well for the presidency, regardless of the fact that he was running against a woman, since every presidential race is a contest of who is "man enough" for the job.[8] Male candidates commonly feminize their opponents in order to win, and for Trump, this goal was easier to accomplish because his opponent was a woman.[9]

APPROACH

We approach our primary question from a democratic perspective, that a persistent gender gap in political representation, one that is especially pronounced with the presidency, poses a threat to the fabric of democracy. The United States falls far behind other countries when it comes to equitable representation of men and women in legislatures and executive offices. Progress in Congress has plateaued, with no more than 20 percent of the seats ever held by women at one time;[10] state legislatures are not much better, with women occupying about 25 percent of the seats.[11] State governors are still mostly men; women currently govern only six states, and since 1925, only 37 women have ever been governors.[12] Most notably, the United States has yet to elect a woman to the presidency, and the 2016 election was the first time a woman had won a major political party's nomination. Female heads of state have lost their novelty in countries across the globe. Germany, Ireland, Latvia, Finland, Brazil, the Philippines, Nepal, Croatia, Kosovo, Chile, Brazil, and nearly 70 other countries have had a woman in the top political leadership position, but not the United States, a country that prides itself as the pinnacle of democracy. The democratic principal of political equality, the idea that citizens have a right to equitable treatment under the law, is compromised when political leaders who are passing and enforcing laws do not reflect the demographic makeup of the population.

The historic exclusion of women in American politics matters because women and men have different legislative priorities and policy processes. Female legislators are more likely than male legislators to put on the agenda issues of concern to many women, such as child support enforcement, funding for women's health issues, and funding for domestic violence programs.[13] Female legislators are also significantly more liberal than male legislators, regardless of their political party,[14] so electing more women in political positions would generate different public policy. The process of governing would also be different if women were equitably represented in government. On average, female legislators take more factors into account than men do when passing policies, so their policy prescriptions are better contextualized.[15] Female politicians also differ from men in approaching policy making through an "ethic of care" that considers how issues are connected. For example, on crime policy, male legislators tend to see criminals as individuals who have chosen to engage in a life of crime, whereas female legislators tend to view criminals within a broader context of poverty and educational inequalities.[16] Gender differences in approach lead to different policy outcomes.

In addition to improving political equality with a more representative policy agenda and process, electing more women to political office would improve democracy by increasing political efficacy and participation. Political efficacy is the belief that a person can make a difference in politics, and female constituents who are represented by a woman in Congress exhibit higher rates of political efficacy and participate in politics at a higher rate than female constituents who are represented by a man.[17] We argue that electing women to the presidency would improve American democracy based on what we know about the governing styles of men and women and the ways the presence of female legislators improves political engagement. There is currently an active and rich debate about the sources of women's underrepresentation in politics,[18] and we contribute to this debate with an examination of whether sex and gender barriers have prevented the election of a female president to date.

METHODOLOGY

In this book, we employ mixed methodology—historical analysis, analysis of original social media data, a wealth of secondary data, and case studies of the 2008 primary, the 2016 primary, and the 2016 general election—to determine the influence of sex and gender. For our historical analysis, we examine the 12 women who have made serious bids for the presidency, beginning with Victoria Woodhull in 1872 and ending with Hillary Clinton in 2008 and 2016. To date, more than 100 women have sought their party's nomination,[19] but only 12 mounted enough resources and party support to be considered serious contenders. For each candidate, we briefly describe her background and look at how her candidacy was discussed in media and public discourse; we find remarkably consistent patterns of gender bias in the past 130 years.

For our case studies, we analyze three elections that prominently featured Hillary Clinton. More specifically, we examined the electoral context, media coverage, and public discourse of the most popular contenders in the 2008 Democratic primary (Clinton and Barack Obama), the 2016 Democratic primary (Clinton and Bernie Sanders), and the 2016 general election (Clinton and Donald Trump). We also examine how masculinity shaped the 2016 Republican primary race. These four case studies shed light on how Clinton was treated similarly to previous female presidential contenders and differently from her male contenders.

We also include a quantitative assessment of an original dataset of Twitter posts during the 2016 primary and general elections to determine whether public discourse about Clinton differed from her male competitors in gendered ways. We measure whether the ways in which users interacted with the candidates varied by candidate sex. Female candidates are typically subject to more negative legacy media coverage, and this is especially likely for women who run for president, but the media environment has shifted in the last decade. Today, political information is frequently consumed and disseminated through social media platforms like Facebook and Twitter. We analyze tweets mentioning Clinton and Sanders the last month of the Democratic primary (June 15, 2016, to July 15, 2016) and tweets mentioning Clinton and Trump the last month of the general election (October 8, 2016, to November 8, 2016). We analyze approximately 250,000 tweets and 5,391,117 words during the primary month, and 310,000 tweets and 5,698,222 words during the general election. We find that Clinton received significantly more negative coverage than her male competitors for the most part, but especially in terms of hashtag use in tweets. Twitter users mostly used hashtags that described Sanders and Trump in positive or neutral terms, but the vast majority of hashtags used in tweets about Clinton in the primary and general were negative.

THE CANDIDATES

The 2016 election pitted Clinton against Vermont senator Bernie Sanders and billionaire reality television star Donald J. Trump. These three candidates came from very different backgrounds. Clinton was raised in a Chicago suburb. Her father was a small-business owner, and her mother was a homemaker. Clinton earned an undergraduate degree from Wellesley College and a law degree from Yale University, and she worked as a congressional legal adviser prior to moving to Arkansas and marrying Bill Clinton. In Arkansas, she became the first chair of the Legal Services Corporation and the first female law partner at the Rose Law Firm. When her spouse was elected governor, Clinton worked on public school reform as first lady. As the first lady of the United States, Clinton advocated for health care reform. After her husband left office, Clinton was elected as a U.S. senator for New York in 2000 and was reelected in 2006. In 2008, she first ran for the presidency but lost to Barack Obama in the Democratic primary. Once elected, President Obama appointed Clinton as secretary of state, a position she held from 2009 to 2013. Clinton left that post after Obama's first term and spent her time giving speeches and writing a book.

Senator Bernie Sanders was elected to the U.S. Senate representing the state of Vermont in 2007. Prior to that, he was a member of Congress, the longest-serving independent in U.S. history. Sanders was raised in Brooklyn, New York, and graduated from the University of Chicago. In his early professional life, Sanders was a Head Start teacher, a filmmaker and writer, a carpenter, and a psychiatric aide. His activism started in college as an organizer for the Congress of Racial Equality, and he has been an avid fighter for civil rights since that time. He got into politics in the early 1980s when he won election for mayor of Burlington, and in 1990, Sanders was elected to Congress. He identifies as a Democratic Socialist, an ideology that advocates for democracy and social ownership of the means of production, typically with a focus on democratic management in the workplace and a living wage. Sanders gained national prominence in 2010 when he filibustered against tax cuts favoring wealthy Americans. Since he has been in Congress, Sanders has voted primarily with the Democrats, and in 2016, he ran for the presidency as a Democrat. He raised more money in individual contributions than any other candidate in history and energized the left wing of the party but lost to Clinton in the Democratic primary.

Donald Trump, a businessperson and television personality, won the 2016 presidential contest—the oldest and wealthiest candidate to do so. Trump was raised in New York City. His father worked in the family real estate business, and Trump's mother emigrated from Scotland and worked as a homemaker. Trump earned an undergraduate degree from the Wharton School of the University of Pennsylvania. Prior to entering politics, he managed a real estate conglomerate that was founded by his grandmother and produced the very popular reality television show *The Apprentice* for 12 years. He gained political prominence in the 2000s as an outspoken proponent of the birther movement, a campaign forwarding the fictitious claim that President Obama was born outside the United States.

Trump entered the Republican primary as one of sixteen candidates and bested his opponents with a campaign playing upon nationalist and anti-politically correct sentiment. He was the first president elected without previous government or military experience and the fifth president to win the Electoral College but lose the popular vote.

THE ELECTORAL CONTEXT

The 2016 election marked a year of insurgent candidates at the presidential level. Sanders and Trump were both candidates who branded themselves as working against the status quo. Sanders built a campaign and attracted large crowds with his pitch for economic populism and disdain for big banks and Wall Street. Trump's campaign actively promoted mistrust of the Republican Party, and he targeted various groups in society with his nativist rhetoric. Insurgent elections occur in the United States with some frequency—for example, Ralph Nader running against the Democratic establishment and Pat Buchanan running against the Republican establishment for several election cycles. The economic crisis of 2008 presaged Sanders's popularity, while the election of the first African American president and subsequent rise of the Tea Party in 2010, a group of white Americans with significantly higher levels of racial fear and racial resentment,[20] portended Trump's rise as the titular head of the birther movement. As Norm Ornstein points out, Trump in particular was able to rile the Republican base, which "had been told that once they got [Republicans] in power, they'd force Obama to his knees. Instead, they got compromises. That [anger] has been fueled by a lot of conservative media."[21] As we discuss in later chapters of this book, the context was ripe for insurgent candidates, so Clinton's extensive political experience did not help her as much as it would have in a typical election year. We also discuss how Clinton was defined in public discourse as an establishment candidate because few voters acknowledged the inherently insurgent nature of a female candidate for the presidency.

CHAPTER SUMMARIES

This book is organized into two distinct parts. The first three chapters present an overview of research on the barriers faced by female political candidates in the United States. It provides a useful primer for lay readers and scholars who are not familiar with this line of research. The remaining chapters focus on the 2016 primary and general elections. We apply theories and findings from the first part of the book to the 2016 election to better explain the historical context and identify trends and patterns in the most recent presidential contest that have been previously observed by scholars.

In chapter 1, we examine three decades of research on barriers to women's political leadership to better understand how sex and gender influence electoral politics in general. We focus on seven documented barriers to women's political leadership: the ambition gap, incumbency advantage, party recruitment bias, gender stereotypes, the sexual objectification of female candidates, and gender bias in media. The ambition gap and party recruitment bias limit the pool of women who run for office, and while women who run for political office win at the same rate as men, this is due to female candidates having significantly more qualifications than male candidates by the time they run. This chapter will provide an empirical basis for understanding the unique barriers women face in obtaining political positions.

In chapter 2, we analyze how the presidency and masculinity are entwined and how contests for the White House are invariably about who is "man enough" for the office. We go back in time to show how masculinity was established as a requirement for the office with the first president, George Washington. We find that, over the years, but especially during times of social unrest, presidents have performed hypermasculinity to appeal to voters who feel unsure about their place in the social order. Presidents Theodore Roosevelt and Ronald Reagan stand out in terms of their masculine personas, and both were responding to the threats to the existing social order from people of color and women, whose rights were advancing. We apply theories about presidential masculinity to the 2016 Republican primary election to show how the race was shaped by this dynamic. The masculine requirement for the White House poses a challenge to female contenders, for whom adoption of a convincing masculine persona is more difficult than it is for male candidates.

Chapter 3 presents the history of 12 women who have made serious bids for the presidency: Victoria Woodhull (1872); Belva Lockwood (1884 and 1888); Margaret Chase Smith (1964); Shirley Chisholm (1972); Patricia Schroeder (1988); Lenora Fulani (1988); Elizabeth Dole (2000); Carol Moseley Braun (2004); Michele Bachmann (2012); Carly Fiorina (2016); Jill Stein (2016); and Hillary Clinton (2008 and 2016). Each of the women who have run for the presidency in the last 130 years has experienced similar barriers in the form of more negative press coverage, greater questioning of her validity compared to male candidates, press and public discourse challenging the seriousness of her candidacy, and stereotypically gendered media coverage. These gender biases establish a clear double standard that undemocratically privileges male presidential candidates.

In chapter 4, we analyze Clinton's primary runs in 2008 and 2016. We employ case study analysis and secondary data analysis to each primary and find implicit and explicit gender bias in both races. Clinton's coverage was significantly more negative in both primaries than that of her male competitors, and her qualifications for the office were challenged more than those of male candidates. We also analyze how conflict between societal gender expectations and a woman running for the presidency cultivated misperceptions of dishonesty and "crookedness" and caused a sizeable number of Americans to call for Clinton to step out of the race prematurely in 2008 and when she was ahead in 2016.

In chapter 5, we analyze data from the 2016 general election and find a double standard in candidate treatment. The press favored Trump in the amount and type of coverage he received, challenged each candidate's fitness to the same degree, and covered scandals using a double standard that played into gender stereotypes of power-seeking women. We also document a volume of openly sexist rhetoric from Trump, his surrogates, and his supporters that has never been seen before in a presidential contest.

In chapter 6, we look at the information environment on Twitter, where millions of Americans turned for campaign information and where candidates themselves communicated directly with the public. While social media has the potential to enable active political discussion and learning and to engage users with social incentives, these platforms have proven themselves to also be a breeding ground and outlet for sexism and anger toward marginalized groups. We explore the discourse surrounding popular hashtags during the 2016 election and analyze the prevalence of sexism and misogyny directed at Clinton, in particular. We find that while social media has created a more hostile electoral environment for all candidates, that is especially the case for female candidates, who are treated more negatively than in legacy and online media.

In our concluding chapter, we examine the impact of sex and gender bias on the outcome of the general election. We summarize gender barriers to the presidency observed in 2016 and the ways persistent media and public opinion bias prevent gender equity in politics. We also look ahead at what our findings mean for women who will run for the presidency in the future and for women's progress in politics and society more broadly. We conclude with a discussion of why gender equity is important in politics, with a focus on women's distinctive style of governing and questions of democratic representation.

* * *

This book makes many bold claims that partisans may dismiss, but we draw upon reams of empirical and historical evidence to painstakingly support each of our major findings. We conclude that sex (sexism) and gender (masculinity) were determinative in the outcome of the 2016 election. This conclusion is based on nearly half a century of research documenting barriers faced by female political candidates, especially those running for the presidency. Masculinity is an intrinsic requirement for the presidency, an expectation for the office that hampered Clinton but buoyed Trump during the 2016 primary and general contests. It comes as no surprise, then, that all of the 12 previous female presidential contenders received press that harmed their electoral chances through coverage that was less substantive, portrayed them as emotional, questioned their viability, focused on their dress and appearance, dropped their professional titles, shamed them for their ambition, asked them to prematurely leave the race, suggested that they were actually interested in the vice presidency, sexually objectified them, judged them for not being masculine enough or being too masculine, and framed them in distinctly gendered and sometimes sexist ways.

Data from the 2016 primary and general election confirm that Clinton received significantly more negative and sexist coverage than both Sanders and Trump over the course of the election. Gendered and sexist discourse aimed at Clinton came from the left and the right, and the press failed to accurately differentiate between the candidates in terms of likeability, fitness, and legitimate scandals. We also find an alarming rate of overt sexism in the 2016 general election from Trump surrogates, his supporters, and Trump himself. They criticized Clinton for her clothing, voice, lack of smiling, excessive smiling, sexual orientation, sexual activity, lack of sexual activity, inability to manage money, getting "schlonged," lack of "a presidential look," and body. Gender slurs were common at rallies, at press conferences, and in social media commentary about Clinton.

We present an original analysis of social media discourse in the 2016 election and find that, in addition to increasing tribalism in the United States, social media has created a more hostile environment for female presidential candidates. We find that Clinton was discussed in far more negative and sexist terms than Sanders was in social media during the primary. In the general election, Trump experienced a high volume of negative sentiment during the last month of the campaign. However, Clinton's social media environment was more hostile when hashtag content and tone are taken into account, and Trump supporters achieved greater message control through Internet bots and "troll labor" that amplified negative messages aimed at Clinton.

We also conclude that, contrary to a popular explanation for the 2016 election, Trump's ascendance was not driven by economic anxiety but was driven by prejudice in the form of racial resentment and sexism. Trump supporters were not economically distinct from other voters but were distinct in their high levels of racial resentment and their embrace of different types of sexism. Furthermore, a significant drop in support for the first female presidential candidate among Democratic men was sizeable enough to affect the election outcome. Our conclusion that sex and gender played a decisive role in the outcome of the 2016 election does not negate the fact that other factors were also determinative, but it does contribute to a more complete picture of what happened in the 2016 contest.

CHAPTER 1

Labyrinths and Glass Ceilings: Barriers to Women's Political Leadership

In the 15th century, a 19-year-old illiterate farm girl led a military effort that reversed the tide of the Hundred Years' War between France and England. On the battlefield, Joan of Arc survived an arrow to her neck, an artillery shell to her head, a crossbow bolt to her leg, and a 70-foot jump to escape imprisonment, but she did not survive gendered norms of leadership. Joan of Arc was charged with heresy and burned at the stake for "cross-dressing"—wearing "men's" clothing and armor and cutting her hair short.[1] She was effectively executed for violating gender norms by donning masculine clothing and power.

Today, women are not burned at the stake for seeking or holding leadership positions, but they continue to encounter significant barriers. The term "glass ceiling" was coined by journalists three decades ago to describe women's persistent exclusion from top leadership positions in businesses and government. This metaphor conjures imagery of an impenetrable, invisible barrier to leadership just below the top level, but Alice Eagly and Linda Carli have produced a more fitting metaphor to explain barriers to women's leadership: a "labyrinth."[2] Rather than one barrier that appears near the top of a career trajectory, the labyrinth metaphor takes into account the numerous challenges women face over the course of their lifetime. This chapter lays out decades of research on various aspects of the labyrinth of women's leadership.

We begin this chapter with an overview of the landscape of women's leadership. We describe the history of women's exclusion from and eventual entry into electoral politics and examine current levels of representation. In the second part of this chapter, we analyze barriers to women's leadership that account for persistent gaps in representation. In the third section, we discuss gender barriers that are specific to the presidency. Women have elbowed their way into politics since the founding of our republic, but progress has been slow and marked by fits and starts. Significant barriers still exist for women's leadership, and this is especially the case for the office of the presidency, which remains virtually impossible for a female candidate to win, for reasons we examine here.

THE LANDSCAPE OF WOMEN'S LEADERSHIP

For the first century of our young 240-year-old country, women were political outsiders who were not allowed to vote, serve on juries, or run for public office. Activists protested women's exclusion at every turn; for instance, Abigail Adams implored her husband, John Adams, to

> Remember the ladies, and be more generous and favorable to them than your ancestors. Do not put such unlimited power into the hands of the Husbands. Remember all Men would be tyrants if they could. If particular care and attention is not paid to the Ladies we are determined to foment a Rebellion, and will not hold ourselves bound by any Laws in which we have no voice, or Representation.[3]

John Adams and the other framers ignored Abigail's entreaty and instead codified women's exclusion from political life and full citizenship in the Constitution. This inspired the first women's movement some decades later. About 300 women and men gathered at the Seneca Falls Convention in 1848 to produce the Declaration of Sentiments, modeled after the Declaration of Independence, demanding women's full participation in U.S. society and politics. This early women's movement brought about passage of the Nineteenth Amendment, which granted women voting rights in 1920. The battle for the vote was prolonged and bloody, and it raised awareness of the democratic implications of the political exclusion of half of the population. It also inspired a wave of women to seek political office. The first woman was elected to the U.S. House of Representatives in 1916 (Jeannette Rankin of Montana), a governorship in 1925 (Nellie Tayloe Ross of Wyoming), and the U.S. Senate in 1932 (Hattie Wyatt Caraway of Arkansas). Progress for women in politics was slow after this early spurt of "firsts," until the next wave of the women's movement.

The second wave of the women's rights movement emerged in the politically turbulent decade of the 1960s and coincided in part with the civil rights movement. It brought more women into state and national political offices, including the first women of color in national leadership positions. Patsy Takemoto Mink (D-Hawaii) was the first Asian American woman elected to the House in 1965, and Shirley Chisholm (D-N.Y.) was the first African American woman in the House in 1969. The second wave of the women's movement brought about rapid growth in female political leadership. The percentage of women in the House and Senate rose from 2 percent in 1970 to 12 percent in 2000, and the number of female state legislators increased fivefold from the 1970s to the present.[4] Despite these gains, women are still vastly underrepresented in all levels of government.

Today, women constitute about 20 percent of the House and Senate and about a quarter of state legislative seats and statewide elective offices,[5] but social progress is rarely linear. Movements that challenge the existing social order are always met with resistance and backlash, and gender justice progress in the United States has never been a steady march forward. Despite major advancements for women in education and employment as a result of the second wave of the women's movement, forward momentum has stalled in obvious and measurable ways in the 2000s. The rapid growth in the number of women in elective office peaked in the late 1990s and then mostly leveled off. Linda C. Babcock states: "I don't think we have come as far as we think we have. We do see some visible women out there at the top of organizations and those with political power, so we just automatically think that everything has changed. But those are really still tokens."[6] This stagnation has occurred at a time when female candidates fare as well as or better than their male competitors in terms of raising money and winning elections.[7] We explore persistent barriers to women's leadership in the next section.

Barriers to Women's Leadership

Social scientists have identified six primary barriers within the labyrinth of women's political leadership: (1) the ambition gap, (2) incumbency advantage, (3) party recruitment bias, (4) gender stereotypes, (5) sexual objectification, and (6) media bias. Some of these barriers are not mutually exclusive—for example, media bias amplifies many of the other barriers— but we discuss each separately and in turn.

The Ambition Gap

Men have higher rates of political ambition than women do and are therefore more likely to consider running for public office.[8] Indeed, 57 percent of men have considered running for public office at some point, compared to only 37 percent of women, and men are twice as likely to have thought about running "many times."[9] The political ambition gap emerges early in life: teen boys are significantly more likely than teen girls to have considered running for office (15 percent compared to 9 percent).[10] The ambition gap translates into fewer women than men "choosing" to run for political office.

The principal origin of the ambition gap is a widely held societal belief that ambition is acceptable for men but not for women, a norm that is conveyed to each successive generation when they are young. Women are expected to act modestly, even if they are highly accomplished, and women are seen in a negative light by both men and women when they violate assumptions of modesty.[11] Boys and girls have similar levels of ambition when they are young, but, as they age, girls grow into women with significantly less ambition as they internalize gender role expectations.[12] It is important to note that women and men have similar life aspirations and ideas about civic duty, so this does not account for the political ambition gap. Both, at roughly the same rates, want to have children, get married, achieve career success, and earn a lot of money, and they are equally likely to want to improve their communities.[13] However, women are less likely than men to see running for public office as a viable option for achieving their personal or civic goals.

Another primary source of the ambition gap is girls' warped perceptions of their abilities. Girls and women have measurably lower self-confidence than boys and men in every country, a gap that grows between the ages of four and fourteen.[14] The confidence gap is even more pronounced in male-dominated activities, like math or politics, where both men and women overestimate men's abilities and underestimate women's abilities.[15] In "male" activities, such as math, both boys and girls think that boys are better at the subject, despite having earned the same grades and scored the same on standardized tests.[16] Similarly, men tend to overestimate their Intelligence Quotient (IQ) while women underestimate theirs, and mothers and fathers inaccurately believe their sons have higher IQs than their daughters.[17] In adulthood, warped perception of skills leads to women thinking they are less qualified to run for political office than men with the same or similar qualifications.[18]

Another cause of the ambition gap is a lack of encouragement and external recognition of leadership abilities. Adults in educational settings more often encourage boys to participate in competitive activities, such as student government or the debate team, than they do girls.[19] Participation in competitive activities significantly increases a person's interest in running for public office and confidence that one has the skills to do so. Anna

Fels finds that girls receive less external encouragement and recognition for being ambitious, and, as a result, they learn that this desire will not be rewarded.[20] Instead, many women settle for "recognition by proxy" through attention for their physical attractiveness or the accomplishments of their husband or children. A girl's childhood ambition of becoming the next president or a CEO of a major company is eventually forgotten and replaced with pursuits that better fit with societal gender expectations of women as sexual objects and the primary caretakers of children.[21]

Encouragement is also important for adults. Family influence is especially important since people who are encouraged to run for public office by at least one family member are 43 percent more likely to have high political ambition than a person who receives no encouragement from family.[22] Unfortunately, few women are encouraged to run for office by their family, friends, or peers. Women receive significantly less encouragement from their support network to run.[23] The ambition gap means far fewer women consider running for office than men, and that has a profound effect on the presidency because the office requires an extensive record of public service, especially for female candidates, who have to be better qualified than male contenders to be considered viable candidates.[24]

Incumbency Advantage

Another barrier to women's political leadership is incumbency advantage.[25] Incumbents typically enjoy higher name recognition, greater access to funders, more attention from the press, and the ability to communicate with voters through franked (free) mailers to constituents. This means that female candidates face steep odds of winning if they run against established incumbents, most of whom are men. Incumbent members of Congress are reelected at a rate of 96 percent.[26] The increasing party polarization in the United States has caused sitting elected officials to stay in office longer, which means that there are even fewer opportunities for female candidates to be elected.[27] The lack of opportunity for nonincumbents in national politics has profound implications for the female candidates since presidents bring an average of 22 years of previous public service experience to the office,[28] and 37 percent of presidents have used Congress as a stepping stone to the presidency.[29]

Party Recruitment Bias

Another barrier to women's political leadership is unequal candidate recruitment by political parties. Party leaders recruit men to run for political office more frequently and more intensely than they do women.[30] Party recruitment is crucial for women since they are significantly less likely than men to consider running for office if they have not been approached by the party.[31] The gender gap in party recruitment has not improved in recent years because elections have become considerably more expensive and because many party leaders and donors inaccurately believe that male candidates can raise more money than female candidates.[32] The party recruitment gap is compounded by the fact that when women are asked to run by the party, they are less likely to agree because they doubt the party will sufficiently support their bid.[33] Party recruitment barriers diminish the number of women in political office at all levels, which limits the pool of female candidates with the proper qualifications to run for the presidency.

Gender Stereotypes

Gender stereotypes present another challenge for women's political leadership. The field of psychology has developed standard characterizations of masculine and feminine traits.[34] In general, feminine attributes are communal and masculine attributes are agency related. Communal characteristics include being affectionate, sympathetic, nurturing, and helpful, and agentic characteristics include being controlling, dominant, forceful, and assertive.[35] Furthermore, communal characteristics are considered more appropriate for those in caretaking professions, whereas agency characteristics are perceived to be better suited to the world of business and politics.[36] These stereotypes about men, women, and gender spill over into the political realm, where studies have looked at how strong these gender stereotypes are and whether or not they have electoral consequences.

Stereotypes about women and men are present in evaluations of abstract women and men in politics.[37] Studies find that hypothetical female candidates are seen as possessing feminine qualities, such as compassion and warmth, and that these perceptions are an effect of the hypothetical candidate's sex. These same studies find that hypothetical male candidates are seen as possessing masculine qualities, such as assertiveness and aggressiveness.[38] Researchers agree that gender stereotypes are prevalent in American politics, with women at a disadvantage because of their association with feminine qualities and characteristics and public perceptions of incongruence between femininity and leadership. According to a meta-analysis of leadership and stereotypes of men and women by Anne Koenig et al., respondents' descriptions of leaders, professionals, and managers are largely masculine. They use words like "aggressive," "competitive," and "independent" to describe hypothetical people in these positions.[39] While women can obviously exude these attributes, this meta-analysis found that respondents rarely use the words to describe women but frequently use them to describe men. That word choice is largely due to gender's basis in maleness and femaleness and the inaccurate but widely held assumption that masculinity and femininity are uniquely performed by men and women, respectively.[40] The perceived overlap between sex and gender, and the perceived overlap between attributes that make a good leader and masculine traits, gives men an inherent advantage when it comes to leadership positions. Koenig et al. report that cultural biases that favor male leadership are found across different domains of leadership.[41]

Monica Schneider and Angela Bos delve more deeply into questions of whether female politicians are beholden to feminine stereotypes since they have already transgressed those stereotypes by entering the masculine realm of politics.[42] They suggest that female politicians may represent a subtype of women—"a new stereotypical category created when perceivers encounter a group that deviates from a larger stereotype category"—for whom stereotypes may be less salient to voters.[43] To test whether female politicians are a subtype of women, Schneider and Bos asked participants to describe "male professionals," "female professionals," "male politicians," "female politicians," "politicians," "men," and "women." From these descriptions, they created a list of adjectives and then asked a different group of participants to indicate which adjectives they thought "people in general" would use to describe the particular groups. Schneider and Bos find that "male politicians" are considered a subgroup of "men" since the traits for both considerably overlap, but "female politicians" are not a subgroup of "women" since the traits diverge. "Caring," "motherly," "feminine," and "emotional" were the most common selected traits to describe women but were rarely used to describe "female politicians." Additionally, Schneider and Bos find that "female politicians are defined more by their deficits than their strengths."[44] This research suggests that stereotypes about women may not be salient in some circumstances when individuals are thinking about women running for political office; however, male politicians are still described in masculine stereotypes.

Gender stereotypes come into play with perceptions of issue expertise. In general, women are seen as more politically liberal than men[45] and are assumed to be more competent on "feminine" issues that involve women or children, such as education, social welfare, and reproductive rights, than on "masculine" issues, such as national security and defense.[46] To overcome the perception that they lack credibility in dealing with issues such as national security or defense, women, especially Democratic women, engage in compensatory strategies to appear more masculine.[47] For example, Michele Swers analyzed congressional sponsorship records and found that Democratic women in Congress are more active sponsors of homeland security bills than men of either political party. Swers points out that gendered stereotypes of women being less capable of handling "masculine" issues "creates a political imperative for women to countervail stereotypes about women's ability to provide leadership on defense issues."[48]

Gendered stereotypes and perception of issue competence can be especially damaging for women with presidential ambitions. Assumptions of men's superiority on "masculine" policy issues are especially limiting for female presidential candidates since the office is symbolically and practically associated with foreign policy, defense, and international conflict.[49] Given the association of the presidency with national security, consideration of "masculine" policy competence is largely unavoidable for candidates seeking this office.[50] The gender stereotype that female leaders are less capable than male leaders when it comes to national security has been a pronounced challenge since the attack in the United States on September 11, 2001. Presidential candidates have increasingly focused on issues of national security, terrorism, and war, likely because of the importance of these issues in the eyes of voters since 2001. In 2002, Gallup polls found that almost half of those sampled indicated that war and terrorism were the most important issues facing the country, compared to around 10 percent expressing that sentiment before 2001.[51] For women with political ambitions, that attention on national security concerns can hurt their credibility in the eyes of average Americans. As Jennifer Lawless notes:

> A clear bias favoring male candidates and elected officials accompanies the war on terror. . . . Citizens prefer men's leadership traits and characteristics, deem men more competent at legislating around issues of national security and military crises, and contend that men are superior to women at addressing the new obstacles generated by the events of September 11, 2001.[52]

Lawless found that 64 percent of respondents think that men are better able than women to deal with military affairs. More evidence of a post-9/11 backlash against female candidates is the Gallup poll, which asks respondents whether they would support a woman for president, if nominated by their party. As displayed in figure 1.1, support for a woman declined considerably after 2001, and Lawless links that decline to gender stereotypes about national security that disadvantage hypothetical female candidates.

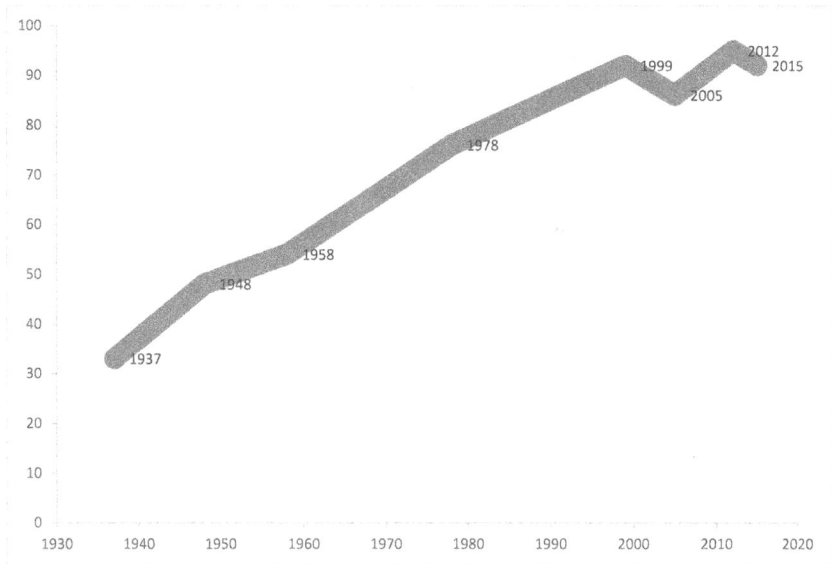

Figure 1.1 Support for Female President: Gallup Polling (Numbers Shown in Percentages)

Source: Gallup.

In addition to holding gender stereotypes, voters also view national security through a partisan lens that disadvantages female political leaders, most of whom are Democratic at the national level.[53] In short, more voters see Republicans, rather than Democrats, as "owning" the issues of national security. Issue ownership is the assumed command of a particular political issue and is usually referred to in the context of political parties; the Republican Party largely has issue ownership of defense and taxes, while the Democratic Party has issue ownership over social welfare issues.[54] This does not mean that Democratic candidates cannot win elections when issues of national security and defense top the agenda, but all things being equal, if a voter has no other information about the candidates, other than their party identification, the Republican candidate is at an advantage, in this circumstance, and a Republican man even more so. Gender stereotypes about national security are compounded with ideas of party issue ownership for female Democratic candidates.

Most research on gender stereotypes in politics uses experiments and hypothetical candidates and elections. Few studies apply this research to actual elections, but one study conducted by Kathleen Dolan and Timothy Lynch does just that. They use a two-wave panel survey to gauge respondent stereotypes and support for equally qualified male and female candidates,[55] then measure their actual vote choice in a congressional race. They find that voters hold gender stereotypes but that gender is a weak predictor of actual vote choice in a congressional race. Partisanship is the most significant indicator of vote choice. We posit that, in particular contexts when issues of national security are particularly salient or a male contender explicitly uses gendered appeals, gender stereotypes may play a bigger role in vote choice.[56] Also, when party identification is irrelevant, such as during primary races, candidate sex is a more potent predictor of vote choice. The 2016 election is a good case for testing whether gender stereotypes influenced the outcome of the election.

Gender stereotypes are at the root of leadership evaluation bias, where women who seek and hold leadership positions are judged more harshly than men. That bias is tied in with gender stereotypes. People view leadership, in both the corporate and political spheres, as a masculine pursuit, and men are viewed as "default leaders," while women are seen as "atypical leaders."[57] Voters tend to assign stereotypically masculine traits to good leadership (toughness, competitiveness, incisiveness, and initiative, and intellectual acuity), while stereotypically feminine traits (conscientiousness, consideration, flexibility, enthusiasm, and dedication) are valued less.[58] It is no surprise, then, that one in four Americans believe that men are better suited for public office than women.[59]

Male and female leaders tend to have different leadership styles and are judged differently when it comes to the authenticity of their leadership. Transformational leadership, a highly effective approach used more often by women than men,[60] produces average higher economic returns in the corporate sector.[61] A recent study of approximately 22,000 companies in 91 countries finds that companies with female CEOs produce higher profits and that having women in top leadership positions significantly increases revenue.[62] Even though female corporate leadership has proven to be more profitable, both men and women continue to prefer male bosses to female bosses.[63]

Researchers have identified role congruity theory (RCT) to explain gendered leadership evaluation bias—traditional gender role expectations for women conflict with leadership expectations in ways that prejudice people against female leadership.[64] Perceptions of role incongruity cause people to both view women as less suited for leadership positions and hold female leaders to a higher standard that inevitably leads to less favorable evaluations of their leadership. Female bosses are evaluated using a harsher (double) standard, so men and women evaluate female leaders more negatively than they do men, and people consistently see women as lacking key leadership skills.[65] People who hold more traditional attitudes about gender roles give female leaders a much more negative evaluation than others do.[66] Leadership evaluation bias presents a steep electoral barrier for women seeking political office, especially in the case of the presidency, the most powerful political position in the world.

One particularly pernicious form of leadership evaluation bias is the double-bind bias, in which female leaders are "damned if they do and damned if they don't" display masculine leadership traits.[67] The higher the political office, the greater the expectation that candidates adopt masculine personas to been seen as legitimate leaders.[68] This expectation inherently disadvantages women because masculine traits are associated with men and voters perceive female presidential candidates as less decisive and weaker than male candidates.[69] The stereotype that male leaders are strong and able to protect the nation caused a statistically significant drop in support for a hypothetical female president post-9/11.[70] The double bind is unavoidable, especially for female presidential candidates, who are under pressure to display masculine traits in order to fill the father-protector role of the presidency, which inherently violates norms of femininity.[71] Sen. Barbara Boxer described facing the double bind as a U.S. senator. "If I was strong in my expression of the issues, I was strident; if I expressed any emotion as I spoke about the environment or the problems of the mentally ill, I was soft; if I spoke about economics I had to be perfect, and then I ran the risk of being 'too much like a man.' "[72]

The double bind of women's leadership has been well documented in the corporate sphere. Female leaders who act in stereotypically feminine ways (e.g., express concern for others and emphasize building good relationships) are rated as less competent, but if they act "masculine" (e.g., they are task-oriented, ambitious, and assertive), they are rated negatively for being "too tough."[73] Victoria Brescoll finds that women are penalized for their anger in workplace settings, but men are not.[74] In her experiment, a female boss was judged more unfavorably than a male boss when both were shown getting angry about losing an account. Research participants awarded the angry male an annual average salary of $38,000, compared to only $23,500 for the angry female.

The double bind of women's leadership makes winning the presidency virtually impossible for female candidates, given the hypermasculinity of the office (discussed below) and the fact that this double bind cannot be skirted or transcended. Female political candidates, and especially female presidential candidates, face conflicting expectations, which no woman to date has been able to effectively navigate.

Sexual Objectification

Recent research has uncovered sexual objectification as another barrier to female leadership.[75] Sexual objectification is the process of representing or treating a person like a sex object, one that serves another's sexual pleasure. In the United States, the widespread objectification of women has become a normal part of life, acceptable to the point that it goes unnoticed by most men and women.[76] The fact that even the most accomplished, powerful women in the world—athletes, politicians, CEOs—are judged by their sex appeal shows how ingrained this measure of worth is for all women.

Sexualizing female candidates hurts their electoral chances.[77] A mention of a female candidate's dress or appearance immediately causes voters to view her as less likeable, less in touch, and less qualified, whether the mention is positive or negative.[78] Using an experiment setting, Nathan A. Heflick and Jamie L. Goldenberg find that voters who were exposed to objectifying images of 2008 vice presidential candidate Sarah Palin viewed her as less competent, less moral, less warm, and even less human.[79] That image had electoral consequence in that Republicans who were primed to focus on Palin's appearance were less likely to vote for the McCain-Palin ticket. Peter Glick finds that female executives who dress provocatively are rated as less competent than their provocatively dressed male counterparts, which demonstrates that sexualization inflicts specific harm to female leaders.[80]

Widespread societal acceptance of women's sexual objectification is one of the primary tools for maintaining gender hierarchy in the United States.[81] It is also a powerful tool for diminishing the viability of a female candidate. The sexualization of female presidential candidates is particularly damaging since mentions of dress or appearance run directly counter to notions of masculinity required for proper presidential leadership. The role incongruence with sexual objectification and presidential masculinity is especially pronounced.

Media Bias

Media bias is another barrier to women's leadership, one that transmits and amplifies many of the barriers examined above. Media coverage teaches little boys to be politically ambitious and little girls to suppress their ambition. Media enhances incumbency advantage when reporters give more airtime to sitting leaders. It reinforces leadership evaluation bias by discussing male and female candidates in different ways and buttresses the double bind through subtle but powerful candidate framing. Press coverage is also a major source of female-candidate sexualization.

Media bias has greatly diminished in the past decade,[82] but for higher political offices, it continues to be the linchpin of women's underrepresentation in politics.[83]

Gender bias in media matters because reporters shape opinions about candidates through the amount and type of coverage they provide. Media coverage does not tell people *what* to think, but it tells people what topics to think *about* through agenda setting and *how* to think about them by focusing on some aspects and not others.[84] Media works against female candidates through subtle framing—overarching labels or narratives that shape public conceptions of candidates.[85] These frames are particularly important for presidential candidates because a frame can be repeated enough that it defines a candidate (e.g., Bill Clinton and the "comeback kid" frame in 1992, George W. Bush and the "decider" frame in 2004; John Kerry and the "flip-flop" frame in 2004; Barack Obama and the "candidate of change" frame in 2008).

Pioneering research from Kim Fridkin Kahn finds that women running for statewide and national office received less coverage and more negative coverage than their male competitors in the 1980s and 1990s and that this bias had electoral consequences, with voters seeing women as less electable.[86] Subsequent research shows that female candidates receive less issue-related coverage than men and that reporters pay more attention to their personality traits, personal lives, dress, and appearance, all of which signals that female candidates are less serious contenders.[87] Female candidates also receive more coverage questioning their viability than male candidates do[88] and are covered as less authentic than their male competitors.[89] Female presidential candidates are twice as likely to be described in emotional terms in press coverage as male candidates, and female candidates today are just as likely as candidates in previous centuries to be portrayed as emotional.[90] Articles about female presidential candidates are also twice as likely to mention their families as those about male candidates—about once in every five articles versus once in every ten articles—and this ratio has remained constant for all female presidential candidates in the past 130 years.[91]

Mainstream media has become much less biased for most political offices in the past decade,[92] but new media and social media have actually increased sexism in public discourse about female candidates. Legacy media (e.g., broadcast television networks, national weekly news magazines, and print newspapers) is rapidly being eclipsed by new media, which includes news blogs, talk radio, and cable news television. New media is more in the realm of infotainment than "hard" news with fewer editorial filters, and it comes with more ideological extremism and character assassinations.[93] Personal prejudices, such as homophobia, sexism, racism, and xenophobia, are more pronounced in new media than in legacy media because of a dearth of editorial filters and rejection of journalistic conventions.[94] Indeed, Meredith Conroy et al. find that female candidates are discussed in significantly more negative terms in new media than in legacy media, and new media coverage contains more overtly gendered insults.[95]

The new popularity of political discourse in social media (e.g., Facebook, Twitter, Instagram) also creates a more hostile media environment for female candidates. Social media was invented in the mid-2000s and was first used by candidates in the 2008 presidential election. By the 2012 presidential election, social media had become a staple of political discourse. This public platform is a source of extreme gender bias in elections because it enables everyday people to express their opinions in public forums, ungoverned by professional journalistic norms or even norms of civil discourse. Social media has become a visible forum for individuals to express bigoted beliefs, fueled by anonymity.[96] Social media is especially powerful when it comes to framing candidates since frames can "go viral," as we explore in chapter 6.

Both new media and social media have exacerbated the presence of gendered and sexist discourse about female candidates in ways that present challenges to their electability.[97] Despite these barriers, women win offices at the same rate as men when they run,[98] because female candidates are, on average, significantly better educated and more qualified than their male contenders.[99] There is only one political office where significant gender barriers remain intact: the presidency.

Unique Barriers to the Presidency

Women face barriers to leadership at all levels of office, but the challenges for women seeking the White House are more intense because of expectations about prototypical citizenship and masculinity. The U.S. president holds singular importance as the symbolic leader of the "free world," and for that reason, access to this office holds incomparable democratic significance. Women's exclusion from this office is both real and symbolic. Public perception of who can legitimately occupy the Oval Office is a measure of the status of different identities and of who gets to count as the prototypical, ideal citizen.[100] We use the term "citizenship" here to refer to cultural practices that indicate one's value in a society, not legal citizenship.[101] The racialization and gendering of citizenship was both explicit and implicit in founding documents and early immigration laws, and even with formal suffrage extended to black men in 1870 and all women in 1920, full citizenship remains aligned with whiteness and with maleness. As such, this excludes certain Americans from "rightfully" holding the presidency in the minds of many. We label this "identity incongruity theory," the idea that public perception of the prototypical citizen causes people to view people of color and women to be less suited for the office of the presidency. This perception leads many Americans to see women and people of color running for or occupying the presidency as fundamentally lacking the right identity to hold the office and therefore to judge them more harshly for the same actions than white men.

The presidency of Barack Obama illustrates the conflation of the presidency and the prototypical citizen. His blackness violated white notions of ideal citizenship, and the race-based backlash in response was measurable. Obama experienced a tide of explicit and implicit racism in social media and from Republican lawmakers during his time in office, and the birther movement effectively framed him as "other," "foreign," and un-American because he is black.[102] As soon as he announced his candidacy, stories started circulating in public discourse questioning Obama's legal citizenship status with claims that he was birthed in another country. This idea quickly moved from the shadows of the fringe to mainstream public discourse, where many Americans channeled fear and anxiety about a nonwhite president into a call for formal documentation of his nativity.[103] Obama responded to birthers by releasing his short-form birth certificate in 2008, but the pressure only intensified, so he released the long-form version in 2011, but to no avail. Today, 72 percent of Republicans still doubt whether President Obama was born in the United States.[104] Birther beliefs "reveal the sustained conflation of citizenship with an ideal or 'hegemonic' form of white racial identity."[105] The raced citizenship origins of the birther story are made more apparent given the relatively scant attention paid to the fact that Sen. John McCain, Obama's opponent in the 2008 race, was born outside the United States (in the Panama Canal Zone). Like the first black president, our nation's first female president will be "othered" because she does not fit the requirements of prototypical citizenship entwined with the presidency. The challenge for a white woman will be even greater than a black man, because the presidential persona is more intrinsically linked to gender than race. Women of color violate prototypical citizenship on both counts and thus face the highest barriers to the presidency. One way to visualize the combined effect of race and gender is to imagine the likelihood of a black woman winning the White House on her first president bid, with just two years of experience as a U.S. senator. A female candidate of color with so little time on the national stage likely would not have been taken seriously by the party or the press. In other words, if candidate Obama were a woman, it is improbable that he would have received such positive press coverage or been considered a serious contender for his party's nomination.

The United States was established on an idea of citizenship that was socially constructed through the exclusion of women as full citizens. During the founding, citizenship was associated with "earning," a predication that barred enslaved peoples and free women.[106] The concept of "citizen" only gained meaning through an interdependent designation of "noncitizen"—"the alien, the slave, the woman"—upon whose labor (both voluntary and forced) the freedom and autonomy required for full citizenship was made possible.[107] The exclusion of women from the polity and full citizenship can be traced back to the canonical writings of John Locke, Jean-Jacques Rousseau, and other Enlightenment philosophers who shaped American political thought by defining the universal, prototypical citizen as male.[108] This notion persists today since the concept of citizenship is predicated on the idea that some people are not fully valued members of society.[109]

Maleness is constitutive of the ideal citizen, so the presidency, an office that symbolizes the prototype, is inextricably entwined with a male occupant. Women who seek this office are inherently seen as outsiders in a sacred grove, as interlopers who have to prove their right to even run. The legitimacy of male presidential candidates with political experience is not questioned by the press and the public, but the legitimacy of female presidential candidates is always already suspect, even if they have cultivated long political résumés. This pattern of bias is ubiquitous but invisible to most voters because, at a core level, women betray the basic requirement that the president embody the prototypical, ideal citizen.

The exclusion of women is a core element of the historical development of the office of the presidency, a masculine institution.[110] Structural barriers work to support this masculinism: party recruitment that favors men, media coverage that favors male contenders, and presidential elections that center around stereotypically masculine issues, such as national security and crime. Presidential power is the manliest power in politics: that of the father-protector of the country. After the terrorist attacks of 9/11, public willingness to support a hypothetical female president dropped to its lowest point in decades.[111]

Female presidential candidates do face higher barriers given the office's unique requirements of prototypical citizenship and masculinity. It is no wonder, then, that women who run for this office are trivialized by the press as inevitable losers, novelty candidates, and less than serious candidates.[112] And those who manage to make it far enough in the process to be considered legitimate contenders are vilified. The ways in which female presidential candidates are discussed in public spheres discourages women from running and hurts the electoral chances of women who do run. Susan J. Carroll writes that in recent elections, "sexism and sexist remarks by journalists and on-air pundits were treated as acceptable—a normal part of political discourse."[113] Media coverage has become less gender biased in the past few decades for most political offices, but sexist discourse has remained a constant for women who seek the presidency. When it comes to this particular office, it is simply not enough for female candidates to be more qualified or, as we saw in the 2016 election, the most qualified candidate in U.S. history. Unique aspects of the office make it virtually impossible for a woman to win the White House.

CONCLUSION

We began this chapter with an overview of women's leadership. The first significant push for women's inclusion in U.S. politics came with the fight for suffrage that culminated with the Nineteenth Amendment in 1920. The second push for women's inclusion came with the women's movement of the 1960s and 1970s. Gender justice advocates pushed for laws against discrimination and harassment in the workplace, for equal pay legislation, and for reproductive rights. This period also saw a rapid increase in the number of female representatives in politics. Despite significant gains in women's political representation in the last half century, women constitute only one in five leaders in national politics, and progress has mostly stalled since the 2000s.

Women face persistent barriers when it comes to political leadership in general. In this chapter, we explored many barriers: the ambition gap that causes women to doubt their own abilities; incumbency bias that benefits male candidates (because they are more likely to already hold office); gendered evaluations of leadership, where women are held to a higher standard than men and therefore are evaluated more negatively; the double bind of women's leadership, where women who exhibit masculine traits associated with good leadership are seen by some as lacking "proper" femininity; the sexual objectification of female candidates, which causes voters to see them as less competent; and media bias in the form of more negative coverage for female candidates.

Women who run for the presidency face additional, distinct barriers. First, because the president is seen as the prototypical citizen in the minds of many Americans, and because the prototypical citizen is seen as male, female candidates face identity incongruence. In short, women are seen by many as lacking legitimacy to hold this office, and as such, their actions receive more scrutiny and more gendered scrutiny than white male contenders. The second barrier unique to women running for the presidency is the expectation of hypermasculinity. Presidential campaigns are fundamentally about who is "man enough" to hold the position, so masculinity is a factor in presidential elections even when women are not in the race. When women run, they face the impossible task of living up to hypermasculine presidential standards that, by definition, they cannot meet in the minds of many voters because of their sex.

Women who run for presidency encounter gendered leadership biases as well as biases that are specific to the office. As we explore in later chapters, most female candidates are not taken seriously by the public and the press, and those who manage some success in the race are vilified. While media and public discourse about female political candidates has improved in the past two decades, it has not improved for women running for the presidency.

In her short life, Joan of Arc's leadership experience exemplified the contemporary labyrinth of women's leadership, fraught with gendered notions of proper ambition, biases in evaluations of her success, the masculinism of political institutions, and the double bind that would ultimately spell her doom. Joan of Arc's strategic abilities and fighting spirit are essential for the contemporary woman who enters the labyrinth, although her sword and mettle have been replaced by thick skin and an iron will. But even these modern tools are not sufficient for women to make significant progress on the leadership front without a more level battlefield.

CHAPTER 2

"The Emperor Has No Balls": Masculinity and the Presidency

In August 2016, after Donald Trump had officially accepted his party's nomination, a guerrilla art collective, Indecline, unveiled a series of life-size Trump statues in New York City, Cleveland, San Francisco, Los Angeles, and Seattle. Indecline entitled the installation *The Emperor Has No Balls*, in reference to Hans Christian Andersen's "The Emperor's New Clothes." The statues, made of clay and silicone, depicted a corpulent, naked Trump with a micropenis and no balls. A multitude of meanings could be drawn from the statue, and many criticized the Indecline installation for being transphobic and fat shaming. The most obvious of Indecline's statements was the assault on Trump's masculinity, a literal trimming of his manhood. This seemingly radical statement was a stark reminder that gender is relevant in American politics, irrespective of candidate sex. Although a dialogue about the role of gender and sex in presidential elections was reinvigorated during Hillary Clinton's long road to securing the Democratic Party's nomination for president, the U.S. presidency has a long history of being entangled with gender, or more specifically, masculinity, whether or not a woman is in the race.

Gender is made relevant in presidential elections in several ways—namely, masculinity is aligned with notions of good leadership in the minds of voters, so candidates commonly invoke masculinity on the campaign trail. The public's underlying notion of good leadership overlaps with ideas of masculinity, which puts women at a disadvantage since they are seen as inherently less masculine than men. It also puts male candidates who are perceived as feminine at a disadvantage. This psychological role of gender is often unconscious, but studies find it to be powerful in shaping preferences. Moreover, public preference for masculinity is maintained by the candidates in the ways they describe themselves and discuss their opponents' shortcomings, demonstrating an empirically observable instance of gender in action in presidential campaigns. These descriptions and discussions tend to be hostile toward femininity, contributing to an environment that is less friendly to women with political ambitions. For instance, the underlying theme of the Indecline installation is that a feminized male is less fit to lead—that a real leader has a large penis and big balls. That Trump is without his balls unwittingly elevates masculinity in the presidential contest at the expense of femininity. These messages motivate both men and women to take on more masculine behaviors and positions, both of which limit who runs for this office and who gets elected.

In this chapter, we examine how gender and the presidency are connected. We begin with an assessment of theories and data on presidential masculinity. Then we describe the history of presidential masculinity in the U.S. context and conclude with a look at masculinity in recent elections, including the hypermasculine 2016 Republican primary. We find that masculinity has been linked to the presidency since the founding and that it becomes more so during times when the social order is shifting and the meaning of masculinity is less stable. We conclude that gender (masculinity) played a significant role in shaping candidate discourse and public perceptions in the 2016 Republican primary.

PRESIDENTIAL MANHOOD

The office of the presidency has long been entwined with masculinity. In the minds of many voters, masculinity is a requirement for winning and successfully executing the duties of the office. Jackson Katz writes that every presidential contest involves competing visions of masculinity, a competition of who is "man enough" to fit the job.[1] He finds that presidential candidates, but especially Republican candidates, project symbols of (white) masculinity as a way to appeal to voters who imagine the presidency in those terms. Instead of focusing on specific policies, presidential candidates make appeals to emotions and fears by creating a "tough guy" persona of someone able to project violence in order to protect the country and traditional ways of life. Candidates seek to become the personal embodiment of the father-protector of the country, ready and able to use violence if necessary. This masculine persona is projected through candidates' physical appearance, speaking style, rhetoric, and even policy positions. Today, candidates routinely feminize their opponents in order to win, even if both contenders are male.[2]

The masculinity of presidential politics is part of a larger bias against women and femininity in U.S. political institutions. Philip Norton and Pippa Norris argue that gender "patterns of domination, subordination, and the exclusion of women are core elements to the historical development of our most basic institutions."[3] Women were formally excluded from participation in political institutions in the Constitution and continue to be informally excluded by biases that still define politics as a masculine, male domain. Cheryl King agrees that political institutions suffer from compulsory masculinist ideology, an ideology that both male and female leaders must adhere to.[4] Societal construction of effective leaders as masculine leaders benefits men and serves to generally exclude women from the highest echelons of power because "it is difficult for women to prove their allegiance to and mastery of the masculinist ideology."[5] The "traditionally masculine schema" of leadership includes being tough, competitive, and incisive and displaying initiative and intellectual acuity.[6] The "traditional feminine schema" traits are conscientiousness, consideration, flexibility, enthusiasm, and dedication, characteristics that run counter to expectations of hypermasculine presidential leadership. Women may wear masculinist ideology, but they cannot embody it because masculinity is seen as an exclusively male prerogative.[7] Georgia Duerst-Lahti writes that "executive political power is arguably the most manly of all areas,"[8] so its default occupant of the White House is implicitly male.

The importance of masculine ideology in American politics is apparent in the important role gender plays in presidential elections, even when both candidates are male. Candidates routinely employ "feminization" of their opponents as a weapon to win, meaning they describe their opponents in feminine terms in order to discredit them. This tactic works because U.S. culture devalues feminine traits and activities. Male identity is gained through a process of socialization whereby little boys learn what it means to "be a man" by rejecting everything that is feminine (e.g., anything pink, dolls), thus creating their identity through the subjugation of the feminine/female. This practice is so common that it is invisible, and boys and girls learn early on that men and masculinity have more social value than women and femininity. Both sexes internalize this to varying degrees, so the feminization of presidential opponents is effective because it exploits preexisting bias against femininity.

Beyond theory, empirical data support the idea that masculinity is linked to the presidency and that the most masculine candidate tends to win. Meredith Conroy examined the gender of adjectives (masculine, feminine, neutral) used to describe the candidates in print news coverage of Democratic and Republican presidential nominees from 1992 through

2012, a proxy measure of their degree of masculinity. Examples of masculine traits are "risk taker," "commanding," and "fighter," and for feminine traits, "compassionate," "cautious," and "caring."[9] Overall, 56 percent of the adjectives used to describe presidential candidates were neutral, while 30 percent were masculine and 14 percent were feminine.[10] The most common masculine traits were "aggressive" and "confident," and the most common feminine traits were "weak" and "inconsistent." Only 31 percent of the feminine traits were positive in tone, compared to 67 percent of masculine traits that were positive. This disparity means that presidential candidates were covered in much more masculine than feminine terms and that masculine traits were used to build up candidates while feminine traits were used to weaken them.

Conroy developed an aggregate gender score for the eight general-election-candidates she examined, ranging from -1 (entirely feminine descriptions) to 1 (entirely masculine descriptions). Figure 2.1 depicts each candidate's score. Conroy finds that in all but one election, the candidate with greater masculine association won the election. The exception was the 1996 Clinton-Dole election in the wake of sexual allegations that saw President Clinton positioning himself as a virtuous man, running from the "manly" label. In other words, the most masculine presidential candidate has won in every election except for one in the past two decades.

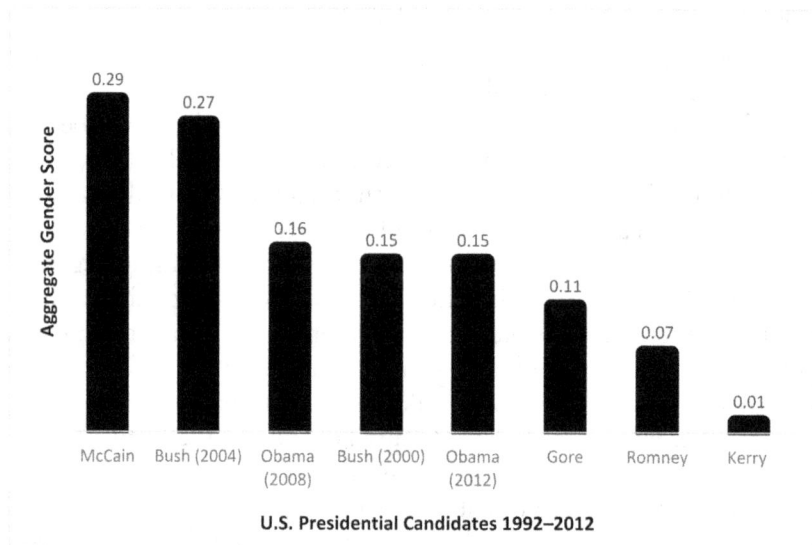

Figure 2.1   Gendered Descriptions of Candidates
Source: Conroy, Meredith. *Masculinity, Media, and the American Presidency.* New York: Palgrave Macmillan, 2015.

As figure 2.1 shows, all of the candidates had a score above zero, which means they were described in gender-neutral terms or masculine terms. George W. Bush (2004) and John McCain (2008) were described in the most masculine terms, while John Kerry (2004) and Mitt Romney (2012) were described in the least masculine terms. Conroy finds that gendered language was often used to invoke conflict between a more masculine candidate and a more feminine candidate. For example, in an article with the headline reading "LIVE FROM MIAMI!" imitating an announcer at a boxing match, a *New York Times* journalist pitted Kerry against Bush:

> In boxing terms, you could say a match-up between John Kerry and George W. Bush is a classic case of a dancer vs. a puncher. Mr. Kerry flicks around the periphery of issues; Mr. Bush pounds right through them.[11]

The reporter draws a contrast between feminine (dancer) and masculine (puncher) fighting styles and casts the masculine approach in more positive terms. When media use gender to contrast two men vying for the presidency, it reinforces a political culture of manliness premised on the notion that feminine attributes are less appropriate for presidential leadership. The conflation of masculinity and the presidency both lays the groundwork for a double standard for female candidates and furnishes a rationalization for exclusive male leadership in the White House.

WASHINGTON, ROOSEVELT, REAGAN, AND TRUMP

Candidates have used masculine personas to win the White House, but this strategy notably intensified with Theodore Roosevelt. As historian Sarah Watts notes, the masculine performance becomes more aggressive during times of social unrest, when the existing social order is shifting in terms of who holds power in society.[12] In other words, during times when the meaning and value of men and masculinity is uncertain, hypermasculine candidates who assuage fears of an uncertain world are more appealing to many voters. Roosevelt, Ronald Reagan, and Donald Trump stand out as the most hypermasculine presidential candidates, and we extend Watts's analysis to note that each rose to power during a time when the elevated position of white men in society was being challenged in profound ways. In this section, we briefly describe how history has revised Washington's masculine mystique, then analyze how Roosevelt, Reagan, and Trump crafted masculine personas to respond to a shifting social order. Their projections of hypermasculinity stand out as the most purposefully and aggressively masculine of the candidates who have run for the presidency.

George Washington entwined masculinity with the presidency simply by being the first to serve in the office and embody the manly ideals of a physically imposing war hero. Eric Garland writes that, as a rebel soldier fighting with guns, George Washington was "one of the original images of manhood in America."[13] The powdered wigs, breeches, silk stockings, and low-heeled shoes worn by Washington would be seen in a radically different light today, but at the time, he embodied the height of manliness. A man known for his humility and truth telling, Washington was more elder statesman than hypermasculine, although his masculine mystique has grown over time to fit the hypermasculine expectations of the presidency today. Satirist Brad Neely pokes fun at hyperbolic imaginings of Washington's masculinity in his animated short *Washington*. In this video, which has been viewed nearly five million times, Neely humorously describes the first president as "six foot twenty fucking killing for fun," having sex with bears, throwing a knife into heaven, and killing with just a stare.[14] The video also refers to Washington having "30 goddamn dicks," aligning presidential masculinity with male genitalia in similar fashion to the Indecline statutes of Trump and discussions of penis size during the 2016 GOP primary. This video resonated with a wide audience because it plays upon common conceptions of Washington as a hypermasculine figure, hyperbolically capable of superhuman physical feats.

A century later, Teddy Roosevelt (president from 1901 to 1909) was the first to explicitly use a hypermasculine persona to win the White House. With rhetorical bravado framing him as a masculine protector, he appealed to voters who felt uneasy in a time of shifting social roles. Watts writes that "Roosevelt emerged as a central purveyor of the cowboy-soldier hero model because he more than any man of his age harnessed the tantalizing freedom of cowboys to address the social and psychological needs that arose from deep personal sources of frustration, anxiety, and fear."[15] The country was going through a transitional period with the abolition of slavery and women's demands for civil rights, both of which posed a serious challenge to the existing social order and unearned privilege of white men.

Roosevelt's masculine persona was anything but natural, which illustrates how gender is socially constructed. Roosevelt grew up a coddled, aristocratic child who was weak and sickly, as he was plagued by asthma. As an adult, Roosevelt led an active life, but it was a far cry from the rugged image of cowboy masculinity he projected. When he first entered politics, winning a seat in the New York legislature in 1883, Roosevelt was mocked by his fellow assemblymen for being effeminate. According to James Bradley, he was a "shrimp-size dandy, dressed in tight-fitting, tailor-made suits, a rich daddy's boy who read books and collected but-terflies."[16] Roosevelt's first speech on the assembly floor elicited laughter because he was sporting a purple satin suit and "being seen as effeminate was a death sentence for an aspiring politician."[17] So Roosevelt had to reinvent himself so he could be an effective politician. He modeled his brand of cowboy masculinity after William Cody's popular *Buffalo Bill's Wild West* show. Roosevelt created a fictional biography of years spent on the frontier, farming, hunting wild animals, and subduing outlaws. In reality, he had occasionally traveled west in luxury train cars to check on investments.[18] Roosevelt used visual mediums to craft his masculine per-sona, planning elaborate photo shoots, which were published in the popu-lar newspapers of the day, showing him as a tough frontiersman, ready and able to fight with weapons in the wild.

Gender is socially constructed, which means that masculinity is always a performance, and for Roosevelt, it was explicitly so. He decided what brand of masculinity he wanted to project and went about skillfully craft-ing and conveying that brand. Roosevelt's presentation of masculinity was notable for its fictional basis, hyperbolic presentation, and effectiveness. His persona allayed the fears of people, especially white men, by providing a hyperbolic presentation of classic masculinity during a time when it was being questioned in many quarters. Similar to the political climate that elevated Trump in 2016, the existing social order during Roosevelt's time was shifting, and white men were no longer unquestionably on top of the pecking order. Like Trump's, Roosevelt's brand of masculinity explicitly reasserted white male privilege in the White House, which was reassuring to his supporters. In 2005, Harvey Mansfield praised Roosevelt's manli-ness in terms that could easily be used to describe Trump's appeal:

> The most obvious feature of Theodore Roosevelt's life and thought is the one least celebrated today, his manliness. . . . TR appeals to some conserva-tives today for his espousal of big government and national greatness, and all conservatives rather relish his political incorrectness.[19]

Like Roosevelt, and later Trump, Ronald Reagan also projected an inflated masculine persona. Reagan cultivated an old-school masculin-ity—aggressive and forceful, a straight-shooting cowboy who tells it like it is instead of being overly intellectual. According to Jackson Katz, Rea-gan's mythic manhood was a calculated response to a rapidly shifting social order brought about by the women's liberation movement, the civil rights movement, the gay rights movement, and the student-led move-ment against the Vietnam War.[20] Reagan's brand of masculinity harkened back to the classic masculinity that Roosevelt conjured, offering a calm projection of stasis in a shifting social sea. Like Roosevelt's, Reagan's masculinity was an intentional performance. Reagan grew up in a small town in Illinois, and his upbringing and life as an actor had little connection to the rugged cowboys he would later play in Hollywood films and the White House.

Katz notes that Reagan was a master manipulator of political symbols who skillfully tapped into the myth of the American cowboy, a strong, silent man who rescues a country that has been emasculated by equality movements and the loss of the Vietnam War. "John Wayne wasn't available. Ronald Reagan was the next best thing."[21] Victoria Bekiempis notes that "cowboy politicians" like Reagan "attract men who are worried about their changing—and potentially waning—place in the United States."[22] Republicans have taken up the hypermasculine presidential persona more so than Democratic candidates in the modern political era, leading journalist Amanda Marcotte to refer to the GOP as the "Party of Anxious Masculinity."[23]

Mass media, and in particular, entertainment media, has also reinforced a heightened masculine norm for the presidency in the modern political age. Numerous films and television shows have buoyed the masculine archetype of the "warrior" president with fictional presidents. For example, in *Independence Day* (1996), Bill Pullman plays a president who uses his fighter-pilot skills to save the world. Harrison Ford's president in *Air Force One* (1997) personally foils a terrorist attempt, as do Jamie Foxx's president in *White House Down* (2013) and Aaron Eckhart's president in *Olympus Has Fallen* (2013). This model of heroic leadership helps to shape the expectations of presidential manliness that permeate the campaign trail leading up to each election.

As we explore throughout this book, like Roosevelt and Reagan before him, Trump made gender (masculinity) a central pillar in his campaign. Trump projected masculine bravado through threats of violence against protesters at his rallies and through a narrative of fictional blue-collar roots. He reinforced his masculinity by deriding Hillary Clinton's "strength" and "stamina" in ways that made the contest about who was "man enough" for the job.[24] Trump used loaded rhetoric on the campaign trail to speak to his base about a shifting social order where immigrants; lesbian, gay, bisexual, and transgender (LGBT) individuals; women; and people of color pose a threat to the existing social and economic structure. He offered a brash reassertion of masculinity during a time in American history when people of color were pushing back against police brutality with new vigor, women were pushing back against sexual harassment and sexual violence with more success, and LGBT individuals had gained considerable new rights through legislation and court decisions.

MASCULINITY IN THE MODERN POLITICAL ERA

The presidency has always been a contest of manhood, but even more so in the post-Reagan mass media era of politics, in which the persona a candidate can craft is more important in determining electoral outcomes than experience or actual traits. The rules of presidential masculinity present a great challenge to a woman running for the presidency,[25] but they also pose a challenge to male contenders. As noted in the first section of this chapter, the more masculine candidate won virtually every election for the past two decades, leading Conroy to conclude that masculinity is a key variable in determining electoral success for the presidency. In this section, we provide examples of how masculinity mattered in the 1988, 2004, and 2012 elections to demonstrate its persistent influence in elections with very different candidates. We selected these three contests because they fall in the post-Reagan era, span different decades, and provide the starkest examples of the importance of masculinity in presidential contests.

The 1988 Election

The 1988 election pitted tough-talking Republican vice president George H. W. Bush against Democratic Massachusetts governor Michael Dukakis. Both candidates performed masculine bravado, and both were feminized in the press. But by the end of the race, Dukakis had effectively been framed as softer and weaker—less presidential—and Bush handily won 53.4 percent to 45.6 percent.[26] Here, we highlight how gender mattered in this election.

Bush's feminization started before he formally announced he was running for president, through constant comparisons to Reagan, with whom he served as vice president. Before the official campaign kicked off, *Newsweek* magazine ran a cover story with a narrative about Bush that was popular at the time: "Bush Battles the 'Wimp Factor.' "[27] Although Bush stood tall at six feet, two inches; played on the baseball team at Yale; was a prisoner of war during World War II; and had been director of the Central Intelligence Agency, he was still less manly than Reagan's projected persona. Bush's wimp label was nothing new. It had emerged years earlier, when Bush was first selected as Reagan's running mate and Garry Trudeau, author of the cartoon strip *Doonesbury*, depicted Bush putting his manhood in a blind trust because he adopted Reagan's more conservative positions (e.g., opposing abortion). Perceptions of Bush as a follower under Reagan's hypermasculine persona made him seem wimpy, incapable of being president, until he was pitted against a competitor who was framed as even more feminine.

Dukakis had a few high-profile events that effectively feminized him in the minds of voters, thus making him unfit for the presidency. First there was the tank ride. In an effort to appear macho against a competitor who fought in World War II and won the Distinguished Flying Cross and three Air Medals, Dukakis participated in a photo opportunity in a tank, riding across rough terrain. This tactic backfired when a video surfaced of the Democratic nominee looking diminutive in the enormous tank, wearing an oversized helmet with his name stenciled across the front. The Bush campaign worked to keep the image in the press, and one popular Bush ad looped the Dukakis tank footage with the message, "Now he wants to be our commander in chief? America can't afford that risk."

Dukakis also had a significant feminizing moment during a presidential debate when the moderator asked him a question about his wife: "Governor, if Kitty Dukakis were raped and murdered, would you favor an irrevocable death penalty for the killer?"[28] Dukakis countered with a campaign-ending response, "No, I don't. . . . and I think you know that I've opposed the death penalty during all of my life." Dukakis was widely criticized for the coldness of his response, but gender also came into play. By not seeking revenge against someone who harmed his wife (after failing to protect her in this hypothetical scenario), Dukakis defied norms of classic masculinity premised on men being the protectors of women. Dukakis was perceived as not "man enough" to fill the helmet or to properly protect or avenge his wife.

The 2004 Election

The 2004 presidential election also pitted the feminine schema against the masculine schema. George W. Bush, the son of the 41st president, was running for reelection against Massachusetts senator John Kerry, a decorated war veteran. As president, George W. Bush had earned historically high approval ratings after the terrorist attacks of September 11, 2001, but by the middle of his reelection bid, his approval ratings had dropped to their lowest point in his presidency, with only 42 percent of Americans viewing him favorably.[29] With waning support for the Iraq War, the election could have gone either way. In the end, Bush won with 53.2 percent of the vote to Kerry's 46.7 percent, another victory for a "macho man" candidate over a feminized one.[30]

President George W. Bush cultivated a masculine cowboy persona reminiscent of Reagan's. During his first term, masculinity was central to his
practice of the presidency. For example, he sold the idea of the Iraq War
using the intensely masculinized rhetoric of strength and dominance to
justify the invasion.[31] Bush also projected the image of "the decider," a
commanding man who makes decisions and does not change his mind.
Bush used military imagery to buttress his presidential masculinity. In
2003, he staged a landing on USS *Abraham Lincoln* to announce "mission
accomplished" in Iraq. Wary of replaying a Dukakis moment, Bush made
sure to remove his helmet as soon as he deplaned.

Bush's competitor in the 2004 election was Massachusetts senator John
Kerry, a decorated Vietnam War veteran. Despite his extensive military
experience and potential for masculine bravado, Kerry was framed as feminine against Bush's macho cowboy masculinity. Kerry's "feminine" communication style of erudite and lengthy explanations during debates made
him look less resolute than "the decider." The Bush campaign framed
Kerry's reversal of support for the Iraq War with the feminizing "flip-flop"
narrative. Many political leaders had changed their position on the wildly
unpopular Iraq War by the 2004 election, so the issue was not Kerry's
newfound policy position but rather the fact that he had changed his
mind at all. In an October 2004 poll, nearly 40 percent of voters reported
that the "flip-flop" charge made them less likely to vote for Kerry.[32] The
Bush camp used rhetoric of the president as a masculine "decider" against
the vision of feminized "flip-floppers" to portray a normal part of politics
(shifting policy positions) as a deal breaker for the presidency, and for
some voters, it was.

The Bush campaign and partisan press also overtly feminized Kerry
through innuendo that he is gay and feminine. Right-wing reporter James
Dale Guckert (who used the alias Jeff Gannon while working in the White
House press corps) published a piece claiming that Kerry "might someday
be known as "the first gay president.""[33] Fox News frequently discussed
Kerry in feminized terms. In the three hours leading up to the first debate,
Fox News commentators discussed Kerry's "pre-debate manicure" five
times and criticized his "fake tan."[34] Popular Fox News host Bill O'Reilly
challenged Kerry's masculinity head-on, asking, "What do you think
Osama bin Laden's going to think about this spray-on tan? Is that going to
frighten him? I don't know if it will."[35] After the debate, Fox News posted
an article on its Web site with made-up quotes in which Kerry refers to
himself as a "metrosexual" and fawns over his nails. Fox issued a retraction and apology, but Kerry's possible gayness continued to be the butt of
late-night talk shows. Senator Kerry fought his "feminization" by staging

sporty photo ops (e.g., windsurfing, snowboarding, tossing a football on the tarmac), but these measures and his battle cry of "bring it on" could not restore his manliness in the eyes of many voters.

The 2012 Election

Masculinity was a key theme of the 2012 presidential election, when Barack Obama ran for reelection against Massachusetts governor Willard "Mitt" Romney. In that election, Romney was the feminized candidate. From the start of the race, he was criticized by other Republicans and in the press as too weak for the office—a wimp. A *Newsweek* headline proclaimed "Mitt Romney: A Candidate with a Serious Wimp Problem." [36] The article compared Romney to Reagan: "A Republican president sure of his manhood [Reagan] has nothing to prove. . . . But a weenie Republican [Romney]—look out." The *Washington Post* ran an article with the headline "Mitt Romney and the Wimp Factor."[37] The *Atlantic* published an article with the title "Growing Concern that Romney's a Wimp."[38] Romney grew up in Detroit, Michigan, where his father served as governor. His social conservatism, blue-collar persona, and Republican partisanship paved the way for him to perform a convincing brand of presidential masculinity, but his primary competitors were successful in feminizing him. When contrasted with former Pennsylvania senator Rick Santorum's fiery rhetoric and masculine persona, Romney's focus on policy proposals made him seem weak.

Romney was running against Obama, a man described during the 2012 campaign in a *Washington Post* headline as "Barack Obama, the First Female President" for his erudite policy focus and "feminine" communication style.[39] But Obama's blackness made it difficult to effectively feminize him. Prevailing stereotypes of men of color as hypermasculine and violent, which are otherwise harmful, can become an advantage with requisite presidential masculinism, but using that advantage necessitates a strategic gender performance that avoids association with what Frank Cooper calls the "Bad Black Man" archetype.[40] In other words, men of color who are presidential candidates are not easily feminized, but they cannot perform hypermasculinity because it will trigger racial stereotypes for some voters. Katz argues that stereotypes of black masculinity helped him fend off concerted efforts from the right to feminize him by labeling him a "lightweight" and a "wimp."[41] Voters in the 2012 election saw Obama as possessing the masculine traits of being elusive and strategic, while Romney was framed in feminine terms as "wishy-washy," reminiscent of Kerry's feminizing "flip-flop" frame in 2004.[42] Obama handily beat Romney 61.7 percent to 38.3 percent in the popular vote.[43]

Masculinity in the 2016 Republican Primary

Gender (masculinity) played a prominent role in shaping candidate interactions in the 2016 Republican primary. The field went from a packed roster of seventeen candidates down to Trump, the GOP nominee who broke the records for Republican votes both for and against him.[44] Trump frequently used feminization against his opponents, as did other candidates. The 2016 Republican primary saw more masculine preening than any other race in modern political history. Candidates attacked one another's appearance, clothing, and penis size and asserted their masculinity in less-than-subtle ways to convince voters they were the manliest in the pack.

Candidates used dress and appearance as weapons to feminize their opponents. For example, Florida senator Marco Rubio was relentlessly feminized by the press and other candidates after photos were published showing him wearing boots with a heel.[45] It all started when *New York Times* reporter Michael Barbaro tweeted a photo of Rubio's boots while covering him on the campaign trail in New Hampshire.

Texas senator Ted Cruz's communications director quickly tweeted, "A Vote for Marco Rubio Is a Vote for Men's High-Heeled Booties," with a link to an article with a photo of Rubio's boots. Another Cruz campaign staffer attempted to characterize Rubio as both feminine and elitist with a tweet saying, "Rubio supports Italian boots on the ground." Former Florida governor and GOP candidate Jeb Bush also capitalized on the opportunity to feminize Rubio, noting that Bush purchased new shoes to brave the New Hampshire snow that were "not high heeled."[46] The press also had a field day feminizing Rubio, giving this nonstory ample airtime in which commentators referred to his footwear as "girly little girl boots"[47] and "straight out of an Austin Powers movie."[48] Rubio's critics insinuated that he was homosexual for adorning himself with fancy boots and dressing like a woman, both of which are unacceptable to a large swath of Republican voters because they defy prevailing norms of heterosexual American manhood. Rubio responded by reasserting his masculinity by letting the press know that he had spent Christmas Eve buying a gun in order to defend his family should it be necessary.[49]

Texas governor Rick Perry asserted his masculinity with Trump in the 2016 election using physical prowess as the measure. Perry emerged as the strongest critic of Trump early in the 2016 race, and Trump responded by calling Perry a "low energy" candidate and questioned whether he had the energy and "brain power" to run a successful campaign. Perry responded by challenging Trump to a pull-up contest at the gym.[50] Perry pitted his cowboy masculinity against Trump's straight-shooter masculinity, challenging him to a physical contest that had nothing to do with executing the office of the presidency. Perry surrogates also needled Trump for the mismatch between his masculine persona and his apparel. One of Perry's senior strategists tweeted, "This is what a Manhattan 'tough guy' wears to the southern border. White golf shoes and a linen jacket."[51]

Trump also used gender-laden language to feminize Texas senator Ted Cruz, one of his most formidable opponents in the 2016 GOP primary. One day before the New Hampshire primary in February 2016, a woman close to the stage at a Trump rally called Cruz a "pussy" because Cruz opposes the torture technique of waterboarding.[52] The audience could not hear her gender slur, so Trump asked her to shout it out. When that did not work in the large auditorium, Trump jokingly told the audience, "She just said a terrible thing . . . she said he's a pussy." The crowd roared with laughter. Trump later repeated this feminizing gender slur at other campaign events. Trump further feminized Cruz by referring to him as a "soft, weak little baby" at a campaign rally in Nevada.[53] Cruz asserted his masculinity at various times during the campaign by making a video of his machine-gun-cooked bacon and by wild-duck hunting in full camouflage gear in Louisiana with *Duck Dynasty* patriarch Phil Robertson.[54]

Male anatomy was prominently featured in the 2016 election in a way previously unseen in presidential politics. For most of the campaign, Trump tried to feminize Rubio by nicknaming him "Little Marco," and in response, Rubio made comments about Trump's physical appearance (telling an audience that Trump doesn't sweat because "his pores are clogged from the spray tan"[55]) and joked about the size of Trump's penis. During a February 2016 rally in Virginia, Rubio implied that Trump had a small penis by remarking, "You know what they say about guys with small hands. . . ."[56] Well before the election, Trump was known to be concerned about his hand size in reference to a *Spy Magazine* article written nearly thirty years ago that described Trump as a "short-fingered vulgarian."[57] Graydon Carter, the author of the article, reports that Trump was very bothered by the description challenging his manhood and that Trump still sends him occasional photos from magazines with his fingers circled. So Rubio was playing upon a Trump insecurity with his insinuation that Trump has small hands and therefore a small penis. Trump defended his hand/penis size at the next presidential debate:

> [Rubio] hit my hands. Nobody has ever hit my hands, I've never heard of this before. Look at those hands, are they small hands? And he referred to my hands, "if they're small something else must be small." I guarantee you there's no problem, I guarantee it.

This was the first presidential debate in U.S. history during which penis size was openly discussed. Candidates have never been so explicit in revealing that the presidential contest is fundamentally a contest of manhood.

Gary Legum notes that the 2016 GOP primary stands out in terms of masculine bravado in presidential elections: "This level of chest-thumping, as if the candidates were competing to see which one of them can be the troop's dominant silverback, would be laughable if it didn't work so well on the GOP base."[58] One young white man interviewed by David Frum explained Trump's masculine appeal:

> We feel masculine traits are devalued everywhere. It's more than just, "Oh, the dad's a jerk in commercials." Rather like gay people a generation ago, young men today feel that they're being treated as if they were born *wrong*. We didn't live through the Reagan years. We've never seen a *man's man* in politics before. Trump offers a sense that someone sees them and cares about speaking to them, even if only as far as it takes to con them.[59]

And indeed it worked. Trump, the candidate who embraced male anxiety as a campaign strategy, a veritable caricature of a "man's man," outmanned the competition and won the Republican primary.

CONCLUSION

Masculinity has been entwined with the presidency since the founding, and that matters for American politics. Gender roles are socially constructed, so there is nothing natural about presidential candidate personas. They reflect strategic decisions, often made over many years. A sickly aristocrat can assume the persona of a rough-and-tumble frontiersman. An actor living a comfortable life can assume a rugged cowboy persona. Especially hypermasculine presidential candidates win elections during times when conventions and traditions are under threat in a shifting social order. At key moments in American history when women, people of color, LGBT individuals, and others have gained more power in society, candidates that caricature classic masculine ideals have ascended to the presidency. Theodore Roosevelt, Reagan, and Trump won the presidency at least in part by assuaging fears of a shifting social order through their masculine performance. Even in times of relatively stable social order, presidential candidates use masculinity to win the office, and the candidate seen as most masculine almost always wins.

The link between masculinity and the presidency is problematic for several reasons. First and foremost, it is a performance, an idea based on stereotypes that appeal to emotions, and is therefore not a good criterion for assessing candidate quality. Candidates are judged on how well they conform to and project a brand of masculinity that fits with voters' fears and concerns of the day. Gender performance on the campaign trail is a facade, a creation meant to form an impression in the minds of voters, and as such, it is always artificial and fundamentally misleading. Judging presidential candidates on how well they perform masculinity is akin to judging actors on their foreign policy leadership, but that is what voters do each and every election.

Masculinity as a criterion for winning the presidency is also problematic in that it presents a barrier for half of American citizens: women. Most Americans associate being masculine with being male and in fact judge masculine women harshly for violating gender norms, which makes it virtually impossible for a female candidate to be seen as properly masculine for the office. The way we discuss men in American politics has a trickle-down effect on women because our discussions contribute to a broader understanding of what characteristics are and are not appropriate for political leadership. When we rely on masculine terms to elevate male candidates and feminine qualities to debase male candidates, we are essentially elevating men and debasing women. The masculine presidency has historically excluded half of the population from holding this office, which is fundamentally undemocratic, and has served to define political leadership in narrow, male terms.

Masculinity linked to the presidency also leads to less than ideal policy making. Elizabeth Debold writes that "Western notions of masculinity, heroism, and leadership have been deeply entwined since before the time that Homer told the story of the *Odyssey*. . . . Therefore, what we value in men tends to describe our ideas of what it means to be a leader."[60] But scholarship on leadership shows that heroic or masculine leadership is not the most effective type. Daniel Goleman identifies six primary types of leadership in the corporate sphere, and those types readily apply to political leadership: "Coercive leaders demand immediate compliance. Authoritative leaders mobilize people toward a vision. Affiliative leaders create emotional bonds and harmony. Democratic leaders build consensus through participation. Pacesetting leaders expect excellence and self-direction. And coaching leaders develop people for the future."[61] The most effective leaders use all six types of leadership instead of sticking with one or two approaches. Adopting a staunchly masculine form of leadership (coercive and authoritarian) is limiting in ways that produce bad policy. For example, had George W. Bush been flexible with his decision-making processes instead of branding himself "the decider," he may have reacted with more flexibility to the burgeoning situation in Iraq and changed course as new information came in. Instead, as "the decider," he was locked into defending his decision, even when it became clear that his invasion and occupation would not achieve their desired goals. Little scholarship exists on how masculine posturing with the presidency compromises effective policy making, but research on corporate leadership shows that leadership that incorporates stereotypically feminine traits is more effective, and women in leadership at high-performing companies who have more social leeway to incorporate feminine leadership traits are rated more favorably than male leaders.[62]

When Indecline was asked whether there were any plans in the works for a Clinton statue, their spokesperson stated, "Hillary doesn't deserve a statue. But now that we're talking about it, we'll probably do one anyway—and give her a huge wiener." This humorous retort buttresses the message that a large penis symbolizes power. The Trump statues attempt subversion but end up recycling the tired, sexist trope that leadership means manliness. In the next chapter, we analyze the treatment of twelve women who have made serious bids for the presidency in the highly masculinized environment of presidential politics.

CHAPTER 3

"A Different Hill Than Men Have to Climb": Women Who Have Run for the Presidency

One of the ways that women who run for the presidency are disadvantaged is through revisionist history that frames their bid as unique or "the first."[1] To date, more than 100 woman have sought their party's nomination,[2] and 12 women have made major bids.[3] The "first woman" narrative has negative electoral consequences because it implies that "women are anomalies in high public office, [and] the public is likely to regard them as bench warmers rather than as an integral part of government."[4] In 2016, Hillary Clinton made it further in the presidential selection process than any previous female candidate, but she faced many of the same challenges of the women who ran before her.

In this chapter, we analyze the presidential runs of the 12 women who mounted major campaigns from 1872 to 2016[5] to see whether there are patterns of gender bias. For each candidate, we briefly describe her background and look at how she was discussed in public discourse. For female presidential candidates through 2008, we rely heavily on Erika Falk's analysis in *Women for President: Media Bias in Nine Campaigns*.[6] Falk examines public discourse about female candidates and similarly situated male candidates using a content analysis of media coverage. We supplement and update Falk's work with additional studies and analysis of the female candidates who ran in the 2012 and 2016 elections. We find remarkably consistent patterns of gender bias over the 130 years women have seriously sought this office.

We begin this chapter with a summary of the patterns of bias experienced by female presidential candidates. In the second section, we describe the experiences of the 12 women who ran for the presidency, in chronological order.

GENDER BIAS IN PRESIDENTIAL ELECTIONS

Female presidential candidates have experienced gendered bias in public discourse (as measured by media coverage) since the first woman sought the office in 1872. This bias comes in five primary forms: (1) higher rates of negative coverage; (2) greater questioning of candidate validity; (3) the casting of women as less serious contenders (through less over-all coverage, less issue-based coverage, and the dropping of professional titles); (4) stereotypically gendered coverage (through "soft sexism," such as ambition shaming, discussing them in emotional terms, mentioning their family, focusing on appearance, and gender marking, and through "hard sexism," such as sexual objectification and openly gendered insults); and (5) double-bind expectations—female candidates are criticized for not being sufficiently "masculine" or for being "too masculine" and defy-ing gender norms. These gender biases establish a clear double standard that undemocratically privileges male presidential candidates.

The first presidential gender bias is negative public discourse about female candidates. The tone of coverage for female presidential candidates is significantly more negative than press about male candidates, a pattern that has held over time.[7] Female presidential candidates from different political parties and professional backgrounds are consistently covered more negatively than similarly situated male candidates, which indicates that this bias stems from gender and not candidate merit.

The second major gender bias is a persistent pattern of questioning the viability of female candidates more than male contenders. All 12 female candidates had their viability questioned in different ways. The first six candidates were outright dismissed as novelty candidates in pub-lic discourse. Elizabeth Dole's bid in 2000 was the first time that any mainstream press covered a female presidential candidate as a serious contender, but Dole and candidates since continue to face questions of their viability. For example, the press frequently suggest that women who run under major party labels are actually running for the vice presidency, implying that the second in command is a more fitting goal for women.

The third major gender bias is a multitude of ways the press implicitly cast female candidates as less serious contenders. One way is to simply cover female candidates less. Falk finds that, on average, male candidates with the same credentials and public support had twice as many articles written about them, and their articles were longer on average.[8] This coverage varies somewhat by election, but the gap has remained over time. The press also signals that female candidates are less serious contenders with the subtle but powerful practice of dropping their professional titles, such as "senator" or "governor." According to Falk, men's professional titles are dropped 11 percent of the time compared to 32 percent of the time for women, and women are more likely to be referred to by their first name, especially in newspaper headlines.[9] Female candidates also receive less issue-based coverage than their male competitors, which signals they are less policy oriented and thus less serious about holding the presidency. On average, male presidential candidates receive 68 percent more paragraphs written about issues than female candidates receive.[10] The amount of issue coverage has declined over time for female presidential candidates but not male candidates, even though female candidates typically run more issue-driven campaigns.[11]

A fourth gender bias comes in the form of covering female candidates in stereotypically gendered ways that diminish their electability. One way is ambition shaming—casting competitive female candidates as unworthy of their frontrunner position because it violates gender expectations. On the two occasions when a female candidate has been truly competitive in a primary (Clinton in 2008 and 2016), she faced unprecedented calls to prematurely exit the race that similarly situated males have never faced.[12] Female candidates are also significantly more likely to be covered in emotional terms than their male competitors, which reinforces stereotypes of women as emotional instead of rational beings. According to Falk, reporters discuss female candidates in emotional terms twice as often as they do male candidates.[13] The emotional stereotype harms the electability of female candidates because it runs against the grain of masculinity expected for the office. Public discourse is also gendered through a disproportionate focus on the family and personal lives of women who run. Female presidential candidates are twice as likely as male candidates to have their families mentioned in news coverage, and this has remained constant over time.[14] Mentions of family and personal life remind voters that women are traditionally aligned with the caretaking roles of wife and mother, feminized roles that run counter to the masculinity associated with the presidency.

Female candidates are also delegitimized through a focus on their physical appearance that reduces perceptions of their agency and power. Falk finds that reporters mention female candidates' dress and appearance far more often than those of male candidates—four times the amount.[15] This ratio has not shifted over time, and female candidates today face the same focus on their physical appearance as candidates did a century ago. Female presidential candidates from 2008 on are also more likely to be sexualized in media coverage than male candidates. Sexual objectification is the process of turning a human being (who acts) to an object (that is acted upon),[16] and voters see sex objects as less competent, moral, and warm.[17] Female candidates have been sexualized in recent campaigns through references to their cleavage and their sexual attractiveness.

Another way public discourse is gendered is the fact that gender is remarked upon for female but not male candidates, especially in headlines. This practice of gender marking may appear neutral, but instead, "women are portrayed as though they are hampered by their gender, whereas men are portrayed as gender-free."[18] The fact that men's gender is unremarkable in presidential contests both is a function of and reinforces the idea that male candidates are the norm and that female candidates are "other." Gender marking also reinforces assumptions that gender matters when it comes to executing the ostensibly gender-neutral office of the presidency.

A fifth major gender bias comes in the form of the double bind where female candidates are judged harshly for not achieving the standard of masculinity required for the presidency or are judged as violating norms of femininity for being "too masculine." One way that women's fitness for the office is challenged is through press framing them as frail or sick, as though they lack the physical stamina to withstand the requirements of the office. The "frail" frame has been especially prominent in recent campaigns, for example, Michele Bachmann's headaches in 2012 and speculation about Hillary Clinton's health in her two presidential bids.

Falk finds that early female presidential candidates faced the double bind through coverage that cast them as violating the "culture of true woman-hood," defined as piety, pureness, submissiveness, and domesticity.[19] As gender roles evolved over time, Falk finds that female candidates continue to be judged in more subtle ways for violating societal expectations of femininity. Republican female presidential candidates are especially prone to the double bind because religious voters hold more conservative ideas about proper gender roles. Evangelical Protestants, Nazarenes, and Southern Baptists vote Republican by sizeable margins,[20] and they all follow the patriarchal religious teaching that wives should submit to their husbands.

The gender biases in presidential campaigns have become more pronounced in the last decade, as female candidates today face a more hostile media environment than candidates of previous eras. Gender bias is plentiful in legacy media, meaning traditional news sources with editorial filters that follow well-established journalistic standards. New media became popular in the early 2000s with the rise of blogs and opinion-driven cable news that has fewer editorial filters. Discourse around female candidates is more sexist in new media than in legacy media,[21] but the sexist content of social media exceeds both legacy and new media. Social media—user-generated content that is shared in multiple platforms (e.g., Facebook, Twitter, Instagram, reader comments on legacy and new media sources)—emerged in the mid-2000s. Today, 62 percent of Americans get news through social media, much of it curated with user opinion.[22] More people report seeing sexism in social media than in new or legacy media,[23] and the discourse around female presidential candidates in new media is rife with sexist descriptions and slurs. For example, the "bitch" frame, a gender slur that epitomizes the double bind, is used as a matter of course for female presidential candidates in social media.

TWELVE WOMEN WHO RAN FOR PRESIDENT

Twelve women have made major bids for the presidency: Victoria Woodhull (1872); Belva Lockwood (1884 and 1888); Margaret Chase Smith (1964); Shirley Chisholm (1972); Patricia Schroeder (1988); Lenora Fulani (1988 and 1992); Elizabeth Dole (2000); Carol Moseley Braun (2004); Hillary Clinton (2008 and 2016); Michele Bachmann (2012); Jill Stein (2012 and 2016); and Carly Fiorina (2016).[24] Eight out of the twelve female presidential candidates ran on a major party label (Smith, Chisholm, Schroeder, Dole, Moseley Braun, Clinton, Bachmann, and Fiorina), while four ran for a third party (Woodhull, Lockwood, Fulani, and Stein). Half of the major party candidates were Democrats (Chisholm, Schroeder, Moseley Braun, and Clinton), and half were Republicans (Smith, Dole, Bachmann, and Fiorina). We describe each candidate and the gender biases she faced in chronological order.

Victoria Woodhull (1872)

Victoria Woodhull (1838–1927) was the first woman to run for president of the United States in 1872—nearly five decades before women won the right to vote. She was "scandalously" married three times and had previously worked as a clairvoyant and fortune teller. Woodhull had may "firsts," including being the first woman to ever petition Congress in person, the first female stockbroker, and the first woman to open a brokerage house on Wall Street (with her sister, Tennessee Claflin). Woodhull was a forceful advocate for the idea that women already had the right to vote under Fourteenth and Fifteenth Amendment guarantees of protection for the rights of all citizens. She petitioned Congress with this claim, and her skillful presentation elevated her to a leadership position in the suffrage movement. Woodhull also ran a national feminist newspaper with her sister.

Woodhull formally announced her bid for the presidency in 1870 with a letter to the editor of the *New York Herald* and was formally nominated by the Equal Rights Party in 1872. Abolitionist leader Frederick Douglass was nominated as her vice president (although he never accepted or acknowledged the nomination and gave stump speeches for the Republican incumbent, Ulysses S. Grant). One Electoral College elector from Texas cast a vote for Woodhull, but she was never taken seriously as a presidential candidate. She attempted to gain nominations for the presidency in 1884 and 1892, but her political career had peaked with her first presidential run.

During Woodhull's candidacy, the press described her presidential bid as "unnatural" and framed her as not viable. In 1872, one columnist wrote: "She is rather in advance of her time. The public mind is not yet educated to the pitch of universal women's rights."[25] Woodhull's press coverage focused extensively on her family life. The press was "obsessed" with her ex-husbands, her current relationships, and her sister. Woodhull actually received more press coverage than her comparable male competitor because the *New York Herald* paid an inordinate amount of attention to her personal life.[26] Erica Falk finds that four in ten articles made mention of Woodhull's family and personal life.[27] Press coverage of Woodhull also mentioned her appearance in gendered ways. For example, an 1872 *New York Times* editorial mentioned her "dainty high-heeled boots."[28]

The press also frequently discussed Woodhull in emotional terms. She was described as part of the "sorrowful sisterhood" of women who neglected their husbands and was said to lack the proper emotions for a woman.[29] Woodhull faced the double bind in that she was described in terms befitting presidential masculinity—"ambitious," "strong minded," "independent," "commanding power"—but these traits were held against her.[30] The press labeled her as "soiled," "naughty," and "notorious" for projecting traits that went against the grain of "true womanhood."[31]

Belva Lockwood (1884, 1888)

Suffragette and educator Belva Lockwood (1830–1917) was one of the first female attorneys in the United States and the first woman allowed to practice before the U.S. Supreme Court. Lockwood ran for the presidency in 1884 and 1888 and was the first woman to appear on ballots. She was nominated by the National Equal Rights Party. Born into a poor family in upstate New York, Lockwood started teaching at age 14, and she protested that her pay was half that of male teachers. She later worked as a principal, peace activist, equal pay advocate, and proponent of temperance. She was initially refused her law school diploma because of her gender, but she appealed to President Grant and received her diploma a few days later. Lockwood effectively lobbied Congress on bills ensuring women equal pay for equal work, equal access to the legal bar, guardianship rights, and equal property rights. She won a $5 million settlement from the government on behalf of the Cherokee Nation, recompense for tribal lands.

Lockwood was never treated as a serious contender for the presidency in public discourse, owing to the fact that she was a woman and was running under a third-party label. She garnered a total of approximately 4,100 votes across the two elections, an unusually high number since political leaders and newspaper editors openly trivialized and mocked her candidacy. For example, the *Atlanta Constitution* called her "old lady Lockwood" and warned its readers of the dangers of "petticoat rule." The *Boston Globe* ran an article titled "Belva in the White House: A Cabinet Meeting of the Period When Women Shall Steer the Ship of State," in which they describe her as being obsessed with clothing and appearance and unable to fulfill her duties because it would interfere with her hairdo.[32] The *New York Times* ran a satirical piece about Lockwood around the "divided skirt question" of whether women should wear full-length pants, which was so taxing on Lockwood that it made her ill.[33] Framing female candidates as physically frail or ill has been a common refrain in presidential elections since.

Lockwood was also cast in stereotypically negative emotional terms, as a fearful, anxious candidate who lacked the constitution for the office.[34] Her femininity was openly mocked at campaign stops by "Belva Lockwood Clubs," groups of men who paraded in dresses, bonnets, and stockings.[35] Lockwood's physical appearance was mentioned frequently in articles; for example, a *New York Times* series questioned the quality of her hair and the color of her underpants, asking if they were "cardinal red."[36] Lockwood was occasionally described in positive terms like "fair" and "pure" but was portrayed as lacking the heroic masculinity expected of presidential candidates.[37]

Margaret Chase Smith (1964)

Nearly a century passed before another woman made a serious attempt at the White House. Margaret Chase Smith (1897–1995) ran for the presidency under the Republican Party label in 1964. The first woman to be elected to both houses of Congress, Smith served in the House for a decade and in the Senate for two decades. She was the first woman to run for a major party nomination. As a young woman, Smith worked a variety of jobs, including teaching and coaching girls' basketball. She became active in the Republican Party in Maine and later handled the schedule, correspondences, and speech writing of her husband, Clyde Smith, when he was elected to the House of Representatives. After her husband suffered a heart attack and died in April 1940, Smith won his seat in a special election and again in a standard election three months later.

During her time in Congress, Smith broke ranks with her party by supporting President Franklin D. Roosevelt's New Deal legislation and, later, by becoming one of the first political leaders to criticize McCarthyism and voting against making the House Un-American Activities Committee a permanent congressional committee. She drafted legislation that created special female military units during World War II and passed the Women's Armed Services Integration Act (1948) to make women a formal part of the armed forces. Unlike those of her male competitors, Smith's stellar congressional record was not enough to garner serious consideration for the presidency.

When Smith announced her candidacy for the presidency in January 1964, she stated, "I have few illusions and no money, but I'm staying for the finish. When people keep telling you, you can't do a thing, you kind of like to try."[38] She failed to win any of the state primaries, but her name was the first woman's name to be placed on the ballot at a major party convention. Smith came in third place with popular votes in the Republican primary, and she received 27 delegate votes at the convention that would eventually nominate Arizona senator Barry Goldwater.[39]

Smith's candidacy was marked by press coverage defining her run as "unnatural." Falk finds that "remarks about the proper sphere for women were more common in 1964" than at any other time because Smith ran during the second wave of the women's movement, when questions of women's roles were hotly debated.[40] Her candidacy was routinely described as not viable by reporters and opinion writers.[41] One reporter stated that Smith "is realistic to know that the country is not quite ready to elect a woman as president."[42] Smith pushed back against the framing that she was not a viable candidate because she was a woman, asking reporters, "If this is not the time for a woman candidate, then when would the time be?"[43]

Press coverage framed Smith's true ambition as the vice presidency rather than the presidency, despite her frequent protestations that she was running to win the presidency.[44] Twenty-one percent of articles suggested that Smith was truly seeking the number two position.[45] For example, the *New York Daily News* wrote, "Sen. Margaret Chase Smith of Maine—who said she'd like to run for President, period, but is believed willing to settle for the Vice Presidential nomination."[46] The suggestion that Smith was seeking the vice presidency was an improvement over the treatment of previous female candidates, who were not considered serious enough for even the second in command, but the "vice presidential" frame also sent a clear signal that Smith was not fit for the presidency.

Smith also faced more subtle gender bias in terms of the amount and type of coverage. She received a third the amount of coverage as an equivalent male candidate in the race.[47] When it comes to issue coverage, Smith received far less than a similar male contender—only 8.6 percent of her coverage discussed policy issues.[48] Smith's physical appearance was mentioned far more frequently than that of her male candidates, with one in five articles mentioning some aspect of her clothing or body.[49]

Smith was also presented in stereotypical ways in public discourse. She was described as emotional, as both a sad and angry candidate.[50] Ideals of womanhood were less rigid by the time Smith ran for office compared to previous candidates, but she was judged using stereotypes of femininity. She was described in both feminine ("charming" and "poised") and masculine ("formidable" and "strong") terms.[51] The double bind is especially pronounced for Republican female presidential candidates, who face an extra challenge appealing to religious voters, who typically hold more conservative ideas about "proper" gender roles. Republican female contenders have uniformly navigated the tension between women's leadership and religiously prescribed gender roles by publicly nodding to their support for tradition. Smith capitulated to more traditional notions of womanhood throughout her campaign; for example, she told reporters, "I view the role of wife and mother as the foundation, the keystone and the basis for women to expand their activities."[52]

Shirley Chisholm (1972)

Author, educator, and politician Shirley Chisholm (1924–2005) ran for the presidency in 1972. She was the first black woman elected to Congress, where she represented New York's 12th District from 1969 to 1983. She was also the first black person to be nominated at a major party convention for president and the first woman to run for the Democratic Party nomination. Chisholm earned her master's degree in elementary education from Columbia University and worked as a teacher and a nursery director, and her expertise in education policy propelled her into politics. She served in the state assembly before winning a seat in Congress with the campaign slogan "Unbought and Unbossed." While in Congress, Chisholm was a founding member of the Congressional Black

Caucus and the National Women's Political Caucus. She expanded the food stamp program and fought for a minimum wage for domestic workers. Chisholm was also a vocal opponent of the Vietnam War and a known supporter of the Equal Rights Amendment to explicitly include rights for women in the Constitution.

Chisholm announced her candidacy for the presidency in July 1971 at a Baptist church in Brooklyn. She received little support from the Democratic Party or her colleagues in Congress. Chisholm faced constant threats against her life from people who felt threatened by a woman of color running for the presidency, and she was awarded Secret Service protection throughout the primary season. Chisholm earned a total of 430,703 primary votes (out of 16 million cast), which gave her 28 delegates to the party convention. She placed last out of seven Democratic contenders in 1972.[53]

Chisholm faced both race and gender biases in public discourse. Despite a proven record of effective public service in Congress, she was openly framed as incompetent by the press.[54] One journalist wrote: "Can't you just imagine a woman being faced with a crisis (Cuba) such as President Kennedy had? The office of President or Vice President is no place for a woman."[55] Another writer opined of her candidacy: "Women are not qualified for this high office. If one is ever elected President, she would have to depend 100% on the advice of the men she appointed to high executive positions."[56] Chisholm's viability was also questioned in more subtle ways. She received half the amount of press coverage as an equivalent male candidate in her race, and his articles were 25 percent longer.[57] Additionally, her comparable male competitor received 17 percent more issue coverage than Chisholm.[58] The press dropped Chisholm's professional title (congress member) more than that of any other female presidential candidate—63 percent of the time.[59]

As with other female candidates, Chisholm's physical appearance was discussed frequently in the press, often with references to her race.[60] The press often mentioned her gender and her race in articles, signaling that both of these identities are important considerations for the presidency. Chisholm was described by the press in stereotypically emotional terms as angry.[61] Reporters described Chisholm as having a "temper," possessing "scathing anger," ranting and raving, and being "fiery."[62] This framing of Chisholm as a stereotypical angry black woman reflects the intersectional bias of women of color who run for the presidency. This framing also demonstrates the double bind that Chisholm faced for projecting masculine strength but violating societal norms of femininity.

Patricia Schroeder (1988)

Patricia "Pat" Schroeder (1940–) represented Colorado in the U.S. House of Representatives for more than two decades (from 1973 to 1997). Schroeder was born into a military family, and she earned a pilot's license and ran her own flight service to pay for college. She was one of just a few women to graduate with a law degree from Harvard in 1964, a place she described as "submerged in sexism."[63] She worked as a field attorney for the National Labor Relations Board and a volunteer counsel for Planned Parenthood before running for Congress. When she first announced her congressional bid, she was diminutively referred to as "little Patsy" by opposition party leaders.

In Congress, she was known for advocacy on issues affecting the work-family balance and was instrumental in passing the Pregnancy Discrimination Act (1978), the Military Family Act (1985), and the Family and Medical Leave Act (1993). When she arrived in Congress, Schroeder was one of only 14 women out of the 435 members of the House, and she told reporters that she faced constant sexism. When a male colleague asked Schroeder how she could be a member of Congress and a mother of two young children, she famously replied, "I have a brain and a uterus and I use both."[64]

Schroeder chaired Gary Hart's ill-fated 1988 bid for the presidency, and she briefly campaigned for the presidency after he dropped out in response to a sex scandal. Schroeder gave speeches in key states, including New Hampshire and Iowa, and raised enough money to receive federal matching funds, but she never formally announced her candidacy. Schroeder withdrew her name from consideration during a tearful press conference three months after ostensibly starting her campaign. She was polling a respectable 8 percent support from voters but felt that she would not get a fair shake in the electoral process.[65]

Schroeder's press coverage was an improvement over that of Smith and Chisholm in that the press often mentioned her extensive political experience, but she was never treated as a serious candidate by the press. Some reporters openly stated that she could not win because of her sex: "Many observers have said that Schroeder, because she is a woman . . . doesn't have a serious shot at the nomination."[66] Similarly, a local politician from Iowa was quoted saying, "I don't think any woman can win."[67] Schroeder pushed against questions of her viability, and for the first time in history, a female presidential candidate was joined by a host of other prominent women and feminist organizations that also challenged the idea that female presidential candidates are not legitimate.[68] Reporters also undercut the seriousness of Schroeder's candidacy with frequent suggestions that she was running in order to gain the vice presidency. Schroeder was adamant with the press that she was not interested in the vice presidency, and she reiterated her disinterest after dropping out of the race.[69]

Schroeder's candidacy was subtly presented as less than serious through media coverage. She received less coverage than a similar male competitor, but most notably, she received far less issue-based coverage. A similarly situated male competitor received 339 percent more issue coverage than Schroeder. [70] She was constantly asked who would care for her children if she won the presidency, a question her male peers were not asked. Schroeder also received more coverage focused on her dress and appearance than her male competitors.[71] As Schroeder put it, a female candidate runs for office "to discuss the issues, and is scrutinized for her hairstyle or her clothing. You'd never hear someone ask 'why is that man wearing the same shirt three days in a row?' "[72]

Schroeder faced the double bind in that she was ascribed feminine traits that made her appear unsuitable for the presidency ("charming" and "gracious")[73] while at the same time her masculine assertiveness was held against her. Reporters described her as an "upset," "fuming," "irked," and "angry" candidate.[74] In the end, a popular, highly qualified candidate dropped out of the running in a tearful exchange about the difficulties of the nominating process. As one reporter who was in the crowd put it, "It was so obvious that she was overcome by the anguish in knowing that a woman had no chance at the White House, only because she was a woman."[75]

Lenora Fulani (1988, 1992)

Psychologist and political activist Lenora Fulani (1950–) ran for the presidency under the New Alliance Party label in 1988 and 1992. She was the first female candidate and the first African American candidate to appear on the general ballot in all fifty states and Washington, D.C.[76] Fulani ran on a platform of social justice for people of color and LGBT individuals. Prior to getting involved in politics, Fulani earned a doctorate in psychology from the City University of New York. She founded the New York Institute for Social Therapy in 1977 and went on to develop youth programs for underprivileged children in New York City, including the All Stars Project. She unsuccessfully ran for lieutenant governor of New York in 1982 and governor in 1990. In 1992, Fulani worked as a grassroots activist for third-party candidate Ross Perot's campaign.

Fulani's 1988 vice presidential candidate was Chicana activist Maria Elizabeth Muñoz. The ticket won nearly a quarter of a million votes in the general election—the most of any female presidential candidate at that time.[77] Fulani was the most successful female third-party candidate to run for the presidency until Jill Stein's 2016 run. Fulani's candidacy was dismissed in the press as not viable, in that she received almost no press coverage. The only headlines she received were for "shouting down Bill Clinton and Jerry Brown" as they gave speeches during the New York primary.[78] This coverage reinforced the "angry black woman" stereotype and framed Fulani's candidacy as only worth discussing when it affected her male contenders. Fulani was barred from participating in the presidential debates because she ran under a third-party label.[79]

Elizabeth Dole (2000)

Harvard Law graduate Elizabeth Dole (1936–) ran on an extensive record of public service in the 2000 presidential election. She served as Richard Nixon's deputy assistant for consumer affairs, Ronald Reagan's secretary of transportation, and George H. W. Bush's secretary of labor. Dole also headed the American Red Cross for a decade. After her presidential run, Dole served in the U.S. Senate from 2003 to 2009, representing the state of North Carolina. During her time in various administrations, Dole was a vocal supporter of women's rights and the Equal Rights Amendment. She was recruited to run by prominent Republicans after she gave a rousing speech at the Republican National Convention on behalf of her husband, Bob, the party's presidential nominee in 1996.

Dole's candidacy marked a distinct break from the past in that it was the first time the press treated a woman as a serious contender.[80] "Dole's race was the first in which there were notable voices arguing that America was ready" for a woman in the White House and the first time gender discrimination was publicly discussed as a barrier to women gaining the office.[81] However, press coverage of Dole was still gendered and sexist in ways that hampered her run. For example, 64 percent of news articles about Dole mentioned her sex as though it were an important consideration for the presidency.[82] She was frequently described with the "first woman" frame, despite the many women who had run before her.[83]

Dole dropped out of the presidential race during the primary because of lack of funds, even though she was polling a close second to George W. Bush. Dole's communications director, Ari Fleischer, attributed her lack of money to sexist media coverage that framed her presidential bid as not viable. Reporters also trivialized her candidacy through constant speculation that she was actually running for the vice presidency, despite her repeated protestations to the contrary.[84] Dole also received significantly less media coverage than comparable male contenders in the primary,[85] and her coverage was more negative.[86] She received more horse-race coverage than her male competitors, and it came at the expense of more substantive policy coverage.[87]

Gender stereotypes were abundant in public dialogue about Dole. Reporters were more likely to mention her family and personal life, and they placed inordinate focus on her dress and appearance.[88] Forty percent of articles written about Dole referred to some aspect of her appearance.[89] For example, one article referred to her as "clad in a violet suit,"[90] while another suggested that "she brought only a skirt" to the election.[91] Dole was also more sexualized in public discourse than her male competitors;[92] for example, a reporter mused that "she looks great naked."[93]

Dole also experienced the double bind. The press described her in highly feminine terms, as a cheerleader and wife who possesses "charm," and in masculine terms as displaying "confident leadership" and being a "bold reformer."[94] Carole Kennedy finds that Dole faced a backlash from conservatives for not being masculine enough to fit the presidency but also for being too aggressive for a woman.[95] Dole experienced an additional hurdle with the pressure to appeal to religious conservatives, who ascribe to more traditional gender roles. Like Smith before her and Republican women to follow, Dole capitulated to the values of religious voters, for example, telling a report that "the most important career a woman can have is that of a mother raising fine young future citizens."[96] Dole, herself not a parent, had little choice but to appeal to Evangelical and other traditional religious voters that populate the Republican Party, but by doing so, she presented an image in conflict with expectations of presidential masculinity.

Carol Moseley Braun (2004)

Lawyer Carol Moseley Braun (1947–), the first African American woman to serve in the U.S. Senate, ran for the presidency under the Democratic Party label in 2004. Before serving in Congress, Moseley Braun was a prosecutor in the United States Attorney's office and a state representative in Illinois. She ran for the Senate against incumbent Alan Dixon because he voted to confirm Supreme Court justice Clarence Thomas after law professor Anita Hill reported that Thomas had sexually harassed her. Moseley Braun held the seat for nearly a decade. During her senate race, Moseley Braun was described by the *Chicago Tribune* in strikingly sexist terms as a "den mother with a cheerleader's smile."[97] She announced her candidacy for the presidency in February 2003 but dropped out in January 2004 after a third-place showing in the Washington, D.C., primary.

Moseley Braun was never taken seriously as a candidate. Her bid received little press coverage, and a similarly situated male candidate in the race had 200 percent more stories written about him.[98] When Moseley Braun received the endorsement of the National Organization for Women, the *New York Times* published an article stating that "there is a place in the American political system for symbolic candidacies," and the *Chicago Tribute* questioned whether her candidacy was symbolic.[99] Chisholm, the other major party candidate who is a woman of color, was similarly characterized in the press as "symbolic,"[100] but it is not clear for whom it was symbolic or who gets to decide whether a race is symbolic. For Chisholm and Moseley Braun, their presidential runs were exhaustingly serious affairs that required all of the temporal and financial resources they could muster.

Moseley Braun's candidacy was framed as not "really" seeking the presidency, as a "spoiler" campaign to siphon off black votes from Rev. Al Sharpton, and as a bid to raise her profile for a run for Chicago mayor.[101] Her candidacy was also trivialized by reporters who focused on whether her last name should be hyphenated and pondered aspects of her physical appearance. On the latter point, a columnist for the *Chicago Tribune* opined: "Someday a woman will be president of the United States. She may be sorry. One day, she will go to the suburban National Naval Medical Center for a three-hour physical. . . . and then the entire world will know her body fat index."[102]

Hillary Clinton (2008)

Sen. Hillary Clinton garnered more votes during her 2008 bid for the Democratic Party nomination than previous female contenders,[103] but she faced towering gender barriers. As with that of previous women, Clinton's coverage was replete with the "first woman" frame,[104] which othered her as a novelty candidate. Clinton was also referred to in more informal terms than her male competitors, which signaled that she was a less serious candidate. News commentators referred to her as "Hillary" 8 percent of the time, compared to 2 percent for "Barack," while commentators almost exclusively used the candidate's last names and formal titles for Republican candidates.[105] Reporters dropped Clinton's professional title of senator 25 percent of the time, compared to 18 percent of the time for Obama.[106] However, Clinton's professional title was used more often than those of previous female presidential candidates, a sign that her candidacy was comparatively taken more seriously.

When it comes to print media coverage, Clinton received a comparable amount to her competitors,[107] a sign of progress, but her coverage was significantly more negative.[108] She also received disproportionate horse-race coverage at the expense of more substantive policy coverage.[109] Clinton also received far more appearance-based coverage than her male competitors in the primary; for example, the *Chicago Tribune* described the candidate at a campaign stop: "Clinton was well-dressed without being overly showy. Pale pink top and jacket."[110] Reporters talked about her "cackle" and cleavage, her pantsuits, and the size of her bottom.[111] Clinton received more subtle focus on her appearance from liberal commentators, but the gloves came off for some Republicans commentators. For example, conservative Michelle Malkin commented that "[Hillary Clinton] looks 92 years old. I think it's going to scare away a lot of these independent voters" during an interview on the popular show *Fox & Friends*. Clinton received less appearance coverage in print media than previous female presidential candidates did,[112] but print media ceased to be an accurate measure of candidate framing with the rise of the new media environment of less filtered online news, editorial television news, and social media.

"Cleavage-gate" illustrates the hostility aimed at female candidates in the new media environment. A widely circulated *Washington Post* piece noted that Clinton "was wearing a rose-colored blazer over a black top. The neckline sat low on her chest and had a subtle V-shape. The cleavage registered after only a quick glance."[113] "Cleavage-gate" became a full-blown "scandal" because MSNBC devoted significant time to the story.[114] The flames of sexism that originated with an online article were fanned by both cable news media and social media, where user-generated videos on YouTube featuring Clinton with digitally altered fake breasts and demeaning scenarios were widely circulated.

Clinton faced a stark double bind in 2008. She navigated this impossible bind by projecting a "soft" image during debates, wearing "feminine" suits and strings of pearls around her neck while standing and speaking with "masculine" force and assuredness. She purposefully projected toughness to be considered a serious contender, especially on issues of national security, but was then judged as not being "human" or feminine enough.[115] Commentators criticized Clinton's one public display of "humanness"— her tears in New Hampshire during the primary race—as an ominous sign of weakness.[116] Ambition framing also came to the fore in unprecedented, gendered calls for Clinton to prematurely exit the primary.[117]

Clinton's run was hindered by gender stereotypes. She was framed as a "nagging wife" in new and social media throughout the 2008 campaign. Fox News commentator Marc Rudov said, "When Barack Obama speaks, men hear 'take off for the future,' and when Hillary Clinton speaks, men hear 'take out the garbage'!" Patrick Buchanan proclaimed that "when she raises her voice, it reaches a point where every husband in America has heard it at one time or another," while MSNBC contributor Mike Barnicle commented, "That look, like everybody's first wife standing outside probate court." Fox host Tucker Carlson commented that "When [Hillary Clinton] comes on television, I involuntarily cross my legs," while MSNBC's Chris Matthews's relentless drub of sexism against Clinton included labeling her "she-devil."

Clinton was also openly called a "bitch" in legacy media, new media, and social media. The "bitch" frame epitomizes the double bind for female presidential candidates. Glenn Beck referred to Clinton as a "stereotypical bitch," musician and conservative columnist Ted Nugent called Clinton a "worthless bitch," Fox Business News' Neil Cavuto discussed Clinton "trying to run away from this tough, kind of bitchy image," CNN's Alex Castellanos referred to Clinton as a "white bitch," and radio host Marc Rudov stated on Fox News, "The woman is not called a B-word because she's assertive and aggressive; she's called the B-word because she acts like one." According to Falk, a search of "Hillary Clinton is a bitch" netted 9,000 hits at the end her bid, with 427 videos linking Clinton with the word, such as "Hillary Clinton: Crazy Bitch" and "Hillary Bitch."[118] During the primary, Republican candidate John McCain fielded a question from a supporter, "How do we beat the bitch?" to which he responded, "That's an excellent question."[119]

The term "bitch" is a gender slur that derives its meaning from reference to a female dog. "The fact that the term *bitch* was the epithet of choice for Clinton reveals the way sexism in modern culture precludes women from leadership."[120] Clinton was commonly referred to as a "bitch" in 1995 when she was a first lady who was active on policy issues, and that slur was also used to describe Geraldine Ferraro, the first female vice presidential candidate of a major party in 1984.[121] Karrin Vasby Anderson writes that "bitch" is used exclusively to frame powerful or assertive women, as a form of containment, one that reinforces the idea that women's power is both threatening and unnatural.[122] Clinton was also referred to as a "cunt" frequently on social media sites, and the Republican political action committee Citizens United Not Timid spelled out the slur. The Facebook group "Hillary Clinton: Stop Running for President and Make Me a Sandwich" attracted more than 40,000 members by the end of the primary,[123] and Clinton was heckled several times at campaign stops by protesters holding signs and yelling, "Iron my shirt."

The extreme sexism experienced by Clinton can at least partially be attributed to the fact that she stood a chance of winning her party's nomination. Female candidates are trivialized in myriad ways, up until the point where they are actually competitive and are then villainized. Another factor that contributed to the extreme sexism faced by Clinton is the new media environment, the new norm for female presidential candidates.

Michele Bachmann (2012)

Michele Bachmann (1956–) was the only female contender of a major party in the 2012 presidential race. A former IRS tax attorney and Tea Party Caucus founder, she represented a district in Minnesota in the U.S. House of Representatives for almost a decade. Bachmann was elevated to assistant minority leader during her time in Congress. Prior to that, she served in the state senate. Bachmann grew up in a Democratic family and volunteered for Jimmy Carter's 1976 presidential campaign, but she switched her party allegiance and worked for Ronald Reagan's campaign in 1980. Bachmann is known for her strong pro-life and anti-LGBT views, and she was wildly popular with Tea Party loyalists when she put her hat in the ring for the presidency.

Bachmann made a strong early showing by winning the Iowa Ames Straw Poll—the first woman ever to win the poll. She formally announced her candidacy in late June 2011 and was one of the leading contenders during the early primary months. Many pundits speculated that Bachmann would win the Iowa caucuses given her strong showing in the straw poll, but she ended up placing dead last in Iowa, with just under 5 percent of the vote, and soon dropped out of the race.[124] Her precipitous fall from frontrunner status can at least partially be explained by gender bias.

From the start of her campaign, influential Republican Party and religious leaders did not take Bachmann's bid seriously, even after her Iowa straw poll win.[125] Some party leaders asked her to drop out of the race, and many sought an alternative in Texas governor Rick Perry or Pennsylvania senator Rick Santorum. Even Bachmann's congressional ally Rep. Steve King did not endorse her.

Bachmann was a colorful candidate. She was one of the early "birthers" on Capitol Hill who challenged President Obama's citizenship, she made an unsubstantiated claim about the HPV vaccine causing cognitive disorders, and she confused John Wayne with John Wayne Gacy. Bachmann's unusual statements and extreme policy positions would have stuck out in a typical election, but they were hardly unique in a presidential field that included Herman Cain, Newt Gingrich, Rick Perry, and Rick Santorum. However, Bachmann was the only candidate of the bunch who was framed as "nutty." For example, a much-debated *Newsweek* cover showed her with "crazy eyes" with the headline "Queen of Rage," and commentator Chris Wallace asked her whether she was "a flake" during an interview on *Fox News Sunday*. Like Palin in 2008, Bachmann presents a challenge for analyzing sexism in presidential politics because she was such an extreme candidate. However, she was in a field of extreme candidates but was treated as a nutty novelty.

Bachmann's political advisers attributed her swift fall to sexism.[126] Similarly, Michelle Goldberg argues that Bachmann's loss in Iowa was due to sexism, pointing out that she stumped as much as Santorum, had staff problems no worse than Gingrich's, and made lesser gaffes than Perry—but Bachmann finished dead last in the state.[127] The extent of Bachmann's defeat in a state known for favoring Evangelical candidates was surprising considering that she was the candidate most known for her Evangelical beliefs and policy positions. Jessica Wakeman notes that Bachmann was presented as a caricature in the press: "It does seem that female politicians get caricatured more harshly than men. They seem to get caricatured more quickly."[128]

Like other Republican female contenders, Bachmann had to appeal to the pronounced double bind with religious voters. Bachmann did walk a strange line in appealing to conservative Evangelicals with her extreme stances on issues they care about the most, but her identity as a woman conflicted with a patriarchal strain of religion that limits women's leadership. The conflict came to a head during a speech when she admitted that she studied tax law because her husband told her to and "wives, you are to be submissive to your husbands.' "[129] This attempt to appeal to Evangelical voters caused a public uproar and speculation about who would actually be in charge if Bachmann were elected president.

Beyond being uniquely framed as "nutty" in a field of comparatively "nutty" candidates, Bachmann was framed as physically weak, which feminized her candidacy in a way that made her inherently unfit for the masculinized presidency. The "frail" frame was introduced by the conservative publication the *Daily Caller*, which reported that Bachmann suffered from migraines that left her unable to handle stress. Previous presidents suffered from migraines (e.g., Thomas Jefferson and Ulysses Grant) and other serious physical ailments (e.g., Franklin Delano Roosevelt), but their diagnoses were not considered points of disqualification for the office.

At the start of the 2016 presidential campaign, Bachmann discussed the sexism female presidential candidates experience by empathizing with Hillary Clinton:

> I really do have great empathy for what Mrs. Clinton is going through, because the hill that she has to climb on—appearance—it's just a different hill than men have to climb. I'm not whining about it. It's just reality. It is what it is.[130]

Jill Stein (2012, 2016)

Medical doctor and activist Jill Stein (1950–) ran for the presidency under the Green Party label in 2012 and 2016. Prior to running for the presidency, she twice ran for the governorship of Massachusetts and received 3.5 percent and 1.42 percent of the vote, respectively.[131] Stein earned her MD from Harvard Medical School and practiced and taught internal medicine for 25 years in Boston. She got involved in politics as an activist in the late 1980s when she noticed a link between pollution and health problems. Stein organized protests against the pollution from coal plants in the Boston area and testified about the public health effects of a proposed trash incinerator. She spent the intervening decades advocating for public health and campaign finance reform.

Stein announced her first candidacy for the presidency in October 2011 with anti-poverty activist Cheri Honkala as her running mate. She became the Green Party's presumptive nominee after a strong showing in the California primary in June 2012. Stein was arrested twice during the campaign—once during a sit-in at a bank in Philadelphia to protest housing foreclosures and again outside of a presidential debate at Hofstra University to protest the exclusion of third-party candidates. Stein received just over 469,000 votes in the general election, making her the most successful female presidential candidate to date at that time,[132] a sign of steady progress for third-party female candidates.

Stein ran for the presidency again in 2016 on the Green Party ticket with human rights activist Ajamu Baraka. She announced her candidacy during a live interview with Amy Goodman on her radio show *Democracy Now*. Stein was arrested once during this campaign for spray-painting a bulldozer during a protest of the Dakota Access Pipeline, an oil pipeline protested by Native Americans in Standing Rock, North Dakota. Stein peaked at 4.8 percent support in national polls and eventually garnered 1 percent of the national popular vote in a four-way contest between Hillary Clinton, Donald Trump, and Libertarian candidate Gary Johnson.[133]

Stein faced gender bias in that she received almost no press attention during the race and significantly less than third-party contender Gary Johnson. In the six months leading up to the election, Johnson was mentioned in twice as many print media articles as Stein.[134] Stein noted that she faced sexism on the campaign trail. In an interview in September 2016, she lamented that female presidential candidates "are dismissed. We are sort of sidelined and we're treated as second-class citizens, not worthy of the debate for example, not worthy of press coverage."[135]

Carly Fiorina (2016)

Businessperson Carly Fiorina (1954–) was the only woman to run in the 2016 Republican primary election. The former CEO of Hewlett-Packard, Fiorina was the first woman to lead a Top-20 company in the United States and was named the most powerful woman in business by *Fortune* magazine five years in a row.[136] Fiorina got her political sea legs as an adviser on Sen. John McCain's 2008 presidential campaign, and in 2010, she ran for the U.S. Senate in California. Fiorina won the Republican nomination but lost to incumbent Barbara Boxer in the general election.

In 2016, Fiorina was one of seventeen candidates in a crowded Republican field for the presidency. She announced her candidacy on May 4, 2015, during an interview on *Good Morning America*. Fiorina was briefly a top-tier candidate in terms of public support after a strong performance in the first few debates. Her polls rose from 2 percent to 8 percent after the first debate[137] and peaked at 15 percent in September 2015. By October, her public support fell to 4 percent, and it continued to slide.[138] On February 10, 2016, Fiorina suspended her campaign.

Fiorina's 2016 candidacy was distinct from those of her male competitors in gendered ways. She was the only woman in the primary, which is remarkable given the number of candidates running. The Republican Party employed Fiorina as an asset because she could attack Hillary Clinton without being seen as sexist.[139] Indeed, she "came out swinging" against Clinton more aggressively than other Republican contenders the day she announced her candidacy.

Despite her strong fourth-place position at one point in the campaign, Fiorina was never treated like a serious contender by party leaders or the press, and she was perpetually seen as a less-than-serious candidate, despite her poll standings. As with many previous female presidential candidates, Fiorina was the only candidate who was consistently discussed as running for the nomination in order to become vice president. Republican strategist Liz Mair penned an op-ed addressing the constant speculation that Fiorina was running for vice president:

> It is also true that at the end of the day, Carly may very well not be the nominee of the Republican Party in 2016. Only one out of what seems like a gazillion GOP candidates will get that honor, and everyone else will collect their bags and go home. But what is also true is that, in countless conversations about her and the field at large, I have yet to hear a single person say of any male candidate that they are "only running for Vice President."[140]

Fiorina herself dismissed talk of her seeking the vice presidency as "sexist" on a Fox News program, stating: "The people who say that I am in this for vice president—that's sexist. I'm in this to win this job. No one talks about the men being veep."[141]

Fiorina faced moments of overt sexism that trivialized her run from both the left and the right during the nine months of her candidacy. At a brunch hosted by the *Christian Science Monitor* in April 2015, Paul Bedard from the conservative *Washington Examiner* stated, "Well, ma'am, I never met a presidential candidate with pink nail polish on," before asking her how she would better represent women than Hillary Clinton.[142] Fiorina replied, "Well there's always a first." Later that month, Fiorina was asked whether hormones should preclude a woman from being president on the show *Fox & Friends*.[143]

During the Republican primary debates, Fiorina was also treated in gendered ways that hampered her campaign. In the first debate in August 2015, Fiorina was referred to as "Carly" by the Fox News hosts while her male contenders were referred to by their professional titles. She was also held to a different standard of debate by her male competitors, all of whom cut one another off during the debates. In September 2015, Chris Christie reprimanded Fiorina during a debate: "Carly, listen, you can interrupt everybody else on this stage. You're not going to interrupt me, O.K.?" During a debate in November, Trump was booed by the audience when he scolded Fiorina for interrupting other candidates, implying that she should not try to jump in when the men were speaking. Fiorina's gender was front and center in the debates in a way that it was not for her male competitors. For example, in December, conservative radio host Steve Deace tweeted, "Wow . . . Fiorina goes full vagina right away," in response to her mention of breast cancer in her opening statement at a debate.

Fiorina's appearance was the focus of comment and ridicule in sexist ways throughout her candidacy. In September 2015, Trump gave an interview in which he said: "Look at that face! Would anyone vote for that? I mean, she's a woman, and I'm not supposed to say bad things, but really, folks, come on. Are we serious?"[144] In a later debate, he attempted to repair the damage of this sexist remark by complimenting Fiorina as "beautiful," which sexualized her and set Trump up as the validator of her worth.[145] In October 2015, the liberal talk show hosts of *The View* referred to Fiorina's face as "demented" and said it looked "like a Halloween mask."[146]

Fiorina used masculinist rhetoric on the campaign trail in order to fit with expectations of what it means to be presidential. First, she refused to acknowledge the sexism she faced from Trump and others during the primary so as to avoid the perception of being a victim. When asked point-blank about the sexist treatment she received from hosts of *The View*, Fiorina told them to "man up" and do combat with her on policy and not personal grounds.[147] She faced the impossible task of addressing blatant sexism without appearing weak in order to fulfill expectations of presidential masculinity.

CONCLUSION

There is no doubt that women have made progress when it comes to winning the White House. Early candidates were treated as novelties and trivialized by the press and the public, but women's groups started pushing back against this characterization starting with Schroeder's bid in 1988. By the year 2000, the press finally treated a female candidate (Dole) as a legitimate contender. In the 2016 election, three women ran for the office—a third-party candidate, a Republican contender, and a Democrat who won the party's nomination. The number of women running in contemporary presidential elections is remarkable, but patterns of gender bias persist that are stark in their longevity across candidates from different parties, backgrounds, and eras.

Public discourse about presidential candidates is marked by gender in ways that harm the electoral success of women who run. Female candidates receive less coverage and less substantive coverage, their viability is questioned, their professional titles are dropped, they are ambition shamed and asked to prematurely exit the race, they are framed as really running for the vice presidency, they are stereotypically portrayed as emotional, the press focuses on their family and appearance, they are sexually objectified, and they are chastised for not being masculine enough or are judged for being too masculine.

Female presidential candidates today face a more hostile environment than candidates of the past because the new media environment has fewer brakes on bigotry. We examine this new media environment in the remainder of this book with an in-depth analysis of Clinton's 2016 run and a comparison of her coverage in legacy media, new media, and social media.

CHAPTER 4

"I Don't Vote with My Vagina": Hillary Clinton's Primary Elections

Hillary Clinton was not an exceptional candidate. When it comes to basic empirical measures, at the start of the 2016 election, she looked remarkably similar to past candidates in terms of likeability, the "cool factor," policy positions, scandals, and ambition. With 34 years of public service experience, she was on the high end for presidential candidates, but virtually all presidential candidates are accomplished public servants. We conclude that, like the 12 women who previously made serious bids for the presidency, Clinton was seen (and continues to be seen by many) as an exceptional candidate—worse at campaigning, more corrupt, more scandalized—because she is a woman. We contend that if she were a man running with the same experience, credentials, and personal traits, she would be considered a standard presidential candidate: an experienced, knowledgeable, somewhat boring policy wonk who occasionally moves a crowd with soaring rhetoric.

Hillary Clinton became the presumptive nominee of the Democratic Party on June 8, 2016—the first woman in U.S. history to represent a major political party in a general election. Clinton handily bested Bernie Sanders with 55.2 percent primary vote support compared to Sanders's 43.1 percent, garnering 16.8 million votes to Sanders's 13.2 million.[1] The race was not close, but as Nate Silver notes, "the media probably exaggerated the competitiveness of the race"[2] in order to maximize the length of the contest and their profits. This was not Clinton's first time at the presidential primary rodeo, having lost to Barack Obama in 2008. In both primaries, Clinton was seen as the likely Democratic nominee until a primary challenge from an appealing political "outsider" entered the race. In 2016, Clinton faced "outsider" Bernie Sanders, a senator from

Vermont who had served in Congress for 25 years. As in 2008, Clinton was again framed as a centrist or "establishment" candidate. In this chapter, we investigate the gender dynamics of the 2008 and 2016 Democratic primary elections.

Many factors contribute to electoral outcomes—what political scientists refer to as "the fundamentals" (the state of the economy, the presence of an incumbent), as well as the voters' predisposition toward the candidates at the start of multiyear campaigns, campaign quality, political events (e.g., terrorist attacks), scandals, the presence of popular minor party candidates, and identity bias (e.g., racism and sexism). In this chapter, we examine the public opinion context for Clinton's bids for the White House. We also analyze legacy media coverage and public opinion using Clinton's 2008 and 2016 primary election experiences as case studies. Legacy media coverage is print or online coverage that follows traditional journalistic standards with editorial filters—for example, major newspapers such as the *New York Times* or the *Washington Post*. We explore new media (blogs with fewer editorial filters, such as *The Drudge Report* or *The Daily Kos*), and social media (platforms driven by user-generated content and sharing, such as Facebook and Twitter).

Our analysis in this chapter reveals the interplay between sexism, legacy media coverage, and public opinion. We begin this chapter with a look at how public support for a female president has shifted over time. In the next section, we examine public opinion of Hillary Clinton over the course of her public life, with particular emphasis on how her poll ratings drop every time she seeks higher office. The remaining sections examine how sex and gender shaped the 2008 and 2016 primary elections.

PUBLIC OPINION OF HILLARY CLINTON

Hillary Clinton has been more admired and more hated than any political woman in the United States. She has ridden a roller coaster of public opinion since she first became a national figure when her husband, Bill, successfully ran for the presidency in 1991. Throughout her political life, from first lady of Arkansas to first lady of the United States to a senator from New York to secretary of state to presidential candidate, Clinton has taken on the double bind of women's leadership head-on, straddling "feminine" and "masculine" personas.[3] She shifted from an ambitious career woman to a supportive spouse during her husband's campaign for the Arkansas statehouse; from perceptions of her as a "bitch" (as she was called by House Majority Leader Newt Gingrich's mother) and a snob (Clinton's comment, "You know I suppose I could have stayed home and baked cookies and had teas, but what I decided to do was fulfill my profession which I entered before my husband was in public life") to a cookie-baking homemaker and mother during the last months of her husband's 1992 presidential campaign; from a spouse "silenced" by her failed health care reform initiative and her husband's infidelities during the Clintons' time in the White House to a "tough" senate candidate from New York;[4] and from a measured and eventually ineffective primary contender in 2008 to a tough secretary of state in the Barack Obama administration.

Clinton has faced sexism since she entered public life as the first lady of Arkansas in the late 1970s. In 1979, a local television station host laid out the ways in which Clinton challenged gender norms:

> You don't really fit the image we have created for the governor's wife in Arkansas. You're not a native. You've been educated in liberal eastern universities. You're less than 40. You don't have any children. You don't use your husband's name. You practice law. Does it concern you that maybe other people feel that you don't fit the image that we've created for the governor's wife in Arkansas?[5]

Hillary hating reached a new intensity when she became an unconventional first lady involved in policy and political decision making. A few years into her husband's presidency, Henry Louis Gates noted that "Hillary-hating" is "one of those national pastimes which unite both the elite and the lumpen."[6] Right-wing and humor publications made evident the national anxiety about Clinton's unconventional first ladyship with covers portraying her as a witch and a dominatrix.

For decades, Clinton has sustained sexist blows. Martin Amis sums up Hillary hating in a 1996 piece in the *Sunday Times*:

> Newt Gingrich called her a bitch. Rush Limbaugh called her a feminazi. One New York weekly called her a scumbag. William Safire, in *The New York Times*, called her a congenital liar. And the President himself, it is rumoured, calls her the First Liability. Rumour goes on to add that Hillary Rodham Clinton is a communist and a carpetbagger, a wowser and a fraud, a floozie and a dyke. It has been repeatedly suggested that she had an affair with her financial conspirator Vincent Foster, who died, mysteriously, in 1993. At this stage, we don't want to know whether Hillary slept with Vincent Foster. We want to know if she killed him.[7]

In January 2014, *Time* continued the long tradition of sexist covers, asking, "Can Anyone Stop Hillary?" It showed an imagined Clinton wearing a pointed heel that is moments away from crushing an emasculated man. Feminists roundly denounced this cover as sexist for stereotyping power-seeking women as a crushing threat to men.[8]

As shown in figure 4.1, Clinton's favorability rating has mostly remained on the positive side for the 25 years she has been in public life, but with gyrations. By the end of the 2016 election, her approval had dipped to the lowest point since she became a public figure, with two-thirds of Americans viewing her negatively. Despite her roller-coaster ratings, Clinton has topped Gallup's list of the most admired woman in the world for a record 21 years (from 1995 to 2016).[9]

Sady Doyle notes that Clinton's roller coaster follows a fixed and predictable pattern: voters loathe Clinton when she "applies for a new position" but love her once she gets it.[10] For example, when Clinton left her secretary of state post in 2013, she was the most popular politician in the United States,[11] fueling speculation that she would run for the presidency in 2016. A year earlier, a meme featuring Clinton on her phone sporting sunglasses went viral and inspired a number of news articles about her "cool factor." Political analyst Nate Silver wrote a piece for the *New York Times* in which he noted that Clinton had "remarkably high

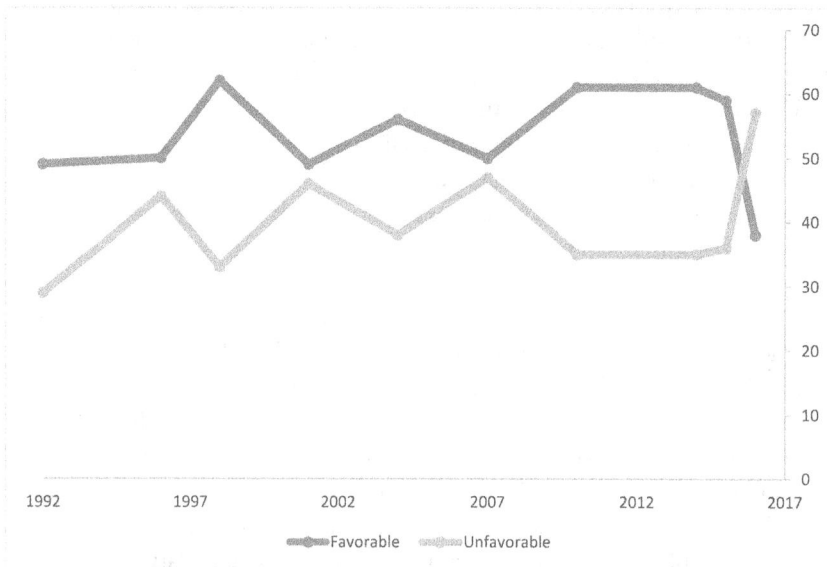

Figure 4.1 Favorability and Unfavorability Ratings for Hillary Clinton: Gallup Polling (Polling Data in This Chart Represent Yearly Averages through 2015 and 2016, at Which Point Monthly Averages Were Used)

Source: Gallup.

numbers for a politician" during a time when political distrust was near all-time highs.[12] Clinton was considered a beloved candidate going into the invisible primary (the year or so before the formal primary election begins), but within months, her approval rating was back in the gutter.

Doyle explains this pattern as "prejudice against women caught in the act of asking for power."[13] It is not a phenomenon unique to Clinton. According to research from Tyler G. Okimoto and Victoria Brescoll, "when female politicians are perceived to be power-seeking, voters react negatively with feelings of moral outrage."[14] Running for higher office is, by definition, a power-seeking act, and the presidency carries the most power one can have in U.S. politics, so millions of Americans displaying moral outrage to Clinton makes sense given this underlying context. Clinton was doing what no woman before her had done, and it incited the largest outpouring of moral outrage against a female politician that we have seen in U.S. politics—greater in volume and scope than the open hatred of vice presidential candidate Sarah Palin during the 2008 election, which is saying something.[15]

THE 2008 PRIMARY ELECTION

When Clinton announced her candidacy for the presidency on January 20, 2007, she was immediately the front-runner for the Democratic nomination. A *Washington Post*–ABC News poll taken shortly after her announcement found that 41 percent of Democrats supported her bid, double that of any potential competitors.[16] Over the course of the invisible primary, she opened a 20-point gap over her closest competitor (Obama). As with the 2016 general election, Clinton was seen as an inevitable victor in the 2008 primary election, but a win was not forthcoming. In this section, we detail the gendered double standards Clinton faced in press coverage during the 2008 primary.

Media Coverage in 2008

As noted in chapter 3, media bias against female presidential candidates comes in five primary forms: (1) higher rates of negative coverage; (2) greater questioning of candidate validity; (3) the casting of women as less serious contenders (through less overall coverage, less issue-based coverage, and the dropping of professional titles); (4) stereotypically gendered coverage (through "soft sexism," such as ambition shaming, discussing them in emotional terms, mentioning their family, focusing on appearance, and gender marking, and "hard sexism," such as sexual objectification and openly gendered insults); and (5) double-bind expectations—female candidates are criticized for not being sufficiently "masculine" or for being "too masculine" and defying gender norms. These biases were evident in the 2008 Democratic primary.

Negative Coverage

Clinton's legacy media coverage in the 2008 primary election was significantly more negative than that of the male candidates in the race, but especially Obama.[17] According to a study from Harvard's Shorenstein Center, her coverage in the first three months of 2007 was 75 percent negative, while Obama's coverage was 60 percent positive.[18] Regina Lawrence and Melody Rose analyzed the 2008 primary and found that Clinton received the same amount of coverage as Obama, which is progress given the attention gap for female candidates in previous presidential bids, but a majority of Clinton's coverage was negative and damaging, while a majority of Obama's coverage was positive.[19] Although Clinton was framed as a less honest candidate in the primary, she was more honest than most of the candidates in the race, including Obama.

Some press displayed open sexism in Clinton's coverage. A content analysis of political cartoons reveals that cartoons featuring Obama were more likely to be favorable, while Clinton's cartoons were significantly more negative.[20] For example, Clinton was frequently presented as hyperbolically small in stature and ugly. She was shown perpetrating violence and being the recipient of gory violence more often than Obama, which fits with the knee-jerk villainization of power-seeking women. This double standard in negative press coverage diminished Clinton's competitiveness because it shaped voters' perceptions of her character.

First Names

When it comes to more subtle gender bias, media commentators were more likely to refer to Clinton by her first name than they were her male competitors. Joseph Uscinski and Lilly Goren analyzed how candidates "branded" themselves (with their first or last names) and how reporters talked about them in the 2008 race.[21] They find that the most watched television news hosts across the political spectrum referred to Clinton as simply "Hillary" 8 percent of the time, compared to using "Barack" just 2 percent of the time. It is worth noting that while Clinton branded her 2016 campaign "Hillary," she did not brand her 2008 campaign with her first name. This study also found that even when male candidates branded their campaigns using their first names (e.g., Rudy Giuliani and Lamar Alexander), reporters still referred to them by their last names. In short, Clinton was referred to in more informal terms than her male competitors of both parties, and both liberal and conservative television hosts referred to her in informal terms. This double standard in name use sent the subtle message that Clinton's candidacy was less serious than her male competitors'.

Exit Talk

During the 2008 primary, Clinton received an unusual amount of pressure to prematurely exit the race. In mid-February, when the race was at its competitive height, reporters and pundits started to call for her to drop out of the race even though it was impossible at that point for either candidate to get enough pledged delegates. Calls for her to drop out came from the left and the right. For example, in February, Republican strategist Pete Snyder appeared on *Hannity & Colmes*, pressing for Clinton to get out of the race. He stated: "Somebody's going to have to go to Hillary Clinton and say, 'get out of this thing.' [S]omeone is going to have to go out there and take her behind the barn." Regina Lawrence and Melody Rose compared "exit talk" in the 2008 primary to previous primaries and found that these calls were exceptional for Clinton and were due to voter discomfort with women seeking power.[22] This double standard in exit talk harmed Clinton's electability because it cast her as an interloper who should not have been in the contest rather than a legitimate contender running neck and neck with Obama.

Gender Stereotypes

In terms of stereotypes, Diana Carlin and Kelly Winfrey find that Clinton's media coverage employed gender stereotypes and reinforced double-bind thinking about women's leadership. They evaluated common stereotypes for professional women—sex object (seductress), mother (nurturing, emotional), pet (weak, naive), and iron maiden (masculine, "bitchy")—all of which are harmful to the electoral prospects of female candidates. Their research shows that Clinton was framed using all of these stereotypes over the course of the 2008 primary election.

Clinton was framed as the antiseductress through exit talk, "the woman who simply wouldn't go away" like the stalker played by Glenn Close in the film *Fatal Attraction*.[23] When it comes to the mother stereotype, Clinton was framed as both a scolding mother and a bad mother for having her daughter as a surrogate on the campaign trail (which is common with presidential candidates). The pet metaphor came into play with coverage framing her as the weaker sex in need of male assistance, which her husband was happy to provide. Many political commentators speculated that Bill Clinton was the master strategist, the brains behind the operation. The iron-maiden trope worked to reinforce the double bind of women's leadership by framing Clinton as too tough and not feminine enough. Ashleigh Crowther analyzed the most common words used to describe Clinton in legacy media and found that she was mostly described in terms that fit the iron-maiden stereotype: "overly ambitious," "calculating," "cold," "scary," and "intimidating."[24] These gender stereotypes reduced Clinton's viability by bringing voter biases against female candidates to the fore in their evaluations of Clinton.

Dress and Appearance

Reporters and commentators also talked about Clinton's physical appearance—her pantsuits, her age, the size of her bottom, her cleavage, her cankles (large ankles), and her cackle. For example, right-wing commentators Rush Limbaugh and Michelle Malkin made sexist comments about Clinton's age on air. Limbaugh asked, "Will this country want to actually watch a woman get older before their eyes on a daily basis?" and Malkin commented, "You all saw the famous photo from the weekend of Hillary looking so haggard and, what, looking like 92 years old. If that's the face of experience, I think it's going to scare away a lot of those independent voters." Fox News' Carl Cameron suggested that Clinton's wardrobe decisions were intended to solve her "likeability" problem: "Wearing bright colors, smiling constantly, as if to deal with what polls say is a likability problem, she has surged 10 points since the Democratic debate." San Francisco radio host Lee Rogers suggested that Clinton had gotten Botox. *Washington Post* writer Robin Givhan called Clinton's cleavage "unnerving" and commented that the last time Clinton wore anything that was remotely sexy in a public setting surely must have been more than a decade ago . . . "it was more like catching a man with his fly unzipped. Just look away!" The double standard here—frequent commentary about Clinton's appearance—harmed her electoral chances through the powerful reminder that she is a woman, that women derive their primary value from their bodies, and that Clinton is not valued for her body.

Overt Sexism

Clinton was the target of open sexism in press coverage and public debate during the 2008 primary election. The Facebook group "Stop Running for President and Make Me a Sandwich" attracted tens of thousands of members, and Clinton faced jeering protesters with signs that read "Iron My Shirt" at multiple campaign stops. Prominent Republican operative Roger Stone created a political organization called Citizens United Not Timid. MSNBC host Tucker Carlson did a segment with a Clinton doll described as having "serrated stainless steel thighs that, well, crack nuts" and commented that "I have often said, when she comes on television, I involuntarily cross my legs." Candidate John McCain responded with laughter during a town hall when a participated asked, "How do we beat the bitch?" Politico's Mike Allen defended McCain, stating: "All right. But what male voter hasn't thought that? What voter in general hasn't thought that?"

Much of the overt sexism aimed at Clinton played upon the double bind of women's leadership that frames her as a "bitch" for being too masculine. An MSNBC panelist used many sexist stereotypes in one segment on Clinton, commenting that "when she reacts the way she reacts to [Sen. Barack] Obama [D-Ill.] with just the look, the look toward him, looking like everyone's first wife standing outside a probate court, OK? Looking at him that way, all I could think of . . . was this fall, if it's [Sen. John] McCain [R-Ariz.] that she's facing, McCain is likable. She's not." All three MSNBC hosts had to take a moment to collect themselves after side-splitting laughter. Fox News host Neil Cavuto stated that Clinton was trying to run away from "this tough, kind of bitchy image." The next day on MSNBC, Pat Buchanan asserted that when Clinton "raises her voice, and when a lot of women do, you know, it's—as I say—it reaches a point . . . where every husband in America . . . has heard at one time or another . . . I know that's a sexist comment . . . but there's truth to it! . . . There's truth to it. . . . It's very difficult for women to reach those kinds of levels effectively, as it is to make them sort of a rally speech. They're not good at that."

In March, Fox News host Bill O'Reilly asked author Marc Rudov, "What is the downside of having a woman become the president of the United States?" Rudov responded, "You mean besides the PMS and the mood swings, right?" O'Reilly responded: "But guys have mood swings, Marc. And you know they have other control issues . . . the main problem I have is if a woman has a female agenda. If she doesn't have a female agenda, if she just wants to be an executive for all the people, then all

I care about is if she's qualified. And I have no qualms about having a female president. But if we take Hillary Clinton, she specifically does have a female agenda." That same month, CNN's Glenn Beck called Clinton a "stereotypical bitch." In April, *Vanity Fair* columnist Christopher Hitchens opined about Hillary Clinton: "[I]f you think of women who really have been put upon by men and by male supremacy, like Benazir Bhutto, as well, you can't imagine her resorting to this kind of self-pity or suddenly decide to feminize herself in the most clichéd way, of such—by welling up and sobbing. I just think that if she knew how it made her look, sort of alternately soppy and bitchy, she'd stop it. But she can't help herself, can she?" Later in April, liberal radio host Randi Rhodes spoke at an event in San Francisco and announced that "Hillary is a big fucking whore."

MSNBC's Chris Matthews's commentary about Clinton was remarkably sexist. He referred to Clinton as "She devil," "Nurse Ratched," and "Madame Defarge." He described male politicians that endorsed Clinton as "castratos in the eunuch chorus." Matthews compared Clinton to a "strip-teaser" and questioned whether she is "a convincing mom." He referred to Clinton's "cold eyes" and the "cold look." Matthews obsessed over Clinton's "Chinese" clapping and her "cackle" and claimed that "some men" say Clinton's voice sounds like "fingernails on a blackboard." He also suggested that Clinton "being surrounded by women" might "make a case against" her being "commander in chief" and once asked a guest if "the troops out there" would "take the orders" from "Hillary Clinton, commander in chief." When the response was, "Why wouldn't they listen to a [female] commander in chief? Sure," Matthews responded, "You're chuckling a little bit, aren't you?" When his guest responded, "No," Matthews couldn't quite believe it, sputtering: "No problem? No problem? No problem?"

Public Opinion in 2008

A poll taken during the invisible primary found that some female voters saw Clinton's gender as an asset. In November 2007, 25 percent of women said they were more interested in the presidential race because a woman was running, and 70 percent of Democratic women backed Clinton.[25] Seven percent of women in the same poll said they would never vote for a female president.[26] Clinton maintained high levels of support until the start of the Democratic primary, when voter support for Obama eclipsed her lead. Clinton suspended her campaign on June 7, 2008, and threw her full support to Obama.

It is impossible to isolate the role that gendered double standards played in Obama's unexpected upset in the 2008 Democratic primary, but it was likely a decisive factor given the decline in Clinton's poll numbers during the formal primary. Voters polled in the middle of the primary reported that sexism was playing a bigger role in the race than racism. According to a CBS poll fielded in March 2008, 39 percent of voters said gender is a greater obstacle to the presidency than race, while 33 percent said race is more of an obstacle.[27] In that same poll, 27 percent of Americans thought Obama was being treated harshly because of his race, while 42 percent said Clinton was being treated harshly because of her gender. When Clinton pointed out sexism in the election, she was then criticized by commentators for playing the "gender card"—the idea that she was trying to gain an unfair advantage in the race.[28]

THE 2016 PRIMARY ELECTION

As in 2008, Clinton entered the 2016 primary race as the most likely candidate to win by a wide margin. As in 2008,[29] she faced a serious challenge from a candidate with whom she shared a strikingly similar voting record but who was effectively framed by opponents and the press as more progressive than Clinton. As in 2008, the primary election was covered in the press as a very tight race, but in the end, Clinton handily won 2,205 delegates over Sanders's 1,894. This happened despite the same level and type of sexism she faced in the 2008 Democratic primary.

Media Coverage in 2016

As in 2008, Clinton received substantially different press coverage than her male competitors in 2016. In this section, we describe double standards in coverage tone and type, scandal coverage, likeability, the "cool factor," the "establishment" frame, the "woman card," and overt sexism.

Negative Coverage

Early in the 2016 primary campaign, the Clinton campaign was openly critical of the press for holding her to a different standard than her male competitors. According to a study from the Shorenstein Center, Clinton was right. During the invisible primary, media coverage was far more negative for Clinton than Sanders. From January through December 2015, Sanders's net coverage was mostly positive, reaching a high point of 60 percent positive in September 2015 and a low of -17 percent in

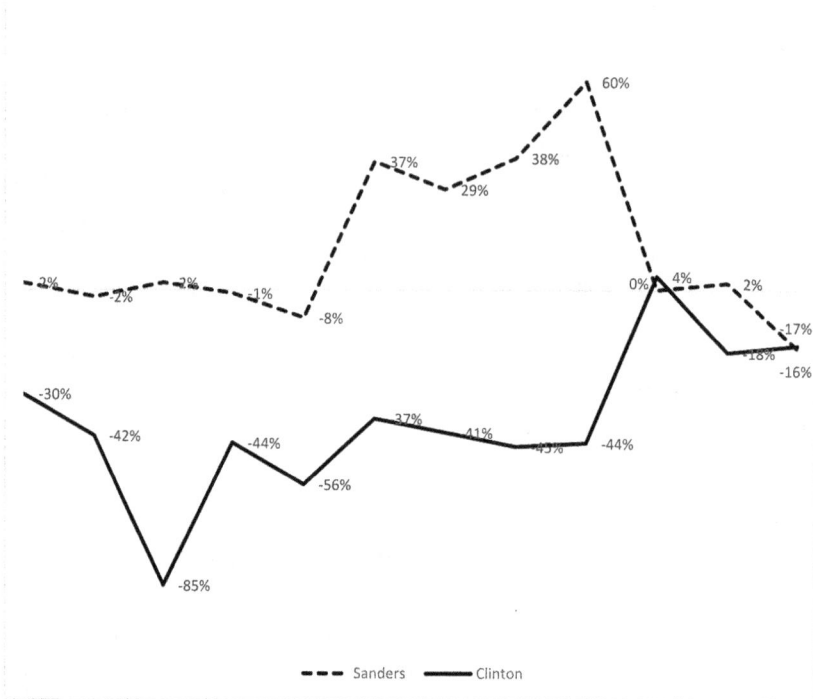

Figure 4.2 Media Tone for Sanders and Clinton during the 2016 Invisible Primary (The Data Represent the Tone of Media Coverage; Each Data Point Is the Percentage of Positive Coverage Minus the Percentage of Negative Coverage)
Source: The Shorenstein Center.

December. Sanders's coverage was positive for eight out of the twelve months of the invisible primary.

Compared to Sanders's, Clinton's negativity is remarkable. She received net positive coverage (of 4 percent) during only one month out of twelve, and the negative tone of her coverage dipped quite low, to -85 percent. Clinton faced a barrage of highly and consistently negative press coverage throughout the invisible primary, while Sanders received quite positive coverage until the very end of 2015.

As noted in chapter 2, previous female presidential candidates received significantly less issue coverage than their male competitors, signaling that they were less serious contenders, but this was not the case in the 2016 primary season. As shown in figure 4.2, Clinton received substantially more issue coverage than Sanders and leading Republican candidates in the invisible primary, so the seriousness of her candidacy was not in question. However, Clinton's policy coverage was significantly more negative than that of the male candidates and 12 times more negative than Sanders's policy coverage.

Along with Clinton's disproportionately negative coverage, reporters rarely mentioned her work in the Senate or as secretary of state, the two periods in her professional life when she was praised by people across the ideological spectrum.[30] Over the course of the invisible primary, high rates of unremitting negative coverage contributed to a steep rise in Clinton's unfavorable rating to over 50 percent, and she entered the Iowa caucus a significantly weakened candidate.

While Clinton was barraged by negative press coverage during the invisible primary, Donald Trump disproportionately benefitted from the press. The Shorenstein Center study finds that Trump was slow to gain popularity in the polls but got a boost from ample and positive press coverage.[31] Press gave Trump the equivalent of $55 million in free advertising during the invisible primary, compared to $36 million for Jeb Bush, $34 million for Marco Rubio, and $32 million for Ted Cruz. The majority of Trump's coverage was positive or neutral throughout the invisible primary, as shown in figure 4.3.

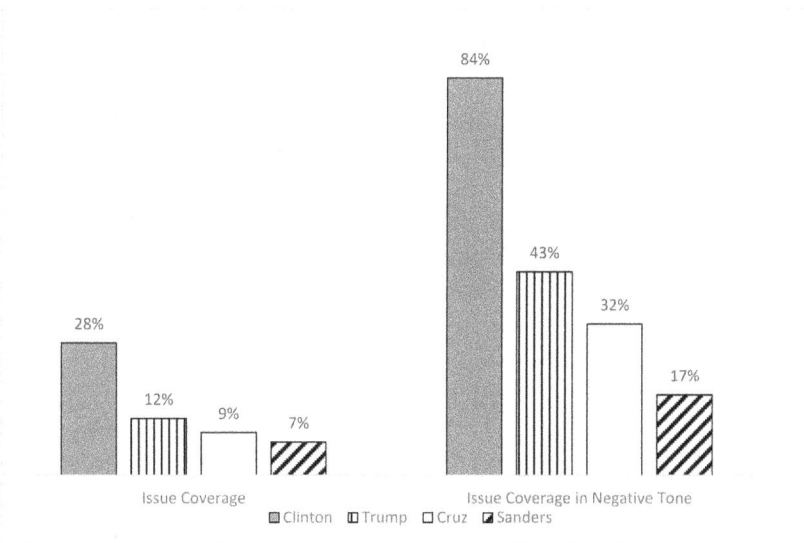

Figure 4.3 Issue Coverage (Percentage of Media Coverage Devoted to Actual Issues) and Tone during the 2016 Invisible Primary

Source: Patterson, Thomas E. "Pre-Primary News Coverage of the 2016 Presidential Race: Trump's Rise, Sanders' Emergence, Clinton's Struggle," Harvard Kennedy School, Shorenstein Center on Media, Politics and Public Policy, June 13, 2016, https://shorensteincenter.org/pre-primary-news-coverage-2016-trump-clinton-sanders/.

This means that while Clinton was being savaged in the press during the invisible primary, which slowly ate away at her lead and weakened her candidacy, leading to a protracted primary (which, in turn, weakened her candidacy for the general election), the press was providing the volume and type of coverage necessary for Trump to clinch the Republican nomination.

Scandal Coverage

There were many valid, nongendered criticisms to be made of Clinton in the 2016 election: that she lacks transparency, voted in favor of authorizing the Iraq War in 2002, and has ties to Wall Street, from whom she has accepted exorbitant speaking fees. However, the primary criticisms she faced in the 2016 primary and general elections involved unsubstantiated "scandals." The ideas of Clinton as scandalous and cor-rupt played upon voter predisposition to moral outrage at power-seeking women who violate gender norms. Clinton's nonscandal "scandals" were believable because they fit well with a villain narrative that in turn fits comfortably with the moral outrage voters direct at power-seeking female candidates. We describe her major scandals (Benghazi, e-mails, the Clinton Foundation), then examine her relative scandal coverage in legacy media.

Benghazi was one major Clinton scandal of the 2016 election. Clinton was held personally responsible for the 2012 terrorist attack on the U.S. Embassy in Benghazi, Libya, that left four Americans dead, including Ambassador J. Christopher Stevens. Republicans in Congress spent more time investigating Benghazi than the terrorist attacks of September 11, 2001, and after 11 different iterations of the investigating committee, the House select committee found no criminal wrongdoing on Clinton's part.[32] This finding did not stop Republicans and right-wing media from using Benghazi to smear Clinton, much to the chagrin of Ambassador Stevens's family. In September 2015, Rep. Kevin McCarthy admitted that the Benghazi and e-mail investigations were part of a Republican "strategy to fight and win" by pulling Clinton's poll numbers down.[33]

The most effective Clinton scandal, also employed to fit the "corrupt" frame, involved her use of a private e-mail server. Media frames are narratives that are embedded in news stories to construct meaning.[34] Framing affects voter perceptions in ways that disadvantage female candidates when they reflect gender bias.[35] For example, the "crooked Hillary" frame, a gendered construct for Clinton in that it plays upon the moral outrage of power-seeking women, effectively maligned her candidacy. Scandals are a reasonable cover for moral outrage against power-seeking women because they provide a seemingly reasonable basis for the moral outrage, one that allows them to villainize a female candidate for a seemingly substantive reason.

Clinton's use of a private e-mail server came to light during the partisan Benghazi committee investigation. The controversy concerned 30,000 State Department e-mails that Clinton acknowledged she wrongfully stored on a private server in Chappaqua, New York, during her time as secretary of state from 2009 to 2013. Clinton's use of a private server may have violated State Department rules that sensitive information should not be transmitted through personal e-mail accounts, although the guidelines allow for exceptions that are not specified.[36] Previous secretaries of state used private e-mail, with John Kerry being the first secretary of state to primarily rely on his state e-mail account. In July 2016, FBI director James Comey publicly announced that Clinton may have violated rules for handling classified information because she received two classified e-mails on her private server,[37] but he ruled that her case was not suitable for prosecution because there was no evidence that Clinton intended to break any laws.[38] Comey publicly weighing in on the matter was a point of consternation, what former Department of Justice spokesperson Matthew Miller called a "gross abuse of power" because Comey violated agency protocol against weighing in on matters that could affect elections.[39] Eleven days before the election, Comey announced that he was investigating additional e-mails; then four days before the election, he announced that nothing new had come from that review. We analyze the crucial influence of Comey's actions on the outcome of the election in the next chapter. Even though Clinton's use of a private e-mail server was a mistake, which she readily admitted, and not an actual scandal, it was covered as major news for more than a year. The digital-media company Shareblue finds that Clinton's e-mails were covered in one or more major publication every day (except four) for 562 days straight, throughout the invisible primary, the primary election, and the general election—rivaling media coverage of the Watergate scandal as the most reported on in political history.[40]

The Clinton Foundation scandal, which came up later in the election, was fabricated by Peter Schweizer, president of the Government Accountability Institute (GAI), an organization cofounded by Steve Bannon and funded by *Breitbart* benefactor and Trump donor Robert Mercer.[41] The "scandal" is the allegation that Clinton used her position at the State Department to engage in lucrative business deals. GAI's model is to build fact-based indictments against Democratic opponents and then use mainstream media to disseminate the allegations. Investigative journalism budgets have been slashed in recent years, making them more receptive to GAI's tactics. Schweizer published the book *Clinton Cash*, and prior to its publication, the *New York Times*, *Washington Post*, and Fox News signed "exclusive agreements" with him to report on specific storylines.[42]

On April 24, 2016, the *New York Times* ran a story based on *Clinton Cash* detailing Russian acquisition of uranium-mining rights from a Canadian company run by Frank Giustra, a large Clinton Foundation donor, with the misleading headline "Cash Flowed to Clinton Foundation amid Russian Uranium Deal." The deal was approved by the State Department, and while the *Times* concluded that there was no evidence that Giustra's donations played a role in the outcome, they wrote, "The episode underscores the special ethical challenges presented by the Clinton Foundation."[43] PolitiFact debunked this scandal, noting that donations to the Clinton Foundation from Giustra came before Clinton knew she would be secretary of state and that nine different agencies had to approve the deal.[44] *Rolling Stone* investigative reporter Janet Reitman notes that "the *Times* allowed itself to be used by GAI to deliver a heavily partisan message went unmentioned. Instead, *Clinton Cash* quickly became both a *New York Times* bestseller as well as the jumping-off point for what is now 16 months of investigations by news organizations into the Clinton Foundation."[45] Reitman also writes: "Not a single one of these investigations has yielded any evidence of a quid pro quo. What the stories have found is evidence of Clinton doing the standard work of a secretary of state: meeting with Nobel Prize winners and corporate titans, some of whom also happened to be foundation donors."[46]

The Benghazi, e-mail, and Clinton Foundation "scandals" are less about substance and evidence and more about Clinton's personal character, a sign that there is a gendered double standard at play. The alleged scandals were a continuation of two decades of right-wing targeting of a woman poised for power with fabricated and hyperbolic attacks. From investigations into cattle futures and Whitewater that netted nothing to conspiracies about Vince Foster's death and speeches to Wall Street, three decades of mostly partisan investigations into corruption have netted nothing concrete on Clinton, and yet she is still widely viewed as a contemptuous, corrupt politician.

The gendered double standard in nonsubstantive "scandals" sticking to Clinton was helped along by a biased press. Clinton received vastly more coverage focused on scandals than other Democratic candidates during the invisible primary. Figure 4.4 shows that over half of her coverage

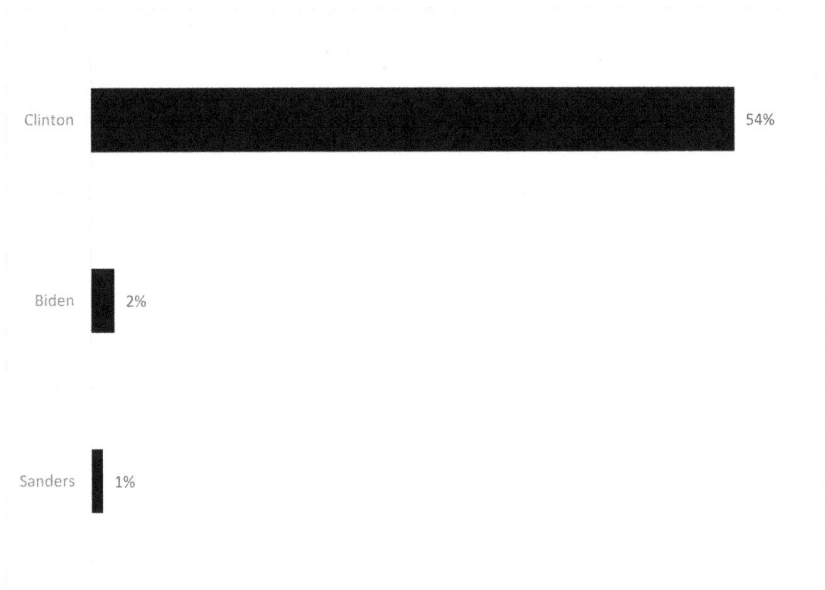

Figure 4.4   Scandal Coverage during the 2016 Invisible Primary (Percentage of Coverage of Candidate That Was about Scandals)

Source: Media Research Center, based on an analysis of the ABC, CBS, and NBC evening news from January 1, 2016, to September 30, 2016.

on national evening news programs pertained to scandals, whereas only a miniscule portion of Sanders's and Joe Biden's coverage was about scandals. This same study found that virtually all coverage of the two male Democratic candidates was positive.

Scandal coverage dominated Clinton's coverage, but Sanders and Biden are not the best points of comparison since neither was the focus of two expensive Republican congressional investigations intended to generate scandals with which to discredit the leading Democratic contender in the next election. Biden had no major scandals in his history, and other than a strange attempt at satire in the 1970s that could be interpreted as an endorsement of rape, Sanders had no major scandals. A better point of comparison for scandal coverage is Trump. In comparison to Clinton's, almost no attention was paid to Trump's scandals during the primary (involvement in 3,500 lawsuits, including a class action claim against Trump University; details of a violent rape in his divorce proceedings with ex-wife Ivana Trump; multiple allegations of sexual misconduct over the years; etc.). Instead, legacy press primarily focused on his activities and events (34 percent of coverage), his electability (21 percent), his issues and ideology (12 percent), and his personal qualities (6 percent).[47] This means that, when it comes to scandals, Clinton was held to a different standard than her male competitors, in terms of both what stuck as a "scandal" and how much attention media paid to legitimate scandals.

The most prominent Clinton narrative of the 2016 primary was the idea that she was a corrupt, deceitful candidate. The "corrupt Hillary" frame was not accurate, in that Clinton was an equally or more honest candidate on the campaign trail and her "scandals" were overblown in ways that worked because of her gender. PolitiFact found Clinton and Sanders to be roughly the same in terms of false or misleading statements (26.1 percent for Clinton compared to 28.3 percent for Sanders).[48] Jill Abramson, the former editor of the *New York Times*, wrote: "As an editor I've launched investigations into her business dealings, her fundraising, her foundation and her marriage. As a reporter my stories stretch back to Whitewater. I'm not a favorite in Hillaryland. That makes what I want to say next surprising. Hillary Clinton is fundamentally honest and trustworthy."[49] Abramson noted the sexism in the many decades of framing Clinton as Lady Macbeth.

Likeability

One of the ways that Clinton was treated differently from Sanders during the primary was a focus on her likeability. From David Brooks's *New York Times* column "Why Is Clinton Disliked?" (she's a workaholic) to Marc Fisher's *Washington Post* piece "Is She 'Likeable Enough?' " (referring to a statement Obama made during the 2008 primary, and the answer is maybe), the candidate's likeability was a major theme of press and public discussion in the 2016 primary.

Pundits discussed Clinton's voice as one aspect that made her "unlikeable." MSNBC host Joe Scarborough dedicated an entire segment with journalist Bob Woodward to discuss why he dislikes Clinton's voice. "She shouts," said Woodward. "There's something unrelaxed about the way she has communicated." After a debate performance in February 2016, Sean Hannity remarked that Clinton "looked angry" and "sounded angry," to which host Geraldo Rivera added, "Why are you screaming like that? . . . When you shriek that way it's such an unpleasant [sound]." During another Fox News segment, conservative radio host Chris Plante remarked, "I find Hillary Clinton's voice to be shrill. It sounds like a cat being dragged across a blackboard." The term "shrill" is associated with women but not men. It has a long history of being used to lecture women "to avoid rhetorical excess and to use their indoor voices" to conform to "proper" gender roles.[50] Fox News's Brit Hume stated that Clinton speaks in a "hard lecturing tone," like "you've been called into the principal's office," and further commented that she has a "radiant smile" but a "not so attractive voice." Sanders, who is known for passionately yelling into the microphone and whose normal cadence is a yell, was not held to the same standard.

Jay Newton-Small argues that the preoccupation with Clinton's likeability is not about Clinton or other female candidates but rather about unconscious sexist bias. "It is a subtle kind of sexism that exists that we don't recognize. When women raise their voices, people tend to get their hackles up. People I talk to at Clinton events put her in a maternal role: Why is she screaming at me? Am I in trouble?"[51] Beyond biases related to maternal expectations, the double bind of women's leadership is also at play with questions of likeability. Female candidates who display the masculine traits that most Americans find to be a requirement for good leadership in general and the presidency in particular are often seen as unlikeable because they defy the "proper" femininity expected of women. This role incongruity means female candidates inevitably start from a position of being unlikeable.

Likeability, or lack thereof, has ripple effects for female candidates. Research from the Barbara Lee Foundation finds that perceptions of being qualified and likeable are not correlated for male candidates, but they are for female candidates.[52] In other words, if a male candidate is not likeable, he can still be seen as qualified, but the opposite is true for female candidates "because qualifications and likeability are so closely linked."[53] This means that female candidates have to be seen as both qualified and liked to earn the support of many voters, and if they are framed as unlikeable, they will be seen as unqualified, despite their experience or record.

During the general campaign, Clinton addressed the likeability issue in an interview with the Humans of New York Web site, noting the gendered nature of her likeability:

> I know that I can be perceived as aloof or cold or unemotional. But I had to learn as a young woman to control my emotions. And that's a hard path to walk. Because you need to protect yourself, you need to keep steady, but at the same time you don't want to seem "walled off." And sometimes I think I come across more in the "walled off" arena.[54]

Clinton addressed the likeability issue again in a press interview in which she acknowledged the double bind of women's leadership at play:

> [When I see male politicians] pounding the message, and screaming about how we need to win the election … I want to do the same thing. Because I care about this stuff. But I've learned that I can't be quite so passionate in my presentation. I love to wave my arms, but apparently that's a little bit scary to people. And I can't yell too much. It comes across as "too loud" or "too shrill" or "too this" or "too that."[55]

Even though Clinton was well aware of the gendered double standard of likeability, she could not navigate the terrain in a way that negated it.

The Cool Factor

Along with being framed as unlikeable, Clinton was framed as anti-"cool." The cool factor that she enjoyed after the 2012 "Texts from Hillary" meme had evaporated when she went for a promotion. Columnist Charles Blow laid out the general sentiment of many Democrats during the primary when he said, "Sanders has become the cool uncle and Clinton has become the cold aunt,"[56] or as political commentator Dasha Burns put it, "for Millennials, Sanders is a grandpa who gets them."[57] On what basis was Sanders considered cool? Burns notes that even though "his white hair is kind of wild, he's awkward, doesn't smile much, he hunches over and waves his arms when he speaks. He campaigns in rolled-up shirtsleeves and has pens in his shirt pocket," Sanders captured the cool imagination by demanding radical change. "And he's doing so loudly, unconventionally, and with a wonky, crotchety nerdiness so uncool it's become completely cool."

It is apparent that Sanders's path to coolness is one that is not open to female candidates. Clinton and other female candidates must at least attempt to straddle the double bind of women's leadership by adhering to polished standards of femininity required to "balance out" the masculine traits needed to run. Clinton would not be considered a legitimate presidential candidate, let alone cool, if she wore unkempt hair and disheveled clothing, slouched over during speeches, and yelled into the mic. This would not make Clinton seem "genuine and refreshing," as Burns describes Sanders, but patently unfit for the job.

The gendered double standard in who gets to be cool is also wrapped up with age. Clinton was 68 and Sanders was 74 during the 2016 Democratic primary, but Americans tend to view women as reaching middle age and becoming elderly much earlier than men.[58] As men age, we tend to view them as increasing in power, but as women age, we view them as getting less attractive.[59] Men in U.S. culture are mostly valued for their prestige and position, while women are mostly valued for their appearance, so as both age, men typically gain social value while women lose value. Republicans played upon this gender gap in the general election by framing Clinton as elderly and frail, but gendered ageism was also a factor in the primary. In short, a candidate cannot be both "old" and "cool." Despite being six years Sanders's junior, Clinton was seen as elderly, while Sanders was able to grasp a youthful mantle that is not accessible to older women. The gendered double standard in coolness diminished Clinton's electability with young voters in particular.

The Establishment Frame

The narrow rules of physical appearance for female candidates also cost Clinton support in the primary from voters who readily saw her as "establishment." As Burns writes, "the well-oiled 'Clinton machine' can at times come off as too measured, inauthentic and conventional."[60] In 2008, progressives were swept up in Obama's message of "hope and change," not Clinton's message of "ready to lead." In 2016, young voters in particular were enamored with Sanders's political revolution message and viewed Clinton's pragmatism with suspicion. Sanders did an artful job of framing Clinton as an establishment candidate, announcing in an early debate that "Secretary Clinton does represent the establishment. I represent, I hope, ordinary Americans who are not that enamored with the establishment."[61] But this framing was not entirely fair. By definition, a female presidential candidate bucks the established political order in a profound way, similar to electing the first black president in 2008. But in order to get to a viably competitive position, Clinton had to follow unspoken but strict rules about self-presentation and demeanor in order to be seen as legitimate.

The establishment rhetoric did not empirically match reality. Clinton and Barack Obama voted the same way 96 percent of the time, placing her on the middle left of the political spectrum, while Clinton and Sanders voted the same way 93 percent of the time during their overlapping time in the Senate. The only divergent votes on major policy were on continuing the wars in Iraq and Afghanistan (which most Democrats, including Clinton, supported and Sanders opposed), bailing out the banks and the auto industry after the financial crash (which Sanders opposed), and offering amnesty to millions of undocumented people (which Sanders opposed).[62] While the two candidates did not differ much on policy positions, Clinton was a far more effective legislator during her eight years in the Senate, sponsoring ten bills that passed compared to Sanders sponsoring just one bill that passed during that time.[63] Furthermore, Clinton successfully passed an average of 8.4 amendments compared to 6.3 for Sanders each year.

On the campaign trail, Clinton stressed gender and racial equality issues, while Sanders stressed economic inequality and checks on capitalism. Each candidate could have empirically been framed as more liberal than the other depending upon which policy issues were emphasized, but Clinton's polished physical presentation made it easier for voters to believe Sanders was the "true" liberal. Additionally, Sanders was first elected to Congress in 1991, which means he has been a formal part of the political establishment longer than Clinton, who was first elected to the Senate in 2000, and the same amount of time if Clinton's years as first lady are included. Granted, Sanders has been pushing against income inequality for the quarter century he has been in office but with little legislative effectiveness since he identifies as a Democratic Socialist and not a Democrat.

The gap between rhetoric and reality about the "establishment" frame became apparent in January 2016 when Sanders referred to Planned Parenthood as part of the "establishment" because the organization endorsed Clinton.[64] Planned Parenthood started as the first birth control clinic in the United States in 1916, and since that time, it has been at the radical forefront of family planning. Planned Parenthood's provision of abortion services makes it a constant target of conservative groups and politicians who want to outlaw abortion in the United States, so Sanders framing this organization as "establishment" for supporting Clinton, a candidate who prioritizes family planning, highlights his campaign's attempts to reframe women's issues as establishment instead of progressive.

The influence of the "establishment" frame was especially acute with younger voters who were unfamiliar with Clinton's record as a feminist trailblazer in national politics. Millennials are highly distrusting of institutions, so Sanders's appeal as the "radical" candidate and his framing of Clinton as "establishment" worked in a way that it could not have were Clinton a man.[65]

Susan Bordo notes that impressions of Clinton as "establishment" were based on her self-presentation for many millennial voters:

> I knew just what one of my graduate students meant when I asked her how millennial feminists saw Hillary and she said "a white lady." A white woman herself, she wasn't referring to the colour of Hillary's skin, or even

her racial politics, but rather what was perceived as her membership in the dominant class, all cleaned up and normalised, aligned with establishment power rather than the forces of resistance, and stylistically coded (her tightly coiffed hair; her neat, boring pantsuits; her circumspection) with her membership in that class. When I looked at Hillary, I saw someone very different—but I understood the basis for my student's perception.[66]

To highlight the gendered double standard at play with the "establishment" frame, let's make Clinton a man (let's call him "Bob Smith"). Like Sanders, Smith would have been seen as a wildly liberal candidate for his highly liberal positions on gender justice, LGBT rights, racial justice, and environmental protection. The "establishment" frame would not have stuck to Smith because he would have presented a more "liberal look"—going without a tie, rolling up his sleeves, and ruffling his hair—without fearing repercussions for his appearance. The "establishment" frame weakened Clinton's general election candidacy because it painted a misleading picture of her policy positions as centrist. We note in the next chapter that Trump picked up this frame in the general election because it was so effective in the primary.

The Woman Card

Another double standard emerged in the 2016 election that was profoundly gendered: the woman card, or, rather, the critique that Clinton was attracting primary voters because of her sex as opposed to merit. Clinton likely did pull votes based on her sex since many Democrats identify as feminists and the election of the first female president would be a historic milestone. The decision for voters involved substantive representation and descriptive representation. Substantive representation means a political leader represents a voter's policy interests, and descriptive representation refers to representing the identity of a voter or some identity they deem important (e.g., race, gender, sexual orientation). If a Democratic voter was satisfied with the issue positions of both Sanders and Clinton, it would be a rational calculus to choose Clinton in order to advance women in politics if a voter prioritized descriptive representation.

Democrats typically have no issue understanding and accepting descriptive politics since they routinely practice it. Within party, black voters are more likely to vote for black candidates than voters of other races.[67] Women are more likely than men to vote for female candidates.[68] Descriptive politics played a key role in the 2008 primary, when many Democrats openly embraced the idea that casting a vote for Obama meant electing the first black president. This position was seen as a universal positive on the left because it meant racial progress in the country. Fast forward to 2016, when voting for the first female president is not only not framed as historic by many on the left but is framed as a bad decision and an illegitimate basis for casting a vote.

During the height of the Democratic primary, actor and Sanders surrogate Susan Sarandon chastised Clinton supporters when she stated, "I don't vote with my vagina."[69] Around the same time, rap artist and Sanders surrogate Killer Mike quoted a supporter saying "a uterus doesn't qualify you to be president."[70] One implication here is that the only basis for voters supporting Clinton was descriptive representation (her sex), with no substantive consideration (her policies). This sentiment, echoed by thousands of Sanders's supporters in social media spaces, also implies that voting for Clinton in order to elect the first female president is a bad thing. To see the gendered double standard here, imagine that, at the height of the 2008 Democratic primary, surrogates for candidate John Edwards chastised Obama supporters, saying, "I don't vote with my skin color" and "rich melanin doesn't qualify you to be president." These words and the shaming of voters who engage descriptive representation in the name of history and progress are unthinkable, but it happened with gender in the 2008 Democratic primary.

Another Woman Frame

Our qualitative framing analysis identified a "new" sexist frame that hinders female presidential candidates. The "another woman" frame was a common refrain during the Democratic primary, an insistence on the part of some voters that they supported female candidates in general, just not Clinton. The "another woman" frame circulated in primary discourse with the popular social media hashtags #JustNotHer, signaling a preference for a female candidate just not this one, and #JillNotHill (Dr. Jill Stein rather than Clinton). Our analysis finds that, although this is a newly identified frame, it is not a new refrain. "Another woman" has been levied against most female candidates since media started treating women as serious presidential contenders in 2000: Elizabeth Dole in 2000 (another woman because she is too robotic), Clinton in 2008 (another woman because she is too shrill), Michele Bachmann in 2012 (another woman because she is too crazy). The "another woman" frame is a nifty way to appear nonsexist by affirming support for a female candidate, but the frame is sexist in that it treats female candidates as interchangeable, it diminished Clinton's candidacy in gendered ways, and it is only applied to female candidates.

The "another woman" frame is patently gendered because it assumes an interchangeability of female candidates based on nothing more than their sex. This is best illustrated by the popularity of the #JillNotHill hashtag campaign. Clinton and Stein have little in common as candidates when it comes to political party, policy positions, or electability, but one is seen as a stand-in for the other because they are both women. The inherent sexism in the "another woman" frame becomes apparent when put in terms of race. Imagine Clinton supporters in 2008 using the "another black" frame to oppose Obama's candidacy in racialized terms. Had they circulated the hashtag #JustNotHim referencing support for another African American candidate, just not Obama, and #BrownNotObama, referring to an African American Green Party candidate whose only shared characteristic was race, observers would have rightfully pointed out the racism.

The "another woman" hashtags were also sexist in that they diminished the seriousness of Clinton's candidacy (as a front-runner with sizeable support and a war chest) by leveling her with a hypothetical candidate and an unelectable minor party candidate based on nothing more than their shared sex. This brings up the double standard of the frame that has only been applied to female candidates. In 2016, primary voters were not comparing Sanders or any of the Republican primary candidates to "better" hypothetical male candidates who may run in the future or minor party men with low electability. Clinton faced a double standard when she was reduced to her sex through comparison to nonexistent or noncompetitive candidates but male candidates were not.

The "another woman" frame is a tidy way to assuage the appearance of sexism, but it enacted sexism by treating Clinton as interchangeable with another woman and reduced the seriousness of her bid by leveling her with hypothetical and unelectable candidates.

Overt Sexism

The sexism Clinton faced from the press in 2008 resurfaced with conservatives in the 2016 primary. During the invisible primary, Fox News host Bill O'Reilly had a panel on the downsides of a female presidency with B-roll of Clinton in which his guests opined about whether a woman would be comfortable using military force, and O'Reilly asserted that women may not be tough enough because "there haven't been that many strong women leaders throughout history."[71] In April 2015, Hannity used sexism to negate Clinton's extensive political experience: "What, are we going to call the president of the United States 'Grandma'?" he asked, adding, "It's nice she can change diapers, feed the baby . . . it doesn't exactly qualify someone to have her finger on the nuclear button."[72] Right-wing talk show host Limbaugh claimed that Clinton's career success was due to her husband: "If she hadn't married the guy, you wouldn't know who she is today."[73] Limbaugh also ridiculed Clinton's age when she used the bathroom during a break at a Democratic primary debate: "Why not wear a diaper? If you can't hold it for two hours get a Depends."[74] In January 2016, Fox News host Andrea Tantaros described Clinton as a "thorough-bred horse" who is "on her way to the glue factory."

The left also aimed overt sexism at Clinton. In early 2016, journalist Charles Blow wrote that "there can be an animatronic plasticity present in her comportment and conveyance that raises questions of ambition versus authenticity."[75] As noted in chapter 2, critiquing ambition for a nakedly ambitious job like the presidency only makes sense when viewed through a gendered lens. Of course Clinton (and every other candidate who runs for the presidency) is, by definition, ambitious. And Blow's emphasis on Clinton's appearance and the suggestion of her being robotic are also uniquely gendered. Overt sexism on the left also appeared on social media during the primary. An analysis of Twitter content conducted by the *Washington Post* during the primary showed that 10 percent of tweets mentioning Clinton that contained gender slurs ("bitch," "vagina," "bimbo," "old hag," "slut," "feminazi," "shrill," etc.) were posted by Sanders's supporters.[76]

The Sanders campaign also directed sexism at Clinton. In October 2015, Sanders's campaign manager Jeff Weaver told a reporter, "Look, she'd make a great vice president. We're willing to give her more credit than Obama did. We're willing to consider her for vice president. We'll give her serious consideration. We'll even interview her."[77] These sentiments are reminiscent of the long-standing strategy of dismissing the seriousness of female presidential candidates laid out in chapter 2. In April, as the race was neck and neck, Sanders told a crowd that Clinton was "unqualified" to be president. That same month, Weaver claimed at a speech that Clinton's ambition would destroy the Democratic Party, and a surrogate speaking at a Sanders rally referred to Clinton and her team as "Democratic whores." The constant focus on ambition, as though it is an odd or bad thing for a presidential candidate, speaks to the gendered way in which we think about ambition and the moral outrage many harbor toward ambitious women.

Sexism also came from Sanders supporters, dubbed "Bernie Bros" by the press.[78] Journalist Robinson Meyer, who first coined the term "Bernie Bro," describes them as mostly white (but not necessarily male) Sanders supporters who see the election in terms of moral righteousness and use sexism in their attacks on Clinton. Bernie Bros were known for going after Clinton supporters in social media (primarily Facebook and Twitter) and for connecting in Reddit, an online forum known for being a safe space for sexism.[79] Amanda Hess finds evidence of Bernie Bro-dom in articles from Sanders supporters discussing Clinton's personality and her appearance, sexist posts in Sanders's Facebook pages (e.g., a post referring to Clinton as "clitrash"), and Sanders supporters assailing other Sanders supporters who call out their sexism.[80] The Sanders campaign was a youth-powered, grassroots effort that channeled new life into the American political landscape, and not all or even most Sanders supporters were sexist toward Clinton or her supporters during the primary, but a tiny minority was active enough to make the Bernie Bros a measurable phenomenon. Primary clashes are nothing new, but what makes the Bernie Bro phenomenon remarkable is that they would not have existed if Sanders's main competitor were male.

There was considerable pushback in social media and the press against the idea that sexism was playing a role in the 2016 election on the left. For example, Glenn Greenwald penned the piece "The 'Bernie Bros' Narrative: A Cheap Campaign Tactic Masquerading as Journalism and Social Activism," in which he challenges the claim that "Sanders supporters are uniquely abusive and misogynistic in their online behavior."[81] However, Sanders affirmed the claims of Clinton supporters that they were being harassed in sexist ways by some of his supporters. When the Bernie Bro phenomenon started receiving media attention, Sanders immediately issued a statement asking his supporters to be respectful. In a January 2016 interview with *Ebony*, Sanders expressed concern about the behavior of some of his supporters: "We have many hundreds of thousands of supporters, and some of them have gone over the edge."[82]

Sanders did not always rein in badly behaving Bernie Bros. In May 2016, Campaign Manager Weaver stirred the ire of Bernie Bros when he claimed that Nevada Democratic Party leaders "hijacked the process on the floor" of the state convention, "ignoring the regular procedure and ramming through what they wanted to do." PolitiFact deemed this claim "unfounded," but in politics, perception can easily become reality for partisans.[83] In response to the perception of wrongdoing by the state Democratic Party, some Sanders supporters started yelling and throwing chairs at Clinton supporters. Clinton surrogate Barbara Boxer told reporters that she felt threatened by the violence. Sanders supporters also made online threats against female party leaders and doxed Chairperson Roberta Lange (publishing personal details, including her home address and the location of her grandchildren's school). Callers left sexist messages on Lange's phone: "Answer the phone you pussy," "You're a cunt," "You fucking stupid bitch! What the hell are you doing? You're a fucking corrupt bitch!" and "You will regret your actions shameful CUNT!"[84] Sanders responded with a condemnation of violence and harassment but did not offer an apology.

Public Opinion in 2016

Sexism no doubt played a part in Clinton's steep plummet in approval ratings over the course of the hard-fought primary. It also likely lengthened the primary and the time it took for Sanders to concede. As shown in figure 4.5, Sanders had a steady climb in approval during the invisible and formal primary seasons. He was a compelling speaker who injected new energy into the Democratic Party, especially among young voters. His improvement in favorability makes sense, but Clinton's precipitous decline, from the 60 percentile for most of the invisible primary to about half that during the formal primary, only makes sense given the sexism she endured in the press and public discourse. Clinton's candidacy faced gendered challenges that Sanders did not face in the form of more negative media coverage, more negative issue coverage, "scandal"

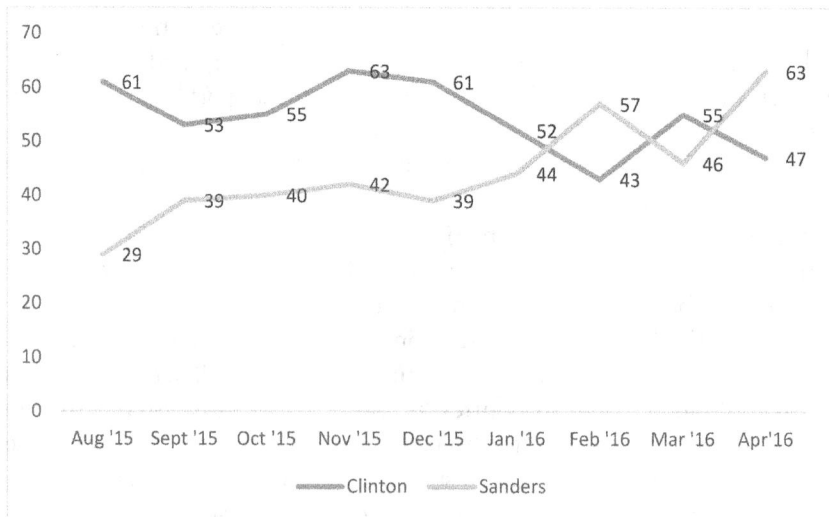

Figure 4.5 Favorability of Clinton, Sanders during the 2016 Primary (Numbers Are Percentages)

Source: Gallup.

coverage, a likeability and "cool factor" double standard, being framed as "establishment," and overt sexism. Had Clinton been Bob Smith, the primary season likely would have been much shorter and Smith would have entered the general election in a stronger position.

Even though the race was far closer in 2008 than 2016, it took Clinton four days to throw her full support behind Obama, but Sanders waited 36 days to endorse Clinton. Sanders may have strategically stayed in the race longer after losing than any other presidential candidate in history in order to move the Democratic Party platform to the left, but doing so with the first female presidential nominee suggests gender may have played a role. We argue that there would have been public outcry over Sanders staying in the race if Clinton were seen as a fully legitimate candidate. Instead, unconscious bias from her ideal citizen incongruity meant that even though she had won, her claim to the title was not seen as entirely legitimate by millions of Americans. Were Clinton a white man, Sanders staying in the race would have seemed peculiar and perhaps offensive, but since Clinton was the first woman to win the nomination, Sanders's unusual decision went virtually unremarked.

CONCLUSION

Sexism during the 2016 Democratic primary meant that the election looked very different than it would have looked with two male candidates. The most current research on gender bias and the presidency finds that, although there is more support for a female commander in chief than at any other point in U.S. history, more than one in ten Americans still hold a strong bias against electing a woman to the White House. That is a significant number given that presidential elections are generally decided within a few percentage points in a handful of swing states in the Electoral College.

Over the course of her public life, Clinton has had to navigate conflicting expectations of the double bind of women's leadership. She has "feminine" and "masculine" personas to avoid harsh evaluations for being too far to one side or the other, but this has not been effective in preventing nearly three decades of gendered vitriol aimed at her in the press and public discourse. Studies of women's leadership show that voters respond with moral outrage to women who are perceived as power seeking, and Clinton has certainly been the target of this outrage. Her approval ratings soar when she is in a position of power but plummet when she seeks a higher office.

Gender dynamics were present in the 2008 Democratic primary election when Clinton ran against Obama. Clinton received far more negative media coverage, her first name was used more often than those of male competitors of both parties, she was asked to step out of the race prematurely, she was framed using negative gender stereotypes, reporters talked about her dress and appearance, and political commentators discussed Clinton in overtly sexist ways that diminished her candidacy. A poll taken after the election found that Americans thought Clinton was treated much more harshly in the election because of her gender than Obama because of his race. Clinton went from being the inevitable party nominee to the Democratic dog in a manger: from a leading policy wonk and leader in human rights to a desperately ambitious candidate who was stubbornly standing in the way of electing the first black president.

Similar gender dynamics emerged in the 2016 Democratic primary. Clinton's press coverage was remarkably more negative in tone than Sanders's, including her issue coverage. Press coverage of Clinton "scandals" that originated in partisan investigations in Congress that found no wrongdoing received inordinate attention, by the left and the right. Clinton also faced hidden but powerful sexism in questions of her likeability and the "cool factor." Clinton was also framed as "establishment" for reasons owing to gender, and many on the left eschewed the historical nature of electing the first female president. Clinton and her supporters also faced a large amount of overt sexism from conservative and liberal commentators and the Sanders campaign. Although Clinton won the 2016 Democratic primary, she officially started the general election later than unusual and in a weakened state.

As noted in the opening of this chapter, a common refrain from Clinton critics is the idea that there is something special about *this* female candidate that makes her uniquely terrible or unlikeable or wrong for the job. But as indicated in chapter 2, the challenges that Clinton faced look remarkably similar to those faced by the 12 women who have previously made serious bids for the presidency. Clinton was exceptional in being one of the most qualified candidates to run for the presidency as measured by years of public service, but she was not an exceptional candidate in terms of likeability, coolness, policy positions, scandals, or ambition. She was treated as exceptional because she was a woman, and given the history of women running for the office, we posit that any woman who gets that close, regardless of political party, will be treated in a similar fashion. We explore the gender dynamics of the general election in the next chapter.

CHAPTER 5

"Such a Nasty Woman": The 2016 General Election

Gender (masculinity) played a bigger role in shaping the 2016 election than in any previous election in U.S. history, and not just because it was the first time a woman was running. Donald Trump gained national recognition as a brash billionaire in the 1980s and became a household name as a reality television star on *The Apprentice* from 2004 to 2015. In April 2016, Republican candidate Trump told an audience that Hillary Clinton was playing the "woman card" and that she lacked the "strength" to be president. Although he had made prior gendered and sexist comments about Clinton, this was the first time Trump explicitly acknowledged his intention to run on gender. Trump raised his political stature as the leader of the birther movement, publicly calling for President Barack Obama to release his birth certificate. Trump's hypermasculinity would have positioned him well for the presidency regardless of his opponent, but especially so in a race against a woman. Trump's unapologetic sexism and misogyny ran counter to historical ideas of how candidates should comport themselves, but it appealed to a sizeable number of Republicans for whom Trump's calls to return to an earlier time in history when people of color and women had little power resonated.

In this chapter, we examine the events of the general election through the lenses of sex and gender with an eye toward the double standards and overt sexism that influenced the outcome of the election. We begin with an examination of how the two candidates were covered in the press, followed by an analysis of overt sexism in right-wing media and from Trump and his surrogates. Particular attention is paid to Trump's conduct during the debates, which were prime moments for sexism.

The Trump-Clinton matchup provides an excellent case study for dissecting sex and gender in a general presidential election. Beyond Trump's almost caricatured presentation of masculinity, the candidates looked very different in terms of experience and policy positions. Based on her years of experience, Clinton was arguably the most qualified presidential candidate in history and certainly was the most qualified in the modern political age. As President Obama put it in a speech to the Democratic National Convention, "there has never been a man or a woman, not me, not Bill, nobody more qualified than Hillary Clinton to serve as president of the United States of America."[1] In contrast, Trump was the only candidate in history without any political or military experience, making him the least qualified candidate the United States has ever seen. If this were a typical presidential election instead of one with a female candidate, we could expect the most qualified candidate in history to be treated as such by the press and the public, and the least qualified to also be treated as such. We could expect the press to be vigilant in pointing out the substantive differences in experience, preparedness, policy positions, and strengths and weaknesses as political leaders. Instead, we find that the press favored Trump in the amount and type of coverage he received, that the press artificially leveled Clinton's and Trump's fitness for the office, and covered unsubstantiated scandals in a way that hurt Clinton. We also find that political leaders and the press effectively framed Clinton in sexist ways that diminished her candidacy.

MEDIA COVERAGE

In this section, we use existing studies to describe media coverage of Clinton and Trump in the general election. We examine the amount of coverage as well as press content about fitness to serve, tone, and frames.

Coverage Amount and Tone

Shortly after the election, Thomas Patterson from the Shorenstein Center at Harvard published an in-depth, quantitative analysis of press coverage of the election. His central finding is that the press failed in their duty to differentiate Clinton and Trump and instead leveled the two candidates in terms of fitness and likability. Patterson finds that, in addition to failing to inform the public about basic differences in candidate qualifications, the press often discussed the election in ways that benefitted Trump. For starters, Trump received a greater volume of press coverage than Clinton throughout the general election (figure 5.1).[2]

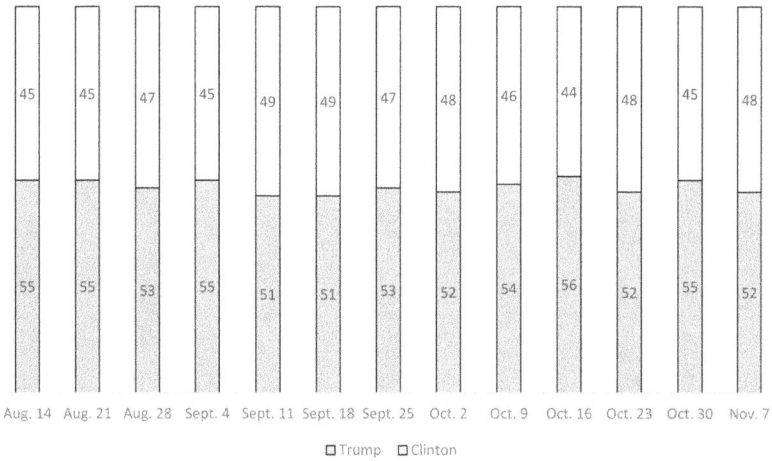

Figure 5.1 Percentage of Press Coverage for Clinton and Trump during the 2016 Election

Source: Data adapted from Harvard Kennedy School, Shorenstein Center on Media, Politics, and Public Policy.

In the primary, Trump's high volume of press coverage propelled him to the top of Republican polls,[3] and in the general election, it established his candidacy as more worthy of attention than Clinton's. Previous research finds that female candidates receive less media coverage than their male competitors,[4] and while sex bias may have played a role in Trump garnering more coverage, his bombastic style and penchant for making controversial statements may also account for it. Voters tuned in to see Trump's latest controversy, and media corporations capitalized on that appeal for profit. Whatever the cause or causes of the gender gap in amount of coverage, it advantaged Trump, especially since the tone of coverage was roughly equivalent for the candidates.

In terms of coverage tone, Patterson finds that the press was highly negative for both candidates—somewhat more negative for Trump during the general election and somewhat more negative for Clinton over the course of the entire election. In other words, the press was overwhelmingly negative toward both candidates and therefore failed to draw meaningful distinctions between Clinton and Trump. As we explore in the remainder of this chapter, Clinton's negative coverage had a distinctly sexist tone in the general election.

CLINTON   Negative ☐   Positive ☐   TRUMP

General Election Coverage   General Election Coverage

Full Campaign Coverage   Full Campaign Coverage

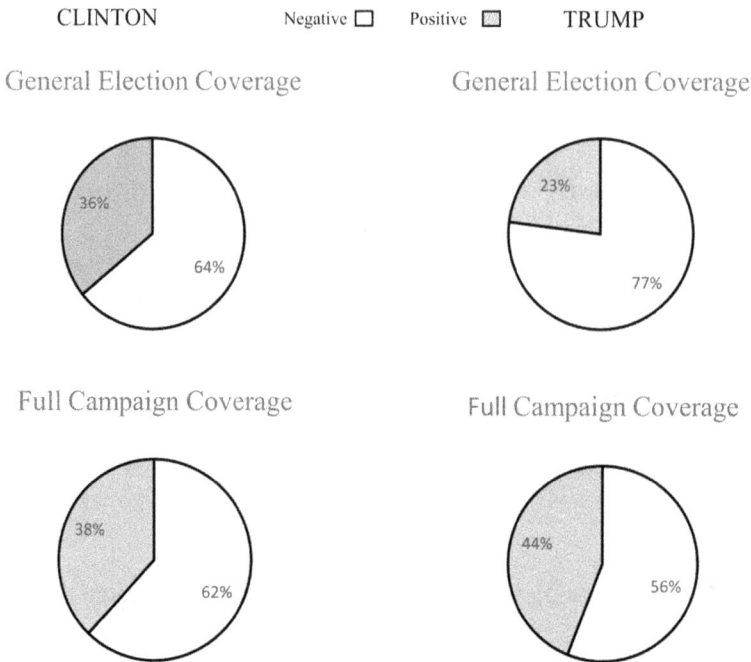

Figure 5.2 Percentage of Positive and Negative Coverage for Hillary Clinton and Donald Trump during 2016 Presidential Campaign

Source: Harvard Kennedy School, Shorenstein Center on Media, Politics, and Public Policy.

Fitness Coverage

The press also covered the candidates' experience in a way that benefitted Trump (figure 5.3). The press was equally negative in covering Clinton's and Trump's fitness for the office. This finding is remarkable given the striking difference in the candidates' political résumés.

On paper, Clinton was the most prepared candidate for the office, while political leaders from Trump's own party were questioning whether or not he was fit to execute the duties of the office. We contend that the overall high rate of challenging Clinton's fitness for the office was due to sexism. As noted in chapter 3, the U.S. press has a long history of questioning the qualifications of female presidential candidates because of their gender. We also argue that the fact that Clinton's fitness was challenged at the same rate as Trump's can be attributed to sexism. It is not a random occurrence that the first female presidential candidate had her fitness questioned at such a high rate, and at the same rate as the least qualified male candidate in U.S. history. Role congruity theory (RCT) explains why Clinton was

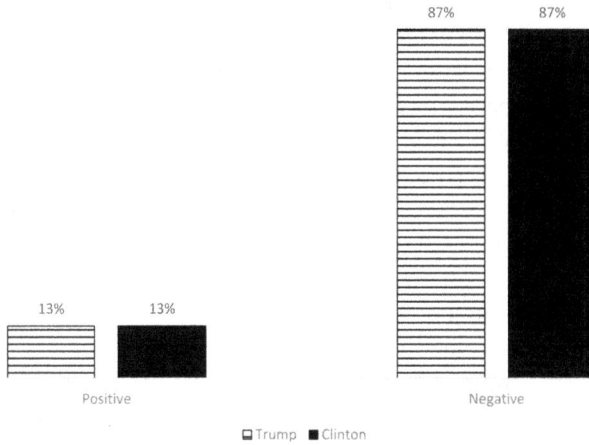

Figure 5.3   Tone of Press Coverage Related to "Fitness" of Office
Source: Harvard Kennedy School, Shorenstein Center on Media, Politics, and Public Policy.

held to a different fitness standard. Traditional gender role expectations for women conflict with leadership expectations in ways that prejudice people against female candidates.[5] This bias causes voters to view women as less suited for the presidency and to unfairly evaluate their fitness for the office. Gender-biased press coverage of Clinton's fitness encouraged voters to evaluate her fitness using a sexist double standard.

Frames

Media coverage and public discourse also disadvantaged Clinton in gendered ways through framing. For example, political reporters often use game frames that employ sports metaphors that disadvantage female candidates because they promote masculine norms.[6] Clinton was defined in public discourse by the "unlikable" frame, the "crooked Hillary" frame, the "frail" frame, and the "woman card" frame, all of which are demonstrably sexist.

The Unlikable Frame

As in the primary, Clinton's likability (or lack thereof) was a frequent topic of press and public discourse in the general election. Her smile and demeanor were frequently discussed by Trump, Republicans, pundits, and the press as proxies for her lack of likability. For example, after a debate on national security in September, Republican Party chair Reince Priebus suggested that Clinton should have smiled more.[7] He also tweeted that Clinton looked "angry" during the debate. Around the same time, conservative commentator David Frum criticized Clinton for smiling too much, tweeting, "Who told Hillary Clinton to keep smiling like she's at her granddaughter's birthday party?"[8] As body language expert Elizabeth Kuhnke notes, Clinton faced an impossible task during presidential debates with her facial expressions, using her "grandmother smile" to appear warm and avoid "resting bitch face," a serious expression that people interpret as women looking angry. Women are expected to smile three times as often as men in workplace settings, and powerful women are expected to compensate even more to avoid being seen as angry, which for women means unlikable. According to Kuhnke, because viewers and voters have been socially conditioned to associate strength with masculinity, powerful women often face a double standard when it comes to smiling: they have to smile to avoid appearing angry, but then smiling makes them appear smug or weak. "No man would ever be at fault for having a serious look on his face. The resting bitch face doesn't exist for me because it is simply a face of authority."[9]

The Crooked Hillary Frame

The "crooked Hillary" frame, a narrative implying that Clinton is corrupt, dishonest, and criminal, was a staple in right-wing media coverage throughout the election. The *Columbia Journalism Review* analysis of 1.25 million stories from April 1, 2015, through November 8, 2016 (Election Day), finds that *Breitbart*, a right-wing blog run by Trump campaign chief strategist and adviser Steve Bannon, was at the center of an active right-wing media ecosystem, surrounded by Fox News, Gateway Pundit, the *Washington Examiner*, The Daily Caller, *Infowars*, TruthFeed, and Conservative Treehouse.[10] Coverage of Clinton in these sources overwhelmingly focused on her e-mails, often with unsupported claims of criminality, followed by the Clinton Foundation and Benghazi "scandals." Trump's coverage was dominated by substantive policy items in right-wing media: immigration, jobs, and trade. Trump's numerous scandals received little attention.

Right-wing media was replete with concocted stories intended to harm the Clinton campaign. For example, the most shared post by Ending the Fed on Facebook in October was "It's Over: Hillary's ISIS Email Just Leaked & It's Worse Than Anyone Could Have Imagined."[11] That same month, *Infowars* circulated the popular article "Saudi Arabia Has Funded 20% of Hillary's Presidential Campaign, Saudi Crown Prince Claims," and *Breitbart* circulated "Clinton Cash: Khizr Khan's Deep Legal, Financial Connections to Saudi Arabia, Hillary's Clinton Foundation Tie Terror, Immigration, Email Scandals Together." These concocted connections were effective in smearing Clinton because they mix verifiable facts with falsehoods that play upon existing biases, including sexism. Much of the anti-Clinton coverage in right-wing media played upon the villainization of power-seeking women, the Lady Macbeth narrative that Clinton has contended with since appearing in national politics in the early 1990s. Salacious conspiracies would find less purchase with readers were the target not already seen as an evil mastermind, a trope that is fundamentally gendered.

Trump's scandal-ridden career and candidacy furnish a stark comparison with which to demonstrate the sexist double standards of the "crooked Hillary" frame. The "scandals" that were used to paint Clinton as crooked (namely, Benghazi and use of a private e-mail server) originated as partisan attacks from congressional Republicans, and extensive investigations into both cases revealed no wrongdoing on Clinton's part. However, Trump had some rather serious scandals that, were he running against a male candidate who was not weakened by gender bias, likely would have spelled his defeat. To illustrate the gendered double standard in public treatment of Clinton's and Trump's scandals, imagine Clinton being a legitimate presidential contender as a woman on her third marriage; having filed for bankruptcy four times; having 3,500 lawsuits filed against her over the years,[12] hiring 200 undocumented Polish workers to tear down a building and exposing them to unsafe working conditions; having settled a housing-discrimination claim with the federal government; having multiple lawsuits for not paying vendors; having a pending lawsuit against Clinton University for violating a litany of laws; and facing claims from 12 men that she engaged in sexually predatory behavior. Imagine Clinton going on to win the Electoral College after bragging about sexually assaulting men on tape and after her husband plagiarized parts of his speech at the Democratic National Convention. It is improbable that she would have even been in the race.

Mainstream media furthered the "crooked Hillary" frame by following partisan cues and focusing disproportionately on Clinton's scandals. Most of the general-election coverage centered on the horse race—who was ahead or behind—but scandal coverage was also a prominent topic of discussion about both candidates.

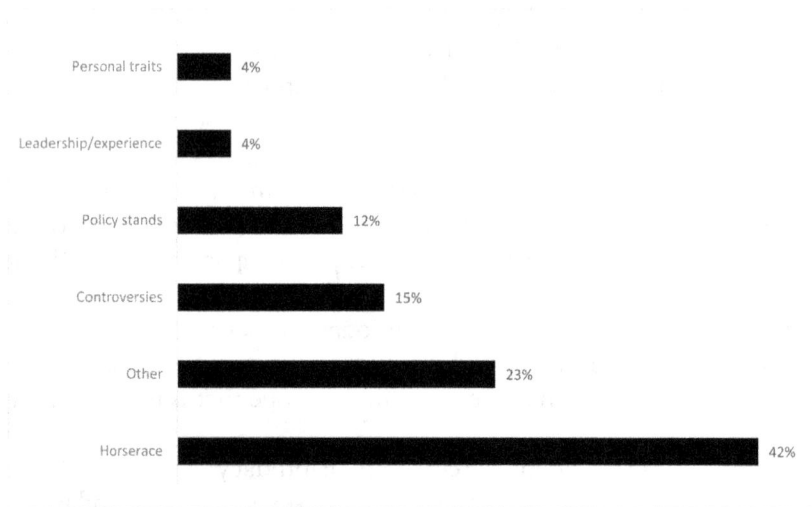

Personal traits	4%
Leadership/experience	4%
Policy stands	12%
Controversies	15%
Other	23%
Horserace	42%

Figure 5.4 Topic of Trump's Press Coverage, 2016 General Election
Source: Harvard Kennedy School, Shorenstein Center on Media, Politics, and Public Policy.

Press coverage was equally likely to focus on the candidates' personal traits, but Trump received more press on his policy positions (12 percent compared to 9 percent) and less press on his controversies (15 percent compared to 19 percent). Patterson points out that the press failed to effectively distinguish between actual and partisan-drive faux scandals. He asks, "Were the allegations surrounding Clinton of the same order of magnitude as those surrounding Trump? It's a question that political reporters made no serious effort to answer during the 2016 campaign."[13]

Clinton's scandal coverage was a decisive factor in the outcome of the election. In the last week of the election, FBI director James Comey sent a letter to Congress announcing that he was reopening the Clinton e-mail investigation, and his retraction four days later did little to revive the dive in Clinton's polls. National support for Clinton dropped 2.8 percent and did not rebound to prior levels by Election Day.[14] Nearly 40 percent of Clinton's coverage in the days leading up to the election was about the private e-mail server "scandal," and 91 percent of her coverage about controversies was negative.[15]

Press coverage of Comey's October 29 letter likely affected the outcome of the election. Political analyst Nate Silver concludes that the Comey letter "probably cost Clinton the election," but the press are reluctant to admit that or the role they played in pushing a salacious but ultimately nonsubstantive story.[16] Poll shifts in Michigan, Pennsylvania, and Florida in response to Comey's letter were enough to alter the outcome in the Electoral College. The "crooked Hillary" frame that circulated in public discourse throughout the campaign plowed fertile ground for undecided voters to believe that Clinton was crooked, and Comey's reversal a few days later did not repair the damage done. Silver cites the press's inordinate attention to and jump to conclusions about the letter as key to poll shifts, arguing that more professional coverage may have caused a measured voter reaction to the letter.

One aspect of the "crooked Hillary" frame is the idea that Clinton is dishonest, and unusually so. In reality, Clinton was far more honest in her campaign remarks than Trump during the election. As figure 5.5 shows, one in four of Clinton's statements on the campaign trail were false in some way (26.4 percent) compared to 69.0 percent of Trump's statements.

The gendered "crooked Hillary" frame harmed Clinton's candidacy, but Trump's bevy of sexist scandals that came out during the campaign had little impact on his popularity. He mocked Carly Fiorina's face ("Look at that face! Would anyone vote for that? Can you imagine that, the face of our next president?!!"); responded to Fox News anchor Megyn Kelly's tough questioning of him during a debate with the comment, "You could see there was blood coming out of her eyes, blood coming out of her wherever"; tweeted that Kelly was a "bimbo"; called supermodel Heidi Klum

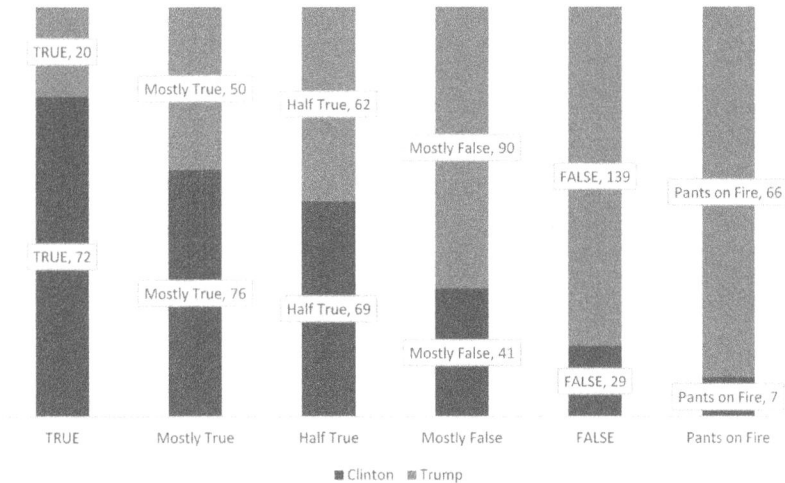

Figure 5.5 Candidate Statements and Rulings: Dishonesty in the 2016 General Election

Source: Politifact.

"fat"; referred to NBC journalist Katy Tur as "little Katy"; and tweeted that Clinton couldn't sexually satisfy her husband. Trump's many previous sexist comments were also brought up during the campaign, including a video in which he tells a 10-year-old that he'll be dating her in 10 years; a 1992 incident in which he told a group of 14-year-olds outside Trump Tower that he would be dating them in the future; his efforts to get Nancy O'Dell fired from hosting a pageant because she was pregnant; his body shaming of Miss Universe Alicia Machado by calling her "Miss Piggy"; his reference to actor Rosie O'Donnell as a "pig"; an incident in which he told journalist Gail Collins that she had the face of a dog; his insults about Cher's plastic surgery; and his remarks calling Arianna Huffington unattractive. Trump also expressed disgust for women's bodily functions, telling an employee that she was "disgusting" for taking a break to breastfeed her child and saying Clinton's bathroom break during a debate was "disgusting." Trump's also made various inappropriate comments about his daughter Ivanka, saying that he would date her were she not his daughter, that "she's got the best body." Trump's off-color comments about gender roles also came to light, including a 1992 *New York Magazine* interview in which he said of women, "You have to treat them like shit" and a 1994 interview in which he said he expects his wife to put dinner on the table and said, "I think that putting a wife to work is a very dangerous thing."

The most serious scandal that emerged during the general election was the release of a tape from 2005 in which he tells *Access Hollywood*'s Billy Bush:

> **Trump**: I moved on her, actually. You know, she was down on Palm Beach. I moved on her, and I failed. I'll admit it.
>
> **Unknown**: Whoa.
>
> **Trump**: I did try and fuck her. She was married.
>
> **Unknown**: That's huge news.
>
> **Trump**: No, no, Nancy. No, this was [unintelligible]—and I moved on her very heavily. In fact, I took her out furniture shopping. She wanted to get some furniture. I said, "I'll show you where they have some nice furniture." I took her out furniture—I moved on her like a bitch. But I couldn't get there. And she was married. Then all of a sudden I see her, she's now got the big phony tits and everything. She's totally changed her look.
>
> **Billy Bush**: Sheesh, your girl's hot as shit. In the purple.

Trump: Whoa! Whoa!

Bush: Yes! The Donald has scored. Whoa, my man!

[Crosstalk]

Trump: Look at you, you are a pussy.

[Crosstalk]

Trump: All right, you and I will walk out.

[Silence]

Trump: Maybe it's a different one.

Bush: It better not be the publicist. No, it's, it's her, it's—

Trump: Yeah, that's her. With the gold. I better use some Tic Tacs just in case I start kissing her. You know, I'm automatically attracted to beautiful— I just start kissing them. It's like a magnet. Just kiss. I don't even wait. And when you're a star, they let you do it. You can do anything.

Bush: Whatever you want.

Trump: Grab 'em by the pussy. You can do anything.

This tape was released on Friday, October 6, 2016. What makes the release date so notable is that within a matter of hours, WikiLeaks released the first of many batches of leaked DNC e-mails—a Clinton scandal. Harry Enten of FiveThirtyEight points out that it is difficult to isolate the effect of the DNC leaks because WikiLeaks released a new batch weekly in the month leading up to the election.[17] Nonetheless, he is able to track the evaporation of Clinton's seven-point lead in the last month of the election and ties it to the Comey letter and the WikiLeaks disclosures. Enten finds that Americans were interested in the leaks and that their release corresponds with a slow but steady drop in Clinton's polls leading up to a final significant dip caused by the Comey letter. Online searches for "WikiLeaks" topped searches for "FBI" during the last month, which suggests that the weekly drip of leaked documents affected her popularity.

We would expect Clinton's poll numbers to drop with the "scandal" of e-mail leaks, even if those e-mails did not actually reveal damaging information or behavior on the part of Clinton. What is remarkable for our analysis is that Trump's boasting of illegal sexually predatory behavior, a bona fide scandal, did not affect his electability. In an NBC/WSJ poll taken shortly after the *Access Hollywood* tape was released, only 32 percent of voters, mostly Democrats, thought it disqualified Trump to be president.[18] In the same poll, 48 percent of voters thought Clinton's handling of her husband's sex scandals in the 1990s was a legitimate concern for her presidency. In other words, voters were more concerned about Clinton's response to her husband's predatory behavior than Trump's actual predatory behavior.

What makes this scandal double standard even more remarkable is the backdrop of mounting sexual harassment, sexual assault, and rape allegations against Trump. By the end of the campaign, a total of nine women had alleged that Trump groped them over the years: Jessica Leeds on a plane (1981); Kristin Anderson at a Manhattan nightclub (1990); Jill Harth at Mar-a-Lago (1997); Karena Virginia outside the U.S. Open Tennis Championship (1998); Mindy McGillivray at Mar-a-Lago (2004); Natasha Stoynoff at Mar-a-Lago (2005); Miss Finland Ninni Laaksonen before an appearance on the *Late Show with David Letterman* (2006); Summer Zervos on the set of *The Apprentice* (2009); and Miss Washington USA Cassandra Searles at a beauty pageant (2013). Three women reported that he kissed them without their consent, including Cathy Heller at Mar-a-Lago (1996); former Miss USA contestant Temple Taggart McDowell (1997); and Trump Tower receptionist Rachel Crooks (2005). Additionally, fourteen beauty contestants reported that Trump walked in on them while they were changing. Many of these contestants were teenagers. Trump's more serious allegations also surfaced during the election, including the description of a violent rape given in a sworn deposition by his first wife Ivana during their divorce proceedings. Author Harry Hurt, who wrote a book referencing the deposition, described Trump confronting his wife after her plastic surgeon botched his scalp reduction surgery.[19] Hurt writes that Trump tore her clothes and raped her in order to mirror the pain of his botched operation.

Another allegation of rape came out during the election from "Katie Johnson," who claims that Trump raped her when she was just 13 years old at a party in 1994 organized by convicted sex offender Jeffrey Epstein. Epstein was convicted of soliciting sex from a minor in 2008 and paid numerous settlements to underage victims over many years.[20] Former president Bill Clinton and Trump were frequent guests at Epstein's parties. Johnson alleges that Trump had sex with her on three occasions but violently raped her a fourth time. (Note that all of these acts of "sex" would be statutory rape.) Johnson's allegations were corroborated by a woman who claims Trump had sex with her at these Epstein parties when she was 12 years old and by "Tiffany Doe," a woman who was 29 years old at the time who was hired by Epstein to procure underage girls for his parties. Doe's sworn declaration states:

> 7. It was at these series of parties that I personally witnessed the Plaintiff forced to perform various sexual acts with Donald J. Trump and Mr. Epstein. Both Mr. Trump and Mr. Epstein were advised that she was 13 years old.
> 8. I personally witnessed four sexual encounters that the plaintiff was forced to have with Mr. Trump during this period, including the fourth of these encounters where Mr. Trump forcibly raped her despite her pleas to stop.

Johnson withdrew her lawsuit against Trump just days before the election because of numerous death threats.

Regardless of whether the claims of Johnson or Doe or Ivana Trump or the two dozen other women who have publicly reported acts of sexual violence from Trump are accurate, what is remarkable is that the sheer volume of the claims, let alone their veracity and Trump's admission of sexual violence in the *Access Hollywood* tape, did not amount to a damaging scandal for Trump's candidacy. Trump's campaign barely responded to mounting allegations of sexual violence, perhaps because he did not need to since these "scandals" did not affect his support. In response to Ivana Trump's allegation, Trump's longtime attorney responded, "You can't rape your wife" (which is inaccurate since spousal rape was illegal at the time in New York), and Trump called the claim "without merit." Trump issued blanket denials for most of the claims as they surfaced, and when former *People* magazine writer Stoynoff came public with a claim of sexual assault in October 2016, Trump responded that he could not have sexually assaulted her because Stoynoff was not attractive enough. He told a crowd: "Take a look. You look at her. You tell me what you think. I don't think so. I don't think so."

Never before has a presidential candidate been plagued with such serious scandals, and yet they mattered little in the election. At the same time, dubious "scandals" against Clinton involving allegations that had been investigated and dismissed and leaks from the DNC that were only loosely associated with the candidate cost Clinton the election. As a female candidate, Clinton would not have been seen as a legitimate contender had she been carrying the scandal baggage that Trump brought into the campaign, and had numerous allegations of sexual violence been lobbed against her or a tape released in which she boasted about sexual assault. The stark difference in the substance and support of the candidates' respective scandals makes this case study of the gender double standard an obvious one. Many voters expect a purity from female candidates that is not applied to their male competitors, a purity that is impossible to achieve in the competitive world of politics. As former *New York Times* editor Jill Abramson put it: "It's fair to expect more transparency. But it's a double standard to insist on her purity."[21]

The Frail Frame

In the general election, another gendered frame emerged that played upon preexisting notions of female physical weakness, pitting Clinton's health at 68 years old against Trump's health at 70 years old. The "frail" frame portrayed Clinton as physically frail and weak—too weak to handle presidential responsibilities. One way this frame appeared was through constant jabs at Clinton's age from politicos. For example, Senate Majority Leader Mitch McConnell described the 2016 Democratic field as "a rerun of the *Golden Girls*."[22] Louisiana governor Bobby Jindal described the Democrats as having "old, tired ideas being pushed by old, tired candidates." Right-wing radio commentator Rush Limbaugh again asked whether voters "want to vote for somebody, a woman, and actually watch a woman get older before their eyes on a daily basis?" Political cartoons of Clinton using a walker were widely shared on blogs and social media.

Partisans also drummed up a health scare on the campaign trail to portray Clinton as unfit. This frame played upon previous efforts to depict Clinton as too physically frail for the presidency. When Clinton was secretary of state, she fell and hit her head at home, which gave her a concussion and a six-month recovery period.[23] Clinton did recover from this serious injury, but not before partisans used it to call into question her fitness for the presidency. As if to ward off gendered health criticisms, Clinton released her medical records during the invisible primary instead of following the usual process of waiting until becoming a party nominee.[24] The report made mention of Clinton's seasonal allergies, hypothyroidism, and precautionary use of blood thinners to ward off clots after her concussion, and deemed her to be in "excellent health." In contrast, in December 2015, Trump issued a bizarre letter from his personal physician, Harold Bornstein, that included few health details and the inaccurate claim that, if elected, Trump "would be the healthiest individual ever elected to the presidency."[25] Bornstein later admitted that he had drafted the letter in five minutes with Trump's limo waiting outside. A few months later, Bornstein issued a more legitimate medical report on Trump that indicated he was overweight, took daily doses of a cholesterol drug and prescription aspirin, and was in "excellent physical health." In other words, the bills of health for Clinton and Trump looked quite similar, but this fact did not prevent gendered framing of Clinton as "frail."

Starting in August, the Trump campaign put out a barrage of claims about Clinton's poor health. On multiple occasions, Trump claimed Clinton "doesn't have the stamina" to be president. For example, during the first presidential debate, Trump pronounced that "to be president of this country, you need tremendous stamina," gesturing that Clinton lacked it. Trump surrogates like Rudy Giuliani and radio host and conspiracy theorist Alex Jones all promoted the unified message that Clinton was physically unfit for the presidency. Giuliani told a Sunday news program: "She has an entire media empire that . . . fails to point out several signs of illness by her. What you've got to do is go online."[26] A quick online search reveals a treasure trove of fake documents and videos to support claims of Clinton's poor health. In early September, Trump campaign cochair Sam Clovis told reporters that Clinton appears "wobbly and a little frail" and needs "longer rest periods," and he questioned her ability to complete a presidential term given health concerns.[27] When asked about the basis for this claim, Clovis made reference to Clinton's ability to board planes and get in and out of vehicles. Clovis went on to describe Trump in very masculine terms, suggesting that the septuagenarian's girth made him an athlete:

> I think the interesting aspect of this will be, I think, the contrast because you know Mr. Trump is a very, he's a big guy. You know, he's big enough to play tight end for the Jets, you know, for the Patriots, and so, he's a big, robust fellow and again Mrs. Clinton will be up on the stage as well. I think it'll be a great contrast physically, but I also think it'll be a great contrast in style.

Not only did Clovis cast Trump as a strapping athlete in comparison to a physically weak Clinton, but he also implied that the sheer size difference between a man and a woman would be an advantage for Trump, playing upon masculine notions of the presidency.

Part of the "frail" frame is a mental fragility that Trump trumped up. In August 2016, he told multiple campaign rallies that Clinton was mentally ill, labeling her "unstable Hillary Clinton" and saying, "I don't think she's all there."[28] Trump advocate Amy Kremer claimed multiple times on CNN that Clinton suffers from chronic traumatic encephalopathy (CTE), a disease caused by repeated blows to the head, and Drudge and Steve Bannon's right-wing blog *Breitbart* pushed the "frail" frame intensely for months.

The "frail" frame reached a fever pitch after Clinton made an abrupt exit from a September 11 memorial event and revealed that she had been diagnosed with pneumonia.[29] Clinton had tried to power through the campaign with the diagnosis, hiding it from most of her staff, the press, and the public, but dehydration coupled with medication brought the illness to light. Presidential campaigns are notoriously exhausting, and in 2004, John Kerry also came down with pneumonia during the election. Clinton's running mate, Virginia senator Tim Kaine, told reporters that he had a hard time keeping up with Clinton and her schedule, and her insistence that she attend the 9/11 ceremony instead of resting is an indication of her refusal to slow down, even for a day or two. After her illness became public knowledge, Clinton released more detailed medical records that confirmed she was in good health. Clinton responded to the "frail" frame with humor, opening a jar of pickles on *Jimmy Kimmel Live* to demonstrate her strength,[30] but the idea that Clinton was too frail to serve as president had already found purchase in the minds of millions of Americans.

In October, the Trump campaign put out an ad claiming that Clinton lacked the "fortitude, strength, or stamina to lead in our world," and it was aired in key battleground states.[31] In the second presidential debate, he announced that Clinton "doesn't have the stamina" to be president.[32] Clinton responded, "As soon as he travels to 112 countries and negotiates a peace deal, a cease fire, a release of dissidents, an opening of new opportunities in nations around the world, or even spends 11 hours testifying in front of a congressional committee he can talk to me about stamina."[33] Trump, the oldest candidate to ever run for the presidency, would repeat this stamina stanza many times until Election Day, at times making the connection to gender overt. For example, at a rally in Pennsylvania, Trump tied Clinton's gender to her alleged frailty, saying: "Here's a woman—she's supposed to fight all of these different things, and she can't make it 15 feet to her car. She's home resting right now. Folks, we need stamina."[34]

Many media commentators noted the double standard at play with Clinton's health on the campaign trail. Dr. Judy Stone points out that Clinton is a healthy woman who happened to get an infection on the campaign trail (pneumonia). She was then "scrutinized and held to standards that no other candidate has been subjected to. The media has been echoing Trump, hounding her to release personal details of her health, which she has done."[35] James Hamblin also points out the role the press played in propping up the "frail" frame.[36] For example, when Clinton had a coughing spell at a rally in Cleveland, NBC published a video of the coughing as a news story with the headline "Hillary Clinton Fights

Back Coughing Attack," which right-wing blogger Matt Drudge picked up under the title "Getting Worse: Clinton Cough Violently Returns. Health Status up in the Air."[37] Reporter David A. Graham labeled the uproar over Clinton's health the "Birtherism of 2016."[38]

What was rarely noted by commentators outside of the feminist blogosphere was the gendered nature of the "frail" frame. One exception is Amanda Hess, who wrote:

> Over the course of his career, Trump has amassed a vast verbal arsenal to wield against women—*pig, dog, slob, bimbo, disgusting, neurotic, ugly*—but when it comes to Clinton, it's all *stamina, stamina, stamina*. The word implies everything Trump has been told he's no longer allowed to say out-right. It strikes a glancing blow at Clinton's sex without his ever having to call her an old lady.[39]

Hess also points out the specifically gendered connotation of the term "stamina"—that it "is a guy thing, and guys know it."[40] Symbolically, the very use of "stamina" as the measure of presidential fitness disqualifies a female candidate at a base level. A poll taken by Marist Institute for Public Opinion in September 2016 found that 53 percent of Americans thought Trump had more stamina, compared to 39 percent for Clinton.[41] Clinton's minor health issues—pneumonia and coughing from allergies— would not have been newsworthy had she been a male candidate because the idea that allergies and infections make a man unfit for the presidency is far-fetched and not newsworthy. In the past, actual serious illness— for example, Franklin D. Roosevelt's progressive polio and John F. Kennedy's Addison's disease—did not disqualify male candidates for the presidency. The "frail" frame worked to discredit Clinton at least in part because of gendered notions of women as "the weaker sex."

The Woman Card Frame

During the 2016 primary, Trump told reporters, "I'm going to be tak-ing a lot of the things that Bernie said and using them. I can reread some of his speeches and I can get some very good material."[42] And indeed he did. Trump used the "woman card" frame that was popular in the primary, stating: "I think the only card she has is the woman's card. She's got nothing else going . . . if Hillary Clinton were a man I don't think she'd get 5% of the vote."[43] The historic track record of challenges faced by female presidential candidates indicates that Clinton actually would have received more of the vote if she were a man. If Clinton were

Bob Smith, a former senator from New York and secretary of state with decades of legal advocacy and policy experience and a $1.2 billion campaign war chest,[44] he probably would have won both the popular vote and the Electoral College. Aside from the literal meaning of Trump's words, as with Sanders surrogates, the intent was to admonish voters for supporting Clinton because of her sex, as though a prioritization of descriptive representation were a bad thing. Trump immediately followed up his "woman card" comment with the gendered "frail" frame, stating, "Hillary does not have the strength or stamina to deal with China or other things." In the span of a few seconds, Trump managed to say both that Clinton was benefitting from her gender and that her gender made her too weak for the presidency.

Clinton responded to Trump's "woman card" comment with the quip, "Well, if fighting for women's health care and paid family leave and equal pay is playing the woman card, then deal me in." Clinton also tweeted a response: "Women still face too many barriers—a president shouldn't be part of the problem. Comments like Trump's set us back."[45] The Clinton campaign circulated the hashtag #womancard and sent paper "woman cards" to donors. Trump used this frame throughout the general election, for example, telling *Today*, "Without the woman's card Hillary would not even be a viable person to run for city council positions."[46]

The "woman card" Frame is sexist. It both discounts the importance of descriptive representation in politics (i.e., electing people who are underrepresented in politics to high office) and inaccurately implies that the only thing the most experienced presidential candidate in history has going for her is her gender. This reductive and misleading critique resonated with many right-wing voters because it played upon broader critiques of identity politics, the idea that certain groups (e.g., women and people of color) are receiving unfair advantages on the basis of their identity. Trump was skillfully tapping into a deep well of resentment about political correctness (PC). Political correctness is the practice of avoiding actions, words, or other forms of expression that may insult or exclude identity groups that are marginalized or that face discrimination, including women and people of color. David French argues that "One has to live and work well outside the core of blue America to understand how frustrated—no, furious—millions of Americans are with the censorious and scolding progressive impulse that is branded under the catch-all category of 'political correctness' or just 'P.C.' "[47] Trump's use of the "woman card" frame tapped into this preexisting resentment with some voters.

OVERT SEXISM

Sexism on the campaign trail was perhaps inevitable with the first female candidate in a general election, given public biases against power-seeking women. This bias was exploited by the press (especially right-wing media), Trump surrogates, and Trump himself. Additionally, public spaces and political discourse were rife with sexism aimed at Clinton from Trump supporters. We explore overt sexism from three different quarters in this section.

The Press

During the general election, Clinton was the target of comments about her voice, her appearance, her character, her health, and her sexuality in conservative media. In September 2016, Brit Hume, a Fox News commentator, made a series of sexist comments about Clinton during the first debate, stating that she looked "smug" and "not very attractive."[48] Earlier in the campaign, Hume had commented on Clinton's voice ("stern, angry, joyless") and criticized her for "shouting angrily" and not smiling enough at campaign events. Fox News's Brian Kilmeade stated that women will vote for Clinton "just because she's a woman" and claimed that Clinton likes to "play the victim card."[49] Fox News's Andrea Tantaros criticized Clinton for "buil[ding] a career on being a permanent victim . . . 'vote for me, I use the same restroom as you.'"[50] Dick Morris, a former adviser to Bill Clinton, wrote several articles in the *National Enquirer* claiming that Hillary Clinton is lesbian who preys on women.[51]

Overall, overt sexism aimed at Clinton in mainstream print and cable news was not as pronounced in 2016 as it was during her 2008 bid, but the media environment had shifted dramatically during that time. The *Columbia Journalism Review* study shows that in 2016 many Americans were getting their news from right-wing sources, with the agenda being heavily influenced by Bannon's *Breitbart News*.[52] Sexism was endemic to right-wing coverage of Clinton. A quick look at headlines indicates that some outlets were not shy about their misogyny. The *Independent Journal-Review* published the piece "Here's What Hillary Looks Like after Paying $600 for a Haircut That Shut Down an Entire Salon," which was picked up by the *New York Post*.[53] The *Daily Wire* published a piece titled "Yes, Hillary Clinton Is Shrill. No, It's Not Sexist to Say So."[54] This outlet also wrote a story with the headline "Hillary Breaks Out the Ugliest Outfit in Human History." The *Daily Mail* put out a piece asking, "Could Hillary Clinton's Smile Cost Her the Election?" after the third debate.

Trump Surrogates

Trump surrogates and GOP leaders also engaged in overt sexism against Clinton during the general election with reference to her sexual practices. Broward County GOP chair Bob Sutton stated that Trump would easily best Clinton in a debate: "I think when Donald Trump debates Hillary Clinton she's going to go down like Monica Lewinsky."[55] In the waning days of the election, former New Hampshire governor and Trump surrogate John Sununu joked that President Bill Clinton was not interested in having sex with Hillary Clinton.[56] The crowd roared with laughter when Sununu asked, "You think Bill was referring to Hillary when he said, 'I did not have sex with that woman'?" Sununu was referring to Bill Clinton's infamous 1998 denial of sexual relations with White House intern Monica Lewinsky. Former New York City mayor and Trump surrogate Rudy Giuliani played upon the gender stereotype of women being bad with money in his defense of Trump after revelations that the candidate avoided taxes for nearly two decades: "Don't you think a man who has this kind of economic genius is a lot better for the United States than a woman?"[57] In other words, a man who skirted taxes due to large business losses is still better than a woman.

Trump

The press and Trump surrogates circulated sexist ideas in the election, but the candidate himself was the most prolific promoter of misogyny on the campaign trail. Trump's persistent sexism made gender the primary theme of the general election. In the early part of the Republican primary, Trump said Clinton "got schlonged" by Barack Obama in 2008, a vulgar Yiddish word for a penis that established his frat-boy approach to his competitor.[58] In September 2016, Trump told a reporter, "I just don't think she [Clinton] has a presidential look, and you need a presidential look."[59] A few days later, he asked a crowd of mostly male supporters in Cleveland, "And she looks presidential, fellows?" These comments are overtly sexist in that they ask people to consider Clinton's physical appearance, a sexist double standard since male candidates are not judged presidential based on their appearance. On a deeper level, Trump was employing dog-whistle sexism to trigger voter biases about the right identity for the president (male). Trump was tapping into the identity incongruity theory, which leads many Americans to see women and people of color running for or occupying the presidency as fundamentally lacking the right identity to hold the office, and for that reason, judge them more harshly for the same actions than they do white men.

Trump's sexism appeared again when he reduced Clinton to her physical appearance after the debate. During a campaign rally in mid-October, Trump described Clinton walking in front of him at the second debate. He chuckled, "When she walked in front of me, believe me I was not impressed."[60] With this comment, Trump dehumanized Clinton by reducing her to a sex object, set himself up in a gendered position of power as a validator of her worth, and deemed her physical appearance undesirable. Trump played upon preexisting biases that women's worth is fundamentally based on their physical desirability, regardless of whatever position of power they achieve in their professional life.

Trump also suggested that Clinton was unfaithful to her husband, a standard to which he does not hold himself. In October, after the release of the *Access Hollywood* tape and a poor debate showing, Trump accused Clinton of cheating on her husband: "Hillary Clinton's only loyalty is to her financial contributors and to herself. I don't even think she's loyal to Bill, if you want to know the truth. And really, folks, really, why should she be? Right? Why should she be?"[61] This gendered line of attack is especially rich given that multiple press outlets reported on Trump cheating on his first wife Ivana with Marla Maples in the early 1990s.

Trump also openly mocked Clinton for "shouting" at campaign events, invoking sexist critiques of her female voice.[62] In April 2016, during an interview on MSNBC's *Morning Joe*, Trump said: "I haven't quite recovered—it's early in the morning—from her shouting that message. And I know a lot of people would say you can't say that about a woman because, of course, a woman doesn't shout, but the way she shouted that message was not. Eww."[63] Later in the campaign, he referred to Clinton's voice as "shrill,"[64] a term with a long, sexist history of telling women to be quiet.[65] Trump defended his comments on MSNBC by saying, "I know men that are shrill."[66]

The presidential debates were a prime time for Trump sexism. According to national polls, Clinton handily bested Trump in all three debates, although his relative performance improved from the first to the third debate. Clinton won the first debate by 35 points (62 percent to 27 percent), the second by 23 points (57 percent to 34 percent), and the third by 13 points (52 percent to 39 percent).[67] In each debate, Trump used sexist rhetorical and physical strategies to assert his masculinity. We recount the most sexist moments of the three debates here.

The First Debate

The first debate took place at Hofstra University in New York on September 26, 2016. One way Trump enacted sexism was his use of Clinton's first name. Clinton responded by referring to Trump as "Donald." Trump also engaged in sexism in the first debate by interrupting. During this exchange, Trump interrupted Clinton 51 times, compared to her 17 interruptions.[68] Trump's interruptions were a mix of petulant nos and talking over Clinton until the moderator jumped in to preserve her allotted time. His frequent and disproportionate interruptions, humorously labeled "manterruptions" in media commentary, are a common experience for women in professional settings. Interruptions in conversation are not inherently sexist, but decades of research show that men interrupt women more frequently than they interrupt men and more frequently than women interrupt men.[69] This gendered pattern of communication is a subtle way of devaluing women's voices, particularly in professional settings. Women from both political parties expressed their concerns to the press about Trump's sexist interruptions during the debate.[70] Reporters Emily Crockett and Sarah Frostenson note that "it was a pretty stunning display, even for Trump," a candidate known for his boorish campaign style.[71]

The Second Debate

The second presidential debate took place on October 9, 2016, at Washington University in St. Louis. At the start of the debate, Trump stated his intention to refer to Clinton as "Secretary Clinton" instead of by her first name as he had done in the first debate, and it seemed that he might be correcting his sexism, but no. Trump interrupted Clinton 18 times compared to Clinton's single interruption.[72] Trump's disproportionate interruptions were particularly egregious in this debate, probably because it was a less formal town hall format. Trump also enacted sexism in whom he invited to attend and in comments about Clinton's body.

This second debate occurred just two days after the release of the *Access Hollywood* tape in which Trump bragged about acts that legally constitute sexual assault. The Trump campaign responded to the tape with the politically bizarre and sexist act of hosting a press conference before the debate with Paula Jones, Juanita Broaddrick, and Kathleen Willey, three women who report sexual misconduct by Bill Clinton. A fourth woman, Kathy Shelton, was also present. Clinton was assigned to represent Shelton's rapist through the University of Arkansas Law School Legal Aid Clinic. Clinton petitioned to get out of defending him, but her request was denied by the judge. After tearing into Clinton for her husband's actions in the press conference, these four women sat with the Trump family in the audience during the debate. Then, during the debate, Trump directly held Clinton accountable for her husband's behavior: "If you look at Bill Clinton, mine are words and his were actions. There's never been anybody in the history of politics in this nation that's been so abusive to women."[73] This tactic is sexist in that it equates Trump's allegations of sexual violence with Clinton's husband's allegations of sexual violence. The number of women who have reported sexual misconduct from Trump and Bill Clinton make it statistically likely that they both engaged in these behaviors, but penalizing Clinton for her husband's actions, and holding her responsible for the sexual violence of a client she was obligated to defend, only makes sense in a society that holds women responsible for the behavior of men in their lives.

Holding women accountable for the misdeeds of their husbands is a common, sexist American pastime that assumes wives are an extension of their husbands instead of independent beings.[74] The notion that Clinton is responsible for her husband's actions derives from the ancient belief that women are inherently secondary to and a part of their husband, their humanity subsumed into his being. The biblical story of Eve being created from Adam's rib epitomizes this idea. This thinking permeated colonial America under *feme covert*, Puritan rules that legally subsumed women under husbands and forced wives to adopt their husband's beliefs. Legal vestiges of this thinking can be found in the not so distant past. Until the 1960s, wives were not allowed to open bank accounts without their husband's approval, and wives needed their husband's signature to obtain a credit card until 1974.[75]

This was not the first time in the election that Clinton was held responsible for her husband's actions. Bernie Sanders enacted this retrograde thinking in the primary when he implied that Clinton was responsible for the North American Free Trade Agreement (NAFTA), a policy that he husband promoted, and Trump did it repeatedly with Bill Clinton's sexual misconduct in the general election. A nonsexist way of considering Clinton's responsibility for her husband is to see her as a distinct human being with a different set of ethical beliefs and moral codes. To do so would make it impossible to equate Trump's misconduct with Clinton's spouse's misconduct.

During the second debate, Trump used his size to lurk over and behind Clinton at many points in what some commentators called "the ugliest debate in U.S. history."[76] Trump edged his way closer to Clinton when she had the floor, at times towering behind her, too close for comfort. Social media lit up with comments about Trump using his size to loom behind Clinton. Viewers created mash-up videos of all the times Trump stood behind Clinton, set to ominous music, several of which went viral.

Trump tried to visually dominate Clinton using his size and body position, a physical performance of hypermasculinity.

The Third Debate

Trump's sexism was on full display in the third debate, which took place on October 19, 2016, at the University of Nevada, Las Vegas. He also interrupted Clinton 37 times to her 9 interruptions.[77] Trump also enacted sexism with the substance of his comments. He called Clinton "extremely upset, extremely angry" over a Supreme Court decision, tapping into the preexisting bias that women in general, and female candidates in particular, are overly emotional and therefore unfit for the rational world of politics. Trump's claim partway through the debate that "nobody has more respect for women than me" elicited laughter from the crowd.[78]

The most stunning moment of sexism in the third debate is the time Trump told viewers "nobody respects women more than me,"[79] then moments later referred to Clinton as "such a nasty woman." Direct insults are exceedingly rare in presidential debates.[80] Trump was responding to Clinton's comment, "I am on record as saying that we need to put more money into the Social Security trust fund—that's part of my commitment to raise taxes on the wealthy. My Social Security payroll contribution will go up, as will Donald's, assuming he can't figure out how to get out of it."[81] Clinton was referencing the revelation that Trump had avoided paying federal income tax for as many as 18 years. Trump's reference to Clinton was explicitly gendered in that he referred to her gender and explicitly sexist in that he labeled Clinton "nasty" because she dared to challenge him. Natasha Geiling points out that the "nasty woman" narrative, in which a woman dares to challenge the patriarchal order, has a long history in literature and life. From Delilah cutting Samson's hair to the witch hunts in colonial America, "nasty women" are punished for their defiance. Trump laid bare his particular umbrage against being challenged by a woman during the third debate.

Rallies

On the campaign trail, Trump emboldened sexism the likes of which has never been seen on the national political stage. Sexism was inevitable with the first female general election candidate, but Trump's rhetoric opened the floodgates of sexism for his supporters on social media and campaign events. Attendees at Trump rallies displayed unbridled misogyny with yells and chants of "tramp," "whore," "Kill her," "Lock her up," and "Trump that bitch."[82] The most frequent chant about Clinton at Trump rallies was "Lock her up," a manifestation of the effectiveness of the "corrupt Hillary" frame.

Trump supporters circulated sexist Clinton slogans in social media, on signs, and on hats, T-shirts, pens, cups, and other merchandise. At the Republican National Convention, Trump supporters were selling items with sexist statements such as "Hillary sucks but not like Monica," "Trump that bitch," and "2 fat thighs, 2 small breasts, 1 left wing." At Trump rallies, supporters were photographed wearing shirts and hats and waving signs that said "Donald Trump, Finally Someone with Balls," "Don't Be a Pussy, Vote for Trump," "Hillary Couldn't Satisfy Her Husband, Can't Satisfy U.S.," "Better to Grab a Pussy Than to be One," "If You Can Read This, The Bitch Fell Off" featuring Clinton falling off a motorcycle being driven by Trump, "Life's a Bitch, Don't Vote for One," "Trump v. Tramp," "I Wish Hillary Had Married OJ," "She's a Cunt, Vote for Trump," and "Trump That Bitch."[83]

Trump also made thinly veiled threats on Clinton's life, a behavior that goes beyond the pale in presidential politics. At a rally in August in North Carolina, he told the audience: "Hillary wants to abolish—essentially abolish—the Second Amendment. If she gets to pick her judges, nothing you can do, folks. Although the Second Amendment people, maybe there is. I don't know."[84] A month later at a rally in Miami, Trump suggested that Clinton's Secret Service detail should stop carrying guns and "see what happens."[85] This is the first time a presidential candidate implicitly called for the assassination of an opponent in public forums. It was an effective way for Trump to assert his masculinity in the contest, and it required a vilified opponent, one whom his supporters saw as worthy of violence or death. The sexist attacks on Clinton's character and preexisting biases against power-seeking women were fertile ground for Trump's assassination suggestions.

CONCLUSION

In this chapter, we analyzed sex and gender in the 2016 general election. Sex (sexism) was a constant theme of the 2016 presidential election, mostly because Trump frequently stressed its importance in holding the office in subtle and not-so-subtle ways. Gender (hypermasculinity) was also a dominant theme, as Trump enacted hypermasculinity in his exchanges about and with Clinton on the campaign trail. This election pitted a highly qualified candidate for the office in the modern political age against the least qualified candidate, a fact that was obscured by a leveling of the candidates in news media, which we attribute to gender biases.

We pulled together postelection studies and moments to get the bigger picture of what happened in terms of press and public discourse during the election. In short, we find that the press failed to accurately inform voters of the differences between the candidates in terms of fitness, likability, and scandals. Trump received more overall coverage, signaling that he was worthy of more attention. Trump and Clinton received about the same amount of negative press coverage and coverage challenging their respective fitness for the office. The press also focused more on Clinton's faux scandals and paid little attention to Trump's actual scandals, especially those involving dozens of allegations of sexual violence levelled against him. Media coverage and public discourse also harmed Clinton's candidacy in sexist ways by framing her as unlikable, crooked, and frail and by suggesting an unfair advantage due to her gender.

The "unlikable" frame is the product of the double bind of women's leadership, where they are expected to appear masculine in order to be seen as legitimate leaders but are then criticized as "bitchy" or unlikable because they violate gender norms of femininity. Sans evidence of deception or actual scandals, the "crooked" frame only sticks with preexisting biases against power-seeking women. Clinton has been marked as Lady Macbeth since she first emerged in national politics, and the 2016 election put the "corrupt" frame on steroids. The sexism at play here is obvious when compared to a lack of attention or framing of Trump's actual scandals, any one of which would have been the end of a female presidential candidate's bid. Mainstream media amplified right-wing media by covering Clinton's partisan-driven, sexism-enabled scandals significantly more than Trump's. The "frail" frame played upon sexist notions of women as the "weaker sex," unable to physically and mentally fulfill the duties of such a masculine office. Even though she released more medical records than Trump, and those records indicate that she was unusually healthy, Clinton was held to a physical standard that no other presidential candidate has been held to. In the middle of the general election, more Americans thought Trump had more stamina than Clinton. The "woman card" frame also diminished Clinton's candidacy by insinuating that the only thing the most experienced presidential candidate in history has going for her is that she is a woman and by treating her sex as an unfair advantage instead of a challenge in presidential politics. Trump effectively used the "woman card" frame to play upon preexisting resentments over political correctness and identity politics.

A particularly egregious double standard in the election was Trump's ability to weather dozens of allegations of sexual misconduct, ranging from sexual harassment to rape, even after the release of a recording in which he brags about engaging in sexual assault. Trump faced little harm from these allegations and admissions, and he was even able to effectively hold Clinton accountable for the sexual misconduct of her husband, a long and sexist practice in the United States. After the release of the Trump sexual assault tape, more voters were concerned about Clinton's handling of her husband's sexual misconduct in the 1990s than Trump's actual alleged sexual conduct.

Overt sexism was also ubiquitous in the 2016 general election in media coverage and from Trump surrogates, Trump supporters, and the candidate himself. People discussed Clinton's clothing, voice, lack of smiling, excessive smiling, sexual orientation, sexual activity, lack of sexual activity, inability to manage money, getting "schlonged," lack of "a presidential look," and body. Trump supporters called her a "tramp," a "whore," a "bitch," a "pussy," and a "cunt" and called for her to be imprisoned, sexually assaulted, and killed. Trump also made thinly veiled threats against Clinton's life. During the presidential debates, Trump constantly interrupted his opponent, physically lurked behind her in an intimidating fashion, deemed Clinton emotionally unfit for the office, and called her a "nasty woman."

CHAPTER 6

#CrookedHillary: An Analysis of Social Media Discourse during the 2016 Election with Eric Vorst

Over the course of the general election, various news outlets referred to the race as the "Twitter Election."[1] The race earned this title because Hillary Clinton and especially Donald Trump frequently took to Twitter to communicate with their followers. Twitter users were highly engaged with election news and content on the digital platform during the election, tweeting the hashtag #Election2016 more than 1 billion times during the election and 75 million times on Election Day.[2] Both candidates used Twitter to criticize each other. The most retweeted[3] tweet during the campaign was a Clinton tweet telling Trump, "Delete your account," in response to his tweet, "Obama just endorsed Crooked Hillary. He wants four more years of Obama—but nobody else does."[4] As of May 2018, Clinton's tweet had been retweeted 550,000 times and liked by 708,500 Twitter accounts. Both candidates targeted one another on multiple occasions on Twitter, but Trump also extended criticism to the overall legitimacy of the election process. He frequently using the term "rigged" to imply that his loss would indicate the election was a fraud.[5] For example, in late October Trump tweeted, "The election is absolutely being rigged by the dishonest and distorted media pushing Crooked Hillary-but also at many polling places-SAD."

Both candidates also experienced Twitter faux pas during the election. For example, in an attempt to connect with Latinx voters, Trump tweeted: "Happy #CincoDeMayo! The best taco bowls are made in Trump Tower Grill. I love Hispanics!" This tweet included a photo of Trump at his Trump Tower desk, grinning and giving a thumbs-up over a large tostada bowl. It was largely met with criticism for reducing political support to eating Latinx cuisine.[6] Clinton also had her share of Twitter gaffes. For example, in August, Clinton asked her followers to use three emojis[7] to describe their student loan debt, which was met with ridicule for diminishing the importance of this pressing policy issue.[8]

The use of Twitter in the 2016 election was unlike anything we have seen in U.S. politics in terms of the volume of citizen participation via social media and of candidate ability to speak directly to their followers at any time and to attack their competitor in real time. This election brought social media, namely Twitter and Facebook, into the political mainstream for the first time in a presidential election. In this chapter, we explore how sex and gender played a role in the new social media political environment. As discussed in previous chapters, female candidates face a more negative legacy media environment than male candidates do, and this is especially true for women who run for president. Our primary question in this chapter is whether female presidential candidates face similar challenges in the social media environment.

We suspect that the public's growing reliance on social media for political news and discussion presents additional hurdles for women competing for political power and influence, given a few studies that find that online political media is more sexist than legacy media. Regina Lawrence and Melody Rose find that during the 2008 Democratic primary, online media was considerably more negative in tone and content about Clinton than legacy print media.[9] Meredith Conroy et al. drew similar conclusions about Sarah Palin's coverage as a vice presidential candidate in 2008.[10] They conclude that "without editorial filters and the outward pursuit of objectivity, the misogyny quotient and negativity in new media is heightened for female candidates . . . new media is worse than old media for female candidates when it comes to negative tone and hard sexism."[11] This chapter contributes original data to burgeoning literature on the question of whether a social media political environment is hostile to female presidential candidates.

We begin this chapter with descriptions of legacy media, new media, and social media. We then review the literature on candidate use of social media. We then provide original analysis of Twitter during the 2016 Democratic Primary and the general election to see whether Clinton's coverage differed in ways that can be accounted for by sex or gender. We find differences in users' treatment of Clinton versus Sanders and Trump in social media that are likely accounted for by her sex and the gender dynamics of presidential elections. We conclude that the new popularity of social media in politics creates an even more hostile environment for female presidential candidates at a time in American history when they are finally starting to be considered serious contenders for the office.

LEGACY MEDIA, NEW MEDIA, AND SOCIAL MEDIA

In this section, we look at the new political environment candidates face as a result of evolving media technology. Hunt Allcott and Matthew Gentzkow write that "American democracy has been repeatedly buffeted by changes in media technology" in ways that make it more challenging for the fourth branch to hold power accountable.[12] They credit cheap newsprint in the 19th century with the spread of partisan balderdash, radio with reducing substantive policy debates to sound bites, and television with debasing the quality of political candidates by elevating those who are "telegenic." The advent of online news sources in the early 2000s and social media in the mid-2000s pose a threat to democratic discourse and citizen ability to make informed electoral decisions. We describe legacy media, new media, and social media in order to understand the new political environment candidates operate within.

"Old" or legacy media are print publications (which today often also have an online presence) that follow professional journalistic ethics, norms of fact checking, and a multilayered editorial process. The journalism code of ethics used today was developed by the Commission on Freedom of the Press, also known as the Hutchins Commission, a group formed during World War II by a group of publishers to determine how media should operate in modern democracy. Victor Pickard notes that the formation of the Hutchins Commission was a response to public criticism about consolidation of media ownership.[13] The commission developed five specific guidelines for the press to follow:

1. Present meaningful news, accurate and separated from opinion;
2. Serve as a forum for the exchange of comment and criticism and to expand access to diverse points of view;
3. Project a representative picture of the constituent groups in society by avoiding stereotypes;
4. Clarify the goals and values of society; implicit was an appeal to avoid pandering to the lowest common denominator; and
5. Give broad coverage of what was known about society.[14]

Since that time, the Society of Professional Journalists has developed multipoint guidelines for journalists to follow that address fact-checking standards, plagiarism, sourcing, permissions, and myriad other topics.

These guidelines are taught in journalism school and enforced in legacy media organizations. Examples of legacy media include the *Washington Post* and the *New York Times*. Print newspapers are a dying breed, so most legacy media sources have moved online and now use paywalls to continue to pursue high-quality journalism. Paywalls make legacy media less accessible than new media.

We define "new" or online media as online blog sites that do not necessarily abide by legacy media guidelines for objectivity fact checking and that have superficial or nonexistent editorial protocols. Most new media sources are online blogs, for example, *Breitbart* and *Infowars* on the right and *The Huffington Post* and *Alternet* on the left. Some new media sources are aggregators, meaning they pool stories from other sites, while others mostly generate original content. New media diverges from legacy media in that it tends to be ideologically extreme or partisan, it rarely involves (expensive) investigative journalism, and editorial control is loose or nonexistent. In the 2016 election, new media sources were the primary purveyors of fake news, meaning stories that are factually incorrect or misleading.[15]

An extreme example of the lack of editorial filters or journalistic standards in new media is the widely believed but patently false Pizzagate scandal. Pizzagate is a story that ties Clinton to a pedophilia ring being run out of Washington, D.C., pizza shop through an e-mail leak from campaign chair John Podesta. The Pizzagate conspiracy originated on an anonymous white supremacist's Twitter account and was quickly picked up by new media blogs, including the *Conservative Daily Post*, which falsely claimed the FBI had confirmed the story.[16] *Infowars* and other right-wing new media outlets hammered the story, and by the end of the election, nearly half of Republicans believed that Podesta's leaked e-mails contained coded messages to "pedophilia, human trafficking, and satanic ritual abuse," and 24 percent of Democrats believed this.[17] Fake news about Pizzagate motivated North Carolina resident Edgar Maddison Welch to travel to D.C. and fire his assault rifle into the Comet pizza shop before he was subdued by police.[18] Welch was sentenced to four years in prison.

Some publications are hybrids of legacy and new media—for example, Politico, founded in 2007, and The Daily Beast, created in 2008. Both of these outlets are only present online, but both use legacy media editorial and fact-checking processes. New media and hybrid outlets often mix "hard" investigative news with "soft" entertainment news to pay the bills and avoid having to put up a paywall. The vast range in types and quality of online news sources makes it difficult for readers to evaluate the quality of the news they are consuming, a challenge that is exacerbated by the dissemination of articles through social media networks that add a layer of confidence to the source because it essentially comes recommended from a "friend."

According to the Pew Research Center, 93 percent of adults in the United States get their news from online sources,[19] and most political information is consumed and disseminated via social media platforms like Facebook and Twitter.[20] Although much of the political content that is shared on these platforms is from legacy press, which are more reputable than new media, the personal commentary that goes along with legacy media articles opens the door for misinformation, rumors, conspiracy hawking, and unsolicited and unsavory commentary. Also, partisan news media that eschews facts and fact checking in order to promote ideological agendas are shared alongside legacy media and trustworthy new media outlets in a way that levels the quality of information in each. Pew Research finds that individuals are less discerning of the quality of the news sources they post, so long as this information confirms their political bias.[21]

Political communication scholars have made a lot of progress toward understanding social media and its broader impact on American politics and democratic values. Much of this scholarship has been directed at how political behaviors online influence offline political behaviors[22] and, more recently, how the mechanisms of online social networking produce political echo chambers, in which users are isolated from attitude-challenging content, and filter bubbles, where content is curated by an algorithm that takes into account viewers' previous behaviors and thus limits the content to which users are exposed in a manner that will bias their information retrieval.[23] With respect to political echo chambers, the expectation is that social media venues enable users to select whom to follow and interact with and that these selections will be politically similar, limiting an individual's exposure to ideologically crosscutting information. Moreover, this exposure can be characterized as incidental; individuals may not be cognizant that their network is politically homogenous and may assume they are getting a broader snapshot of political news from their feeds than they truly are. Filter bubbles, on the other hand, affect the content in users' news feeds on Twitter, Google News, and other news applications. If a user clicks on a story about former vice president Joe Biden, stories about Biden will likely be toward the top of the user's news queue when she or he refreshes the application.

On Twitter, filter bubbles affect whom users are recommended to follow, the tweets displayed on the Twitter "discover" option and "search" tab, and the Twitter "moments" that are displayed. Elanor Colleoni and colleagues find that users on Twitter are more likely to interact with other ideologically similar users than users with different ideologies.[24] Similarly, Michael Conover et al. find significant ideological segregation in retweets but ideologically crosscutting interactions in tweets that mention other Twitter users.[25] This finding suggests that Twitter users do engage people with dissimilar political beliefs but do so in critical ways. These researchers find that "the content of political discourse on Twitter remains highly partisan" and that the "fractured nature of political discourse seems to be worsening."[26]

With Facebook, a similar pattern of ideological bubbles and filters that limit citizen exposure to diverse political ideologies is found. Eytan Bakshy et al. analyze the content of the various ways Facebook users obtain their political news—namely, through their personal feeds and through the Facebook "news" tab. They find that news accessed from personal feeds is more politically homogenous than information accessed from Facebook's news feed, meaning that users may get exposure to diverse news but not from the choices they make about whom they follow.[27] This means that, unless Facebook users go beyond their network to access content from the Facebook news feed, they are seeing news, information, and commentary that mostly conform to their ideology.

Beyond partisanship, social networking sites breed misinformation and the spread of rumors. Jieun Shin et al. find that Twitter facilitated the spread of false information, especially rumors about candidates the user opposed, during the 2012 presidential race.[28] Shin and colleagues also found that reputable fact-checking accounts were not successful in debunking Twitter rumors or reducing their spread. In fact, partisan Twitter users selectively share fact-checking messages that disparage the opposition and promote their own candidate, and fact-checking messages receive more hostile comments from partisans whose candidate or party is being checked than other Twitter posts do.[29]

When online networking and social media first emerged in the mid-2000s, scholars were optimistic about its potential to advance political knowledge, democracy, dialogue, and political participation.[30] Some scholars were concerned that political leaders and institutions would use online communications to manipulate citizens[31] and would likely be used in this manner by totalitarian governments.[32] But most scholars who tackled the subject anticipated that online technology would enhance democracy through greater access to information[33] and provide spaces for democratic debate.[34] Instead, social networking sites have increased political partisanship and tribalism and made it more difficult to practice thoughtful learning about and analysis of politics.[35] Partisan online media and social media have contributed to a polarized political environment rife with misinformation, conspiracy theories, and partisan rancor. This new political reality is more hostile to all political candidates than was the previous environment shaped mostly by legacy news organizations. Our question is whether it is equally hostile to male and female candidates.

CANDIDATE SEX AND SOCIAL MEDIA

A burgeoning body of work examines how male and female political candidates navigate the new social media environment.[36] Male and female candidates plot their courses differently in terms of the issues they mention,[37] the tone of their messages,[38] and the degree to which they personalize their content.[39] For example, Heather Evans and Jennifer Hayes Clark find that female candidates are more likely than male candidates to attack their opponents on Twitter. Additionally, female candidates are more likely than male candidates to discuss policy issues in their tweets. The authors conclude that women who run for office strategically use social media tactics to combat pervasive stereotypes about women as weak and feminine[40] and to compensate for lower levels of issue coverage in legacy press.[41]

Researchers also find that people interact differently with male and female candidates in social media. Shannon McGregor and Rachel Mourão analyze sex differences in candidate network centrality (how centrally featured they are in networks surrounding their campaign), rhetorical share (how often the candidate's message is being shared by others), and interactivity (how frequently the candidate interacts with people in her or his network). They find that sex alone does not predict differences in these three variables but that having a male opponent does. In other words, few differences were found between male and female candidates within their social network, but when paired with a male contender, female candidates have less centrality, sharing, and interactivity.[42]

Existing scholarship on candidate sex and social media suggests that men and women have divergent strategies for utilizing online platforms as campaign tools and are positioned somewhat differently within a related network, depending on the sex of their opponent. The missing piece is whether social media users discuss candidates differently because of sex and gender. In the next section, we introduce analysis of an original data set that tackles this question.

SOCIAL MEDIA DISCOURSE IN THE 2016 ELECTION

As we have documented in this chapter, female candidates are hindered by sexism in legacy media, but new online media is even more sexist. Given these findings, combined with recent scholarship on social media that finds these spaces to breed partisanship and misinformation, we suspect that social media may up the sexist ante even further. In this section, we analyze original data from Twitter discourse in the 2016 primary and general election. We test whether tweets that mention Clinton are more negative and less positive than tweets that mention Sanders and Trump and analyze the tone of the hashtags that accompany tweets that mention each candidate. For example, is Clinton more likely to be mentioned when positive hashtags, like #ImWithHer, are tweeted? Or is Clinton more likely to be mentioned when negative hashtags, like #LockHerUp, are mentioned? We address these questions using a sample of tweets collected over one month during the primary and the final month of the general election.

Methodology

Twitter is a social networking site and information-sharing platform. Twitter has 317 million monthly users, and 24 percent of Americans use Twitter.[43] Among Twitter users, 71 percent use the app multiple times a day. Women and men are equally likely to use Twitter, but users vary from the general public in that they are more educated and in that their average income is higher.[44] On Twitter, users, from their unique handle, tweet posts that have a restriction in the number of characters used. Though Twitter increased the character limit to 280 in November 2017, a 140-character limit was in place at the time of the election. Users can also "thread" their tweets. A thread is a sequence of tweets where users convey longer messages, despite the character limit. Tweets may contain original information, links to the Web, unique pictures and video, and mentions of other twitter users' handles. Users are exposed to tweets from those they follow in their personal feed, but they can also access others' feeds and respond to and share tweets from individuals outside their network. Additionally, hashtags bring users together surrounding a particular topic. For instance, #CrookedHillary was a frequently used hashtag by those who opposed Clinton during the 2016 race; users who searched for the hashtag would be taken to a unique feed of tweets that mention it. Feeds surrounding hashtags can be organized chronologically or by popularity, where the "top" tweets are mentioned first. Users can also filter hashtagged tweets to feature only those that include photos or videos, or posts from verified news organizations.

Our analysis draws upon an original data set gathered using the NodeXL Excel template[45] to access the Twitter API. We performed daily searches of tweets mentioning Hillary Clinton and Bernie Sanders from June 15, 2016, through July 15, 2016, and Clinton and Donald Trump from October 8, 2016, through November 8, 2016, creating individual data sets for each candidate on each day. In other words, we analyzed tweet discourse about the candidates during the last month of the primary election and the last month of the general election. In terms of sample size, the primary data set includes approximately 250,000 tweets and 5,391,117 words, and the general data set includes approximately 311,529 tweets and 5,698,222 words.

It should be noted that a limitation of using the Twitter API for data collection is that the results returned for high-frequency search terms represent a sample of approximately 1 percent of all tweets during the specified search time frame. According to Twitter, these results are "a statistically relevant sample." Such a vague explanation is somewhat bedeviling to social scientists because it limits the ability to establish the extent to which this ostensibly "random" data is representative of the larger population. It should be stressed that such limitations apply to any scientific study using high volumes of data acquired via the Twitter API. Given that Twitter operates as a publicly traded for-profit business, it is likely that Twitter has a financial motivation for not allowing potential business competitors to have insight into the nature of their randomization models or any other type of proprietary algorithms or code. Twitter API is the preferred method for social media researchers.[46]

The primary tool for conducting sentiment analysis is Lexicoder 3.0, a software application.[47] The Lexicoder Semantic Dictionary draws upon a set of approximately 5,000 commonly used words with designated positive and negative sentiment. We processed tweets for each day in the primary and general-election data sets, which produced daily scores for positive and negative sentiment for each candidate. We then calculated the candidates' overall percentage of words with positive sentiment and negative sentiment. For example, a daily positive sentiment rate of .032 means that 3.2 percent of all the words from that day's sample were positive.

Tweets in the 2016 Democratic Primary

In this section, we test whether Sanders and Clinton faced differences in how they were discussed on Twitter that can be attributed to candidate sex. We examine three things: the negative sentiment in tweets about each candidate; the positive sentiment in tweets about each candidate; and hashtag use in tweets about the candidates. We find that social media discourse about Clinton had more negative sentiment, less positive sentiment, and more overt sexist content than social media discourse about Sanders.

Negative Sentiment

Figure 6.1 presents the negative sentiment in tweets mentioning Sanders and Clinton from June 15 through July 15, 2016. The Y axis indicates negative words as a percentage of all words, while the X axis is specific dates in the last month of the primary election.

We find that tweets mentioning Clinton were significantly more negative than tweets mentioning Sanders during the final month of the primary. On average, 2.7 percent of all words in tweets mentioning Clinton were negative, compared to 1.9 percent of all words in tweets that mentioned Sanders. In other words, the average negative sentiment in tweets mentioning Clinton was 43 percent higher than the average negative sentiment in tweets mentioning Sanders. This is similar to Thomas Patterson's finding that Clinton faced more negative legacy press coverage than Sanders during the primary.[48]

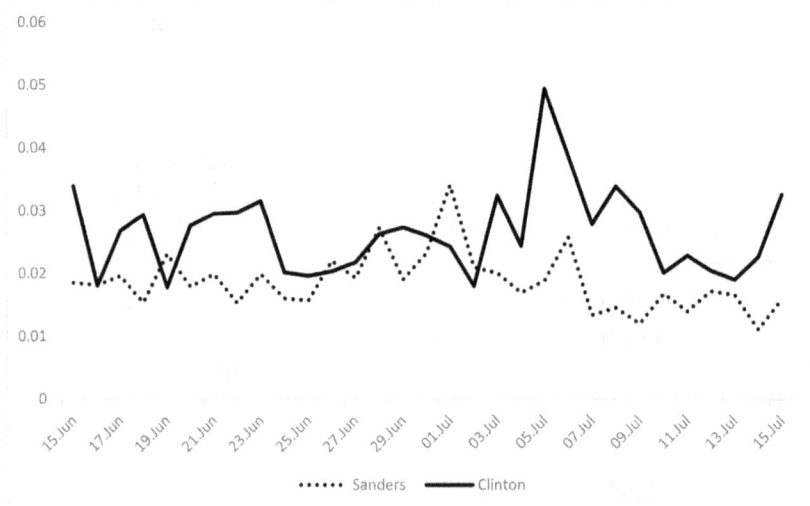

Figure 6.1 Negative Sentiment in Tweets, Primary Election
Source: Analysis of the authors.

July 7, 2016, saw the largest gap in negative sentiment between the two candidates, caused by a spike in negative sentiment in tweets mentioning Clinton. That was the day that Attorney General Loretta Lynch announced that Clinton would not face criminal charges over her use of a private e-mail server. In response, tweets mentioning Clinton were highly negative, including "Hillary Clinton's Hit Men Target Bernie Sanders at Blue Nation Review," "I'm a lawyer specializing in security clearance cases. Hillary Clinton got off easy," and "Hillary Clinton lawyers deleted info to hide what she did!"

This positive news for Clinton, that her actions did not amount to criminal behavior, did not translate positively in public discourse. Instead, it inspired the most negative discourse about her during the last month of the primary.

Positive Sentiment

Next, we analyze the amount of positive sentiment for Clinton and Sanders in the final month of the primary. Figure 6.2 shows the percentage of positive sentiment for each candidate for specific days. The Y axis indicates positive words as a percentage of all words, while the X axis represents specific days during the last month of the primary election.

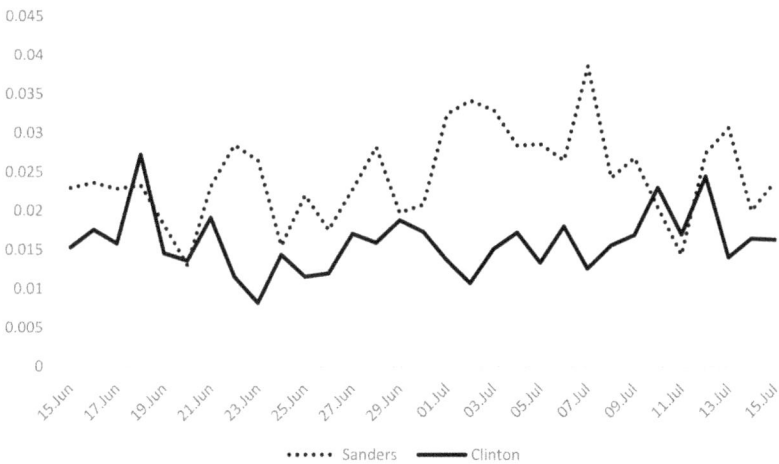

Figure 6.2 Positive Sentiment in Tweets, Primary Election

Source: Analysis of the authors.

Tweets mentioning Sanders were significantly more positive than tweets mentioning Clinton. On average, 2.6 percent of all words in tweets mentioning Sanders were positive, compared to 1.6 percent of tweets mentioning Clinton. Overall, positive Twitter discourse about Sanders was 48 percent higher than positive Twitter discourse about Clinton.

Hashtag Use

Our third measure of social media discourse is the use of hashtags in tweets that mention the candidates. As an analytical tool, hashtags can gauge common themes in popular discussions. As a practicality, hashtags enable users to contribute to a community without necessarily following the users in the community. For our analysis, we extracted all hashtags from tweets that mention Sanders and Clinton to compare their tone. Figure 6.3 shows the top 10 hashtags for Clinton during the final month of the primary.

Of the ten, one shows positive support for a Clinton candidacy (#ImWithHer), three are neutral identifiers (#Hillary, #HillaryClinton, #Clinton), and six are negative or trolling of Clinton (#Trump2016,

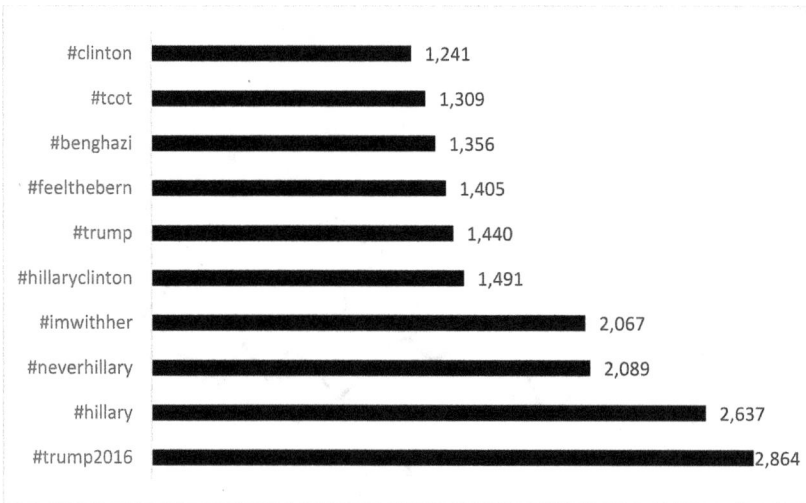

Figure 6.3 Top Ten Hashtags in Tweets Mentioning Clinton, Last Month of Primary Election (Note: "tcot" Stands for Top Conservatives on Twitter; This Hashtag Is Typically Used to Indicate a Tweet Is from an Influential Conservative on Twitter)

Source: Analysis from the authors.

#NeverHillary, #Trump, #FeelTheBern, #Benghazi, #TCOT). (Trolling is a practice of making a provocative post in order to demean or anger, such as hashtagging a post about Clinton with #Trump.) The most-used hashtag in tweets mentioning Clinton was #Trump2016, which means that Trump supporters often invoked Clinton in their tweets. At this point in the election, Trump had secured his party's nomination and Clinton was still fighting for her nomination. The frequency of the Benghazi hashtag during the primary suggests that this "scandal" was a major part of social media discourse about Clinton.

While we can generally classify hashtags as positive, negative, and neutral for a candidate, sometimes they are used in more complicated ways. For example, the hashtag #ImWithHer generally conveys support for Clinton, but Twitter users who opposed Clinton also used this hashtag—for example, the tweet "Remember folks @GenniferFlowers was Hillary Clinton's husbands's admitted mistress. #Millenials #ImWithHer #Trump." Another example is use of the hashtag #FeelTheBern in tweets mentioning Clinton. On occasion, Clinton supporters used the hashtag to reach Sanders supporters, a strategy that Michael Conover et al. refer to as "content injection." In this strategy, Twitter users use a hashtag to reach those who disagree with the tweet, who are drawn to it because the hashtag fits their worldview.[49] For example, one social media user tweeted, "Bernie Sanders just gave an amazingly condescending interview about Hillary Clinton - #FeelTheBern #ImWithHer," in an apparent effort to inform Sanders's supporters of the opinion that their candidate was talking down to Clinton. It is important to keep in mind that while we can generally assess the tone of a hashtag as applied to specific candidates, hashtags are sometimes used in ways that do not neatly fit those boxes.

Chart 6.4 shows the top 10 hashtags used in tweets about Sanders in the final month of the primary. Of the ten, five show positive support for Sanders' candidacy (#FeelTheBern, #BernieOrBust, #StillSanders, #NeverHillary, #SeeYouInPhilly, #OurRevolution), two are neutral identifiers (#BernieSanders, #Bernie), one is negative (#ImWithHer), and one references a scandal (#Guccifer2).

The only overtly negative hashtag in Sanders's top 10 is #ImWithHer, which would indicate that a respondent did not support Sanders. For example, one social media user tweeted, "Exit Polls, and Why the Primary Was Not Stolen From Bernie Sanders https://t.co/NgvPqnkg7T #BernieOrBust #ImWithHer." This tweet challenges speculation that the primary was rigged against Sanders, and #ImWithHer is used to convey support for Clinton, while #BernieOrBust was likely used to draw in Sanders's supporters with "content injection."

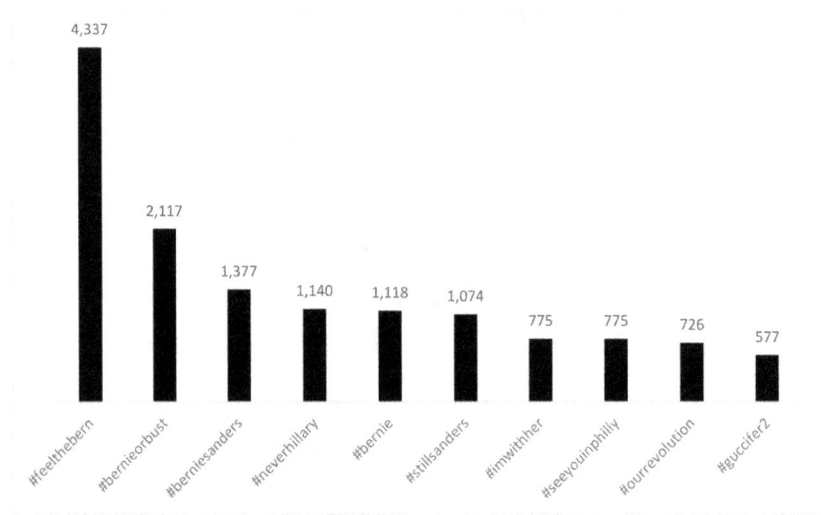

Figure 6.4 Top Ten Hashtags in Tweets Mentioning Sanders, Last Month of Primary Election (Note: "Guccifer2" Refers to Guccifer 2.0, a Persona Who Alleges He or She Hacked the Democratic National Committee Computer Network and Is the Source of the Leaked Emails)

Source: Analysis of the authors.

It is important to again note that hashtag use is more complicated than the positive, negative, and neutral boxes we put them in. Some tweets use #FeelTheBern in ways that disparage Sanders. For example, one person tweeted, "Multiple stabbings and assaults by Bernie Sanders supporters in #Sacramento. I guess this is what they mean by #FeelTheBern." We can draw general conclusions about hashtag use, but sometimes they are used sarcastically or ironically.

We find striking differences in hashtag use by candidate. Overall, the most popular hashtags in tweets about Sanders were far more positive than hashtags used in tweets about Clinton; six out of ten were positive for Sanders compared to the one in ten that were positive for Clinton. Furthermore, the Benghazi "scandal" made Clinton's top 10 most used hashtags, and the Guccifer 2.0 "scandal" made Sanders's top 10; both of those scandals are negative for Clinton. Three of Clinton's top hashtags expressed open support for her competitors (Sanders and Trump), while only one of Sanders's top hashtags expressed support for his competitor. In short, as public discourse is measured using hashtags, Sanders was discussed in far more positive terms than Clinton during the final month of the primary.

Tweets in the 2016 General Election

We also measured negative sentiment, positive sentiment, and the tone of hashtags in the final month of the 2016 general election.

Negative Sentiment

The rate of negative sentiment in tweets mentioning Clinton was about the same in the primary and the general election, but tweets mentioning Trump were even more negative. On average, 3.2 percent of all words in tweets mentioning Trump were negative, compared to 2.5 percent of all words in tweets that mentioned Clinton. This means that average negative sentiment for Trump was 29.8 percent higher than the average negative sentiment for Clinton. As figure 6.5 shows, in the days leading up to the election, Clinton and Trump received roughly the same rate of negative sentiment in Twitter discourse, a spike in Clinton's negatives that fits with the timing of the Comey announcement about reopening the e-mail investigation, an announcement that was retracted days later.

Positive Sentiment

When it comes to our second measure of social media discourse, positive sentiment, we find that rates of positive sentiment in tweets about Clinton looked roughly the same in the primary and general elections. And as in

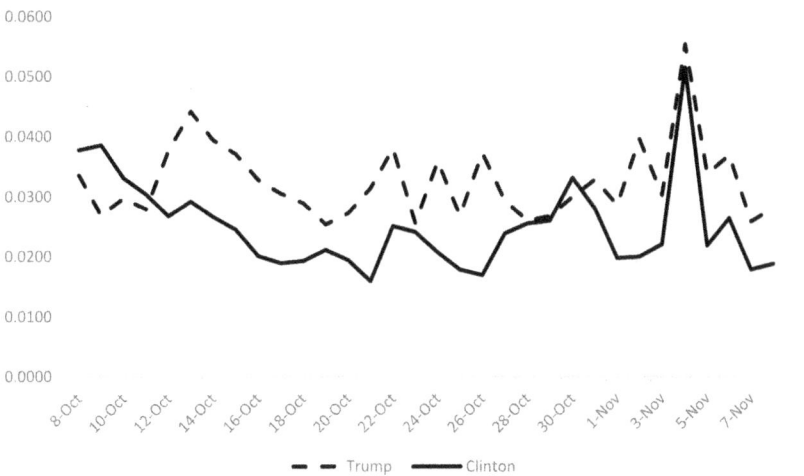

Figure 6.5 Negative Sentiment in Tweets, Last Month of General Election
Source: Analysis of the authors.

the primary, Clinton's competitor in the general election garnered more positive sentiment in tweets. On average, 1.8 percent of all words in tweets mentioning Trump were positive, compared to 1.7 percent of all words in tweets that mentioned Clinton. The average positive sentiment in tweets mentioning Trump was 6.8 percent higher than the average positive sentiment in tweets mentioning Clinton.

As figure 6.6 shows, the most positive day of tweets about both Trump and Clinton was on October 20, one day after the third and final televised debate. According to a national poll, Clinton won the debate 52 percent to Trump's 39 percent, but both candidates received the same amount of positive sentiment in tweets about them.[50] It is also important to note that Trump's positive sentiment was significantly better than Clinton's in the final days of the election. He saw a spike in positive sentiment that held through Election Day.

Hashtag Use

Our third measure of social media discourse is hashtag tone. Figure 6.7 presents the 10 most frequent hashtags in tweets mentioning Clinton during the final month of the general election. One of the top 10 hashtags is positive or supportive (#ImWithHer), while three are neutral identifiers

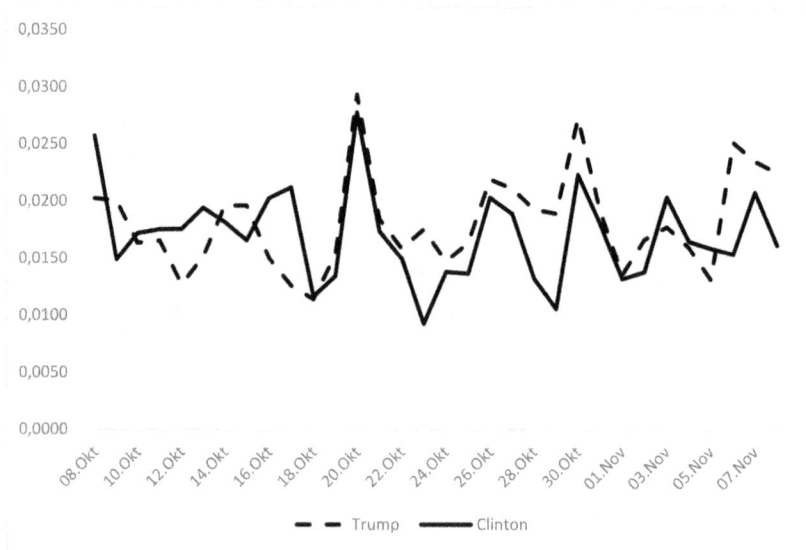

Figure 6.6 Positive Sentiment in Tweets, Last Month of General Election
Source: Analysis of the authors.

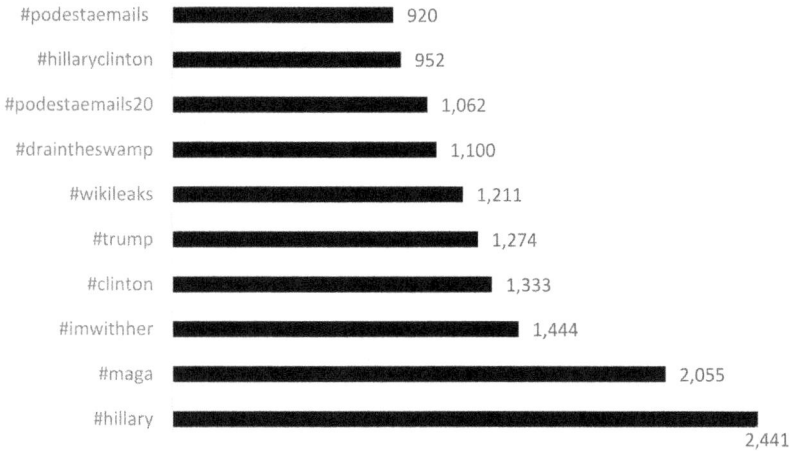

Figure 6.7 Top Ten Hashtags in Tweets Mentioning Clinton, Final Month of General Election

Source: Analysis of the authors.

(#Hillary, #Clinton, #HillaryClinton), and six are negative for Clinton (#MAGA [the abbreviation of Trump's campaign slogan, Make America Great Again], #Trump, #WikiLeaks, #DrainTheSwamp, #PodestaEmails, #PodestaEmails20). In other words, a majority of the most popular hashtags in tweets about Clinton were negative in the last month of the general election.

#WikiLeaks refers to the release of a cache of e-mails from the nonprofit organization that disseminates documents from leakers and anonymous sources. #PodestaEmails and #PodestaEmails20 refer to e-mails leaked from Clinton campaign manager John Podesta. #DrainTheSwamp refers to a saying Trump popularized during the election to refer to a campaign promise to rid Washington of political insiders who fail to represent the interests of everyday Americans.

As in the primary, many of the hashtags mentioning Clinton include reference to scandals, such as the WikiLeaks release of e-mails from the Democratic National Committee. People using Twitter used more scandal-related hashtags in tweets about Clinton in the general (three) than in the primary (one) election. Another noteworthy finding is the high frequency of #MAGA and #DrainTheSwamp, which means Trump supporters were mentioning Clinton in tweets in which they also conveyed support for Trump and his message.

Figure 6.8 shows the top 10 most used hashtags in tweets mentioning Trump in the final month of the general election. Four of the top 10 hashtags are positive or supportive (#MAGA, TrumpPence16, draintheswamp, #Trump2016), while four are neutral identifiers of the candidate or some aspect of the election (#Trump, #ElectionDay, #Debate, #DonaldTrump) and two are negative (#NeverTrump and #ImWithHer). Hashtag use in Trump tweets is more positive than in Clinton tweets (four to one) and less negative (two compared to six). Overall, hashtags used in tweets about Trump are twice as likely to be neutral or positive as tweets about Clinton (eight compared to four).

To summarize the findings of social media discourse in the general election, tweets about Trump had more negative sentiment than tweets about Clinton during the last month of the general election. Clinton received less positive sentiment in tweets about her than Trump during the last month of the general election, and this was especially pronounced in the last few days of the election, when his sentiment was far more positive than hers. In terms of hashtag use, tweets about Trump were far more likely to include positive or neutral hashtags than tweets about Clinton.

Combining our primary and general-election analysis, we find that Clinton was treated more harshly overall in social media discourse than her primary and general-election competitors. Her tweets had higher

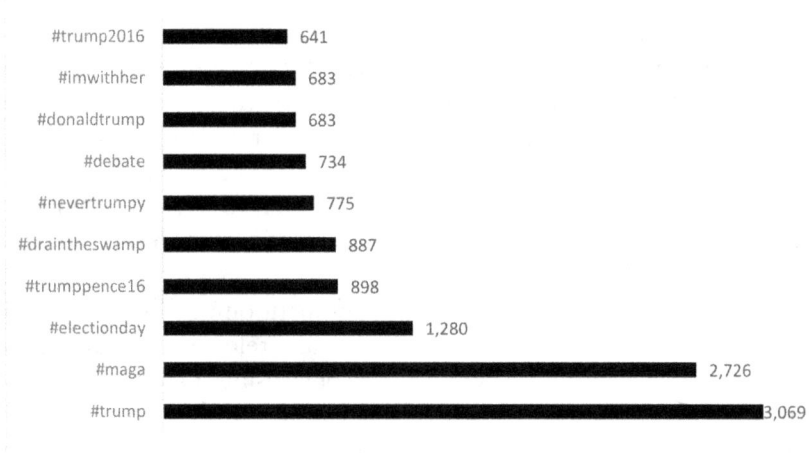

Figure 6.8 Top Ten Hashtags in Tweets Mentioning Trump, Last Month of General Election

Source: Analysis of the authors.

levels of negative sentiment than Sanders's tweets but less negative sentiment than Trump's tweets. However, both Sanders and Trump received
more positive sentiment in tweets about them, and both male candidates
had far more positive hashtag use in their tweets than Clinton did. In
short, social media discourse was significantly more negative for Clinton
when she was running for her party's nomination, and when she faced
the presidential candidate with the highest unfavorable ratings in polling history,[51] he garnered more negative sentiment on Twitter but also
more positive sentiment and far greater use of hashtags with a positive or
neutral tone.

CONCLUSION

This chapter delves into the question of whether female presidential
candidates face gendered challenges in the new political environment
dominated by social media. We know that female presidential candidates
are covered more negatively than male candidates in legacy media, and
even more so in new online political blogs, but little is known about
how social media users discuss female candidates. We began with a brief
description of legacy media, new media, and social media to better understand the new electoral environment.

When social media technology was new, scholars saw great potential to
advance democracy through greater access to information, spaces to discuss
politics, and dialogue across the political spectrum. Instead, social media
platforms have accelerated hyperpartisanship and tribalism in the United
States. Instead of being sites for true exchange of ideas, Facebook and
Twitter limit user exposure to diverse ideas using ideological filter bubbles.
Facebook and Twitter limit what users see based on their friends and past
behavior, meaning that users will see content they mostly already agree
with. That filtering is especially the case after the divisive 2016 election,
where social media users unfriended and unfollowed people on the opposite side of the political aisle in great numbers.[52]

In addition to increasing political tribalism in the United States,
social media has also contributed to a media culture that breeds false
information and conspiracy theories. Popular social media sites were the
nexus for false information during the 2016 election, and fact-checking
accounts were not effective. Social media has created a more hostile
electoral environment for all candidates, one marked by heightened
partisan rancor and candidate attacks in real time. We addressed the
question of whether this new environment is equally hostile to male and
female candidates.

We measured the hostility of the social media environment by looking at rates of negative sentiment, positive sentiment, and hashtag tone in tweets about Sanders, Clinton, and Trump. We find stark differences in the social media environment faced by Clinton and Sanders in the 2016 Democratic primary. Tweets that mentioned Clinton were more likely to convey negative sentiment than tweets about Sanders. Also, tweets that mentioned Sanders had more positive sentiment than tweets about Clinton. The tone of hashtags associated with Clinton was more negative than that of hashtags used in tweets about Sanders. Six out of the 10 most popular hashtags for Sanders were supportive, compared to only one of the top 10 for Clinton. Some of Sanders's most popular hashtags implored him to continue to fight for the Democratic nomination (#StillSanders, #SeeYouInPhilly), even though his chances of winning at that point in the race were quite slim. Twitter users also referred to Clinton "scandals" in their hashtag use. In short, Sanders was discussed in far more positive terms than Clinton was during the final month of the primary. Clinton faced a more hostile electoral environment than Sanders as measured by social media during the 2016 primary.

Our analysis of the 2016 general election tells a more complicated story. Differences in sentiment between Clinton and Trump were smaller. Tweets about Trump had more negative sentiment but also more positive sentiment, especially in the final days of the content, when Trump's positive sentiment spiked. Our analysis of hashtags shows that tweets about Trump were unequivocally more positive than tweets about Clinton when hashtag content and tone are accounted for. Comparing the top 10 hashtags used for each candidate, we find that eight were positive or neutral for Trump while four were positive or neutral for Clinton. Additionally, hashtags about Clinton often discussed controversies, scandals, and conspiracies, but Trump's most common hashtags for the final month of the campaign did not include any references to scandals. This is a remarkable finding considering that the time frame of our analysis included the release of the *Access Hollywood* video.[53] Although the hashtag #TrumpTapes was used on social media after the release of the video, it was not used often enough to make the list of the top 10 hashtags used for Trump in the final month of the election. For comparison, four hashtags related to the DNC e-mail leak (#WikiLeaks, #DrainTheSwamp, #PodestaEmails, and #PodestaE-mails20) made Clinton's top 10 list. It appears that Trump supporters on Twitter were more organized around common hashtags and themes and were able to drown out supportive Clinton voices and hashtags. Investigative reporter Ben Schreckinger concludes that the Trump side was able to accomplish greater message control using Internet bots[54] and "troll labor" (people paid to promote certain stories and hashtags).[55] Overall, Clinton faced a more hostile social media environment, whether organic or bot-generated, than Trump did. Lee Rainie et al. argue that online hostility toward women who run for office is a new fact of political life, as these spaces stay above regulation.[56]

In social media, we find differences in citizen treatment of Clinton versus Sanders and Trump that are likely accounted for by her sex and the gender dynamics of presidential elections. Trump faced greater negative sentiment on social media in the last month, but overall, Clinton's environment was more hostile. She was hammered for "scandals" in a way Trump was not. Trump went into Election Day with significantly higher positive sentiment on social media, and he managed to escape a strong social media rebuke after the *Access Hollywood* tape was released. Social media matters more than ever in U.S. elections, and while the 2016 election furnishes only one case study—not enough to draw firm conclusions—it appears that this form of media presents yet another sex-based challenge for female presidential contenders. Social media makes the political environment more hostile for candidates overall, but especially for women, during a time when female presidential candidates are finally being taken seriously.

CHAPTER 7

Conclusion: "Within Spitting Distance"—Barriers to a Female Presidency

The primary question of this book is how sex (male/female) and gender (masculine/feminine) mattered in the 2016 presidential election. To address this question, we employed mixed methodology with analysis of original data, secondary data, historical evidence, and case studies. We assessed legacy media coverage of the candidates, the ways they were discussed in social media, the rhetoric candidates used to describe their competitors, candidate interactions at debates, and supporter rhetoric at campaign rallies and online. With regard to sex/sexism, we find that public discourse applied a double standard to the female presidential candidate in terms of negative framing, consideration of scandals, and evaluations of fitness for the office. Clinton also faced an unusual amount of blatant sexism and framing of her as a villain, common responses to power-seeking women. As Susan Bordo put it, "the Hillary Clinton who was 'defeated' in the 2016 election, was, indeed, not a real person at all, but a caricature forged out of the stew of unexamined sexism, unprincipled partisanship, irresponsible politics, and a mass media too absorbed in 'optics' to pay enough attention to separating facts from rumors, lies, and speculation"[1]

Gender also played a role in the election given that hypermasculine bravado was a pillar of Donald Trump's campaign. He stoked fears of a feminizing, "politically correct" culture on the campaign trail. He also challenged Clinton's "strength" and "stamina" in ways that tapped into voter bias for masculine presidents who are "man enough" for the job.[2] Through his own words and the words of his surrogates, Trump also injected the election with a level of misogyny previously unseen in presidential politics. This message resonated with many Trump supporters, who promoted unabashed misogyny on T-shirts, signs, and social media. Trump's performance of masculinity through misogyny was important because it played upon the longstanding association of masculinity and the presidency.

We conclude this book with a detailed assessment of how public opinion and voting patterns in the 2016 election reveal the influence of sex and gender. We begin with an assessment of gender stereotypes in the election. Then we compare 2016 election voting demographics to recent previous elections to show how this election looked different because a female candidate was in the race. We also introduce findings of postelection studies that find that sexism was indeed a crucial factor in vote choice for Trump. We conclude this chapter with a look ahead at what the 2016 presidential election means for female candidates, voters, and democracy.

DEFYING STEREOTYPES

Hillary Clinton seemed to defy gendered policy stereotypes in her 2016 bid for the presidency. For example, Clinton was seen as more competent on many national security issues than Donald Trump. According to an ABC News/*Washington Post* poll administered several times between November 2015 and November 2016, Clinton was seen as more trusted to handle terrorism (figure 7.1). This sentiment was likely due to Trump's

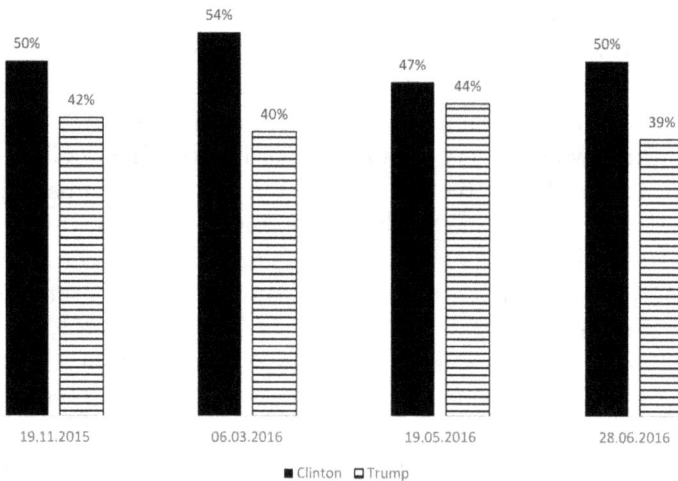

Figure 7.1 Trust in Candidates to Handle Terrorism
Source: ABC News/*Washington Post.*

personal temperament, which drew negative evaluations,[3] and Clinton's record of experience, first as a senator serving on the Armed Services Committee from 2003 to 2009 and later as secretary of state from 2009 to 2013. This unusual circumstance of a female candidate with extensive foreign policy experience running against a male candidate with no military or government experience allowed Clinton to overcome a major barrier that previous female presidential candidates have faced. Clinton's formidable foreign policy experience, especially relative to her opponent's, positioned her well for being seen as "properly masculine" and sufficiently competent on national security issues.

On perception of personal character, preliminary analysis suggests perceptions of Trump did reflect gender stereotypes about men, while perceptions of Clinton did not reflect gender stereotypes about women. Trump was described in masculine, albeit negative, terms like "arrogant," a "bully," and "selfish." Respondents described Clinton using gender-neutral and masculine traits but rarely in terms of feminine traits.[4] Respondents saw her as "experienced" and "strong," as well as "untrustworthy" and "self-serving," none of which invoke feminine stereotypes. This finding means that when they enter the masculine realm of politics, female candidates are not seen in traditionally feminine terms. It also shows that when women enter this masculine domain, the drive for power is seen as incongruent with traditional gender roles in the minds of many voters who see power-seeking behavior in a negative light (e.g., "self-serving").

Data from the American National Election Study (ANES) sheds more light on perceptions of the 2016 nominees' personal character. ANES has asked respondents to rate candidate knowledge, morality, compassion, and leadership in every presidential election year since 1980. Previous research finds that candidate ratings on these measures of character influence vote choice.[5] While morality and knowledge are gender neutral, compassion is considered a feminine trait and leadership a masculine trait. The literature on gender stereotypes would expect Clinton to excel on compassion and Trump to excel on leadership if voters were only considering their sex. However, voters had at their disposal a plethora of information and evidence with which to rank the candidates, and we find that Clinton again defied conventional stereotypes.

Figure 7.2 shows the relative advantage of each candidate. (The 2016 ANES included the traits "speaks mind," "even-tempered," "honesty," and "morality" in addition to "knowledge," "leadership," and "compassion.") Clinton held an advantage on perception of leadership and compassion and was perceived as much more knowledgeable and even-tempered than

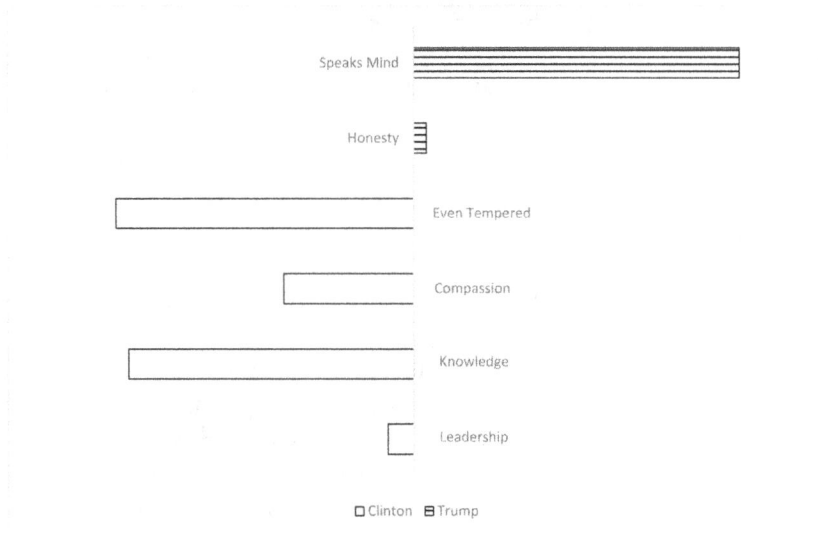

Figure 7.2   Public Perceptions of Candidate Character (Bars Represent Relative Advantage)

Source: The American National Election Studies.

Trump. Trump was seen as more honest and more likely to speak his mind. Although many factors come into play when voters make their choice, Trump made honesty a salient factor in the election, encapsulated in the rally cry and hashtag campaign #CrookedHillary. And although Clinton was more honest on the campaign trail according to PolitiFact, events surrounding Clinton's campaign, like her use of a private e-mail server, provided voters with a salient example of her dishonesty, and this event was a constant feature of her media coverage and discourse on social media. If Clinton and her campaign could have effectively made the election about candidate competence, she would have had an edge, in terms of candidate character.

THE ELECTION OUTCOME

The outcomes of presidential elections are typically determined by incumbency, voter perceptions of the state of the economy, war, scandals, and candidate personalities.[6] At an individual level, presidential vote choice can be predicted by party identification, political ideology (the conservative-liberal spectrum), and evaluation of salient policy issues, government performance, and evaluation of candidate characteristics.[7]

It is virtually impossible to isolate and measure the relative impact of all the decisive variables in any given election, but postelection analysis of exit polls and public opinion polls confirms that sexism was a factor in Trump's unexpected victory. In this section, we organize our analysis in terms of the effect of the Comey announcement, the male vote, the white vote, the Democratic vote, education and vote choice, and the role of economic anxiety versus prejudice in vote choice.

The Comey Announcement

Gender bias against power-seeking women caused some voters to view Clinton with suspicion, and this image played a crucial role in the outcome when James Comey announced that he was further investigating Clinton's e-mails just 11 days before the election. Hillary hating reached an all-time high by the end of the campaign, which millions of Americans explained away with the justification that she was particularly corrupt and dishonest, even though 30 years of investigations had netted nothing and in spite of Clinton's rating as the most honest of all the candidates in the race. Preexisting gender bias against female leaders made fertile ground for sexism framing that was so effective that Clinton, an unremarkable candidate save for her sex, was viewed as negatively as Trump, a candidate remarkable for his extreme rhetoric, who disaffected major swaths of the American public with divisive comments, and who had offered to pay the legal fees of supporters who were violent with protesters at his rallies. By the end of August, Clinton's favorability rating was identical to Trump's, with 60 percent of voters rating the two candidates negatively.[8]

In July, FBI director James Comey found that Clinton had been "extremely careless" with handling classified information on her private e-mail server but that "no reasonable prosecutor" would bring a criminal case against Clinton.[9] Then, 11 days before the election, Comey sent a letter to Congress informing them that he was reopening the Clinton e-mail investigation, and his retraction of that statement four days before the election did not undo the damage to her electoral support. The second Comey letter was one of many factors that affected the outcome of the 2016 presidential election. Even though Comey essentially issued a retraction just days before the election, the damage had been done. Clinton polls dropped 2.8 percent in reaction to news of further investigation into her e-mails, a drop that did not fully rebound to prior levels by Election Day.[10]

Trump managed a political upset on Election Day, garnering votes from 19.5 percent of the electorate compared to Clinton's 19.8 percent (while

2.2 percent voted for a minor party candidate and 29.9 percent did not vote).[11] Nearly 66 million Americans voted for Clinton compared to just less than 63 million for Trump, but Trump won 306 votes in the Electoral College to Clinton's 232 votes, giving him the presidency. In this section, we analyze how the voting patterns in the 2016 election looked different from presidential elections of the recent past to determine whether and how the sexism aimed at Clinton in the primary and general elections affected the outcome.

The Male Vote

The first notable shift from previous elections was a sharp increase in men voting Republican. The gender gap emerged in 1980, and since that time, women have voted more Democratic than men. The gender gap in 2016 was the largest in history—24 points, besting the previous 20-point chasm in 2012, when President Barack Obama lost men by 8 points and won women by 12 points.[12] The gender gap was the widest of record in 2016 because men, but especially white men, moved to the right. In 2012, male voters favored Mitt Romney by 7 percentage points, and in 2016, they favored Trump by 12 points.[13] Women voted Democratic at about the same rate as in recent presidential races, but men increased their Republican support by five percentage points. In light of the analysis above and

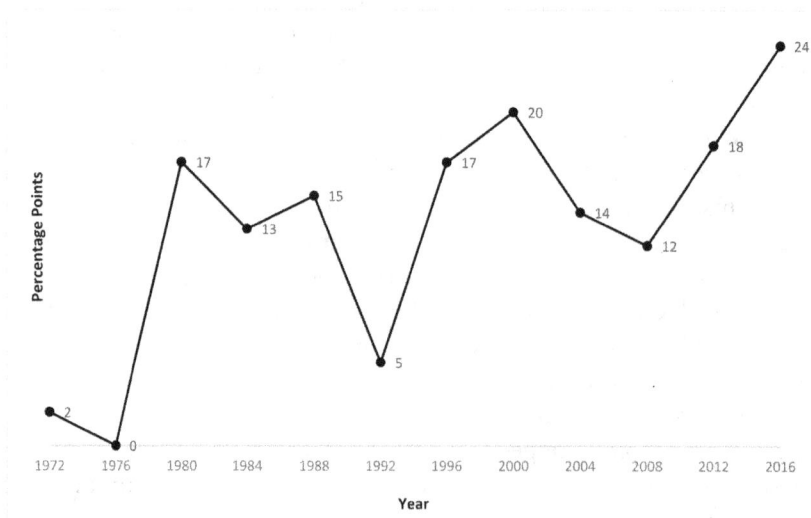

Figure 7.3   The Gender Gap in Presidential Elections over Time, 1972–2016
Source: Edison Research, *Washington Post.*

this dramatic shift in voting along gender lines, it seems likely that men's gender bias against the first female presidential candidate played a significant role in shifting the outcome of the election. With this said, it is not possible to know the precise cause(s) of this dramatic shift in Democratic male voting patterns.

The White Vote

The story of the gender gap in 2016 is complicated. Exit polls indicate that a majority of white men and women voted for Trump, but that nothing new. White voters have voted majority Republican since the 1960s when President Lyndon B. Johnson signed the Civil Rights Act (1964) and the Voting Rights Act (1965).[14] In response, many white voters fled the Democratic Party in droves, especially in the South. After the 2016 election, some commentators seemed surprised that so many white women voted Republican, but that is also nothing new. Party identification remains the most prominent predictor of vote choice in elections,[15] and a majority of white women have voted for the Republican presidential candidate since the 1960s. Overall, the long-standing trend of white people voting Republican held firm in the 2016 election.

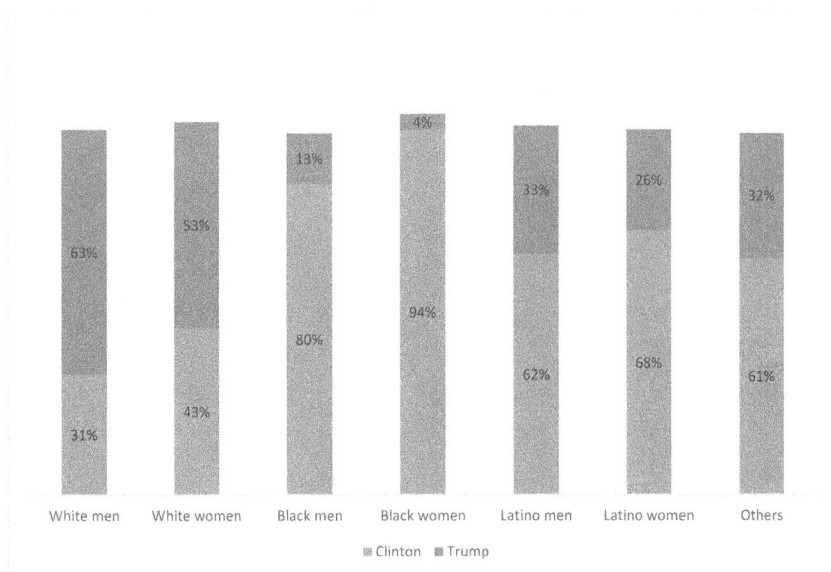

Figure 7.4 Race, Gender, and Vote Choice in the 2016 Election
Source: CNN Exit Polls.

The Democratic Vote

But something did shift with gender and voting patterns on the Democratic side that reflects the influence of sex and gender in the election. Contrary to popular postelection news narratives, women did not abandon Clinton, but they also did not rush to support her. Clinton did slightly better than the typical Democratic candidate with white women, pulling more support with this group than Obama did in 2012. Clinton also attracted a majority of college-educated white women, who typically break for the Republican candidate in presidential elections.[16] As the table below shows, there was a significant shift in the voting patterns of men who typically vote Democratic. Overall, women of all races exhibited similar support for the Democratic candidate in 2016 as they did in 2012. There was a decline in support among Latinx women and an increase in support among white women, but female voting patterns on the Democratic side held overall. However, support among men of all races in the Democratic coalition dropped an average of 4 percent. In other words, men who typically vote Democratic were significantly less supportive of the first female presidential candidate nominated by their party than women who vote Democratic were. This shift on the left suggests that the heated, sexist Democratic primary likely influenced the outcome of the general election.

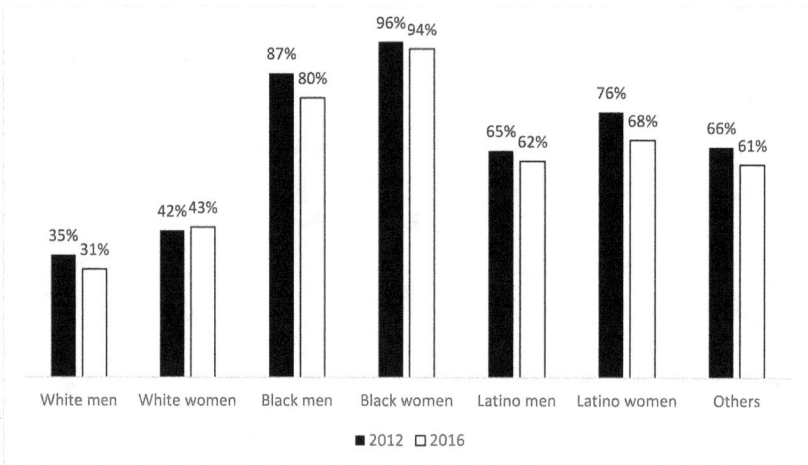

Figure 7.5 Shift in Democratic Voting 2012 to 2016 by Race, Gender
Source: ABC Exit Polls.

The numbers also indicate that the brutal primary in which Clinton's candidacy was weakened through sexism did affect the outcome of the general election. Only 74.7 percent of people who voted or caucused for Sanders in the primary voted for Clinton in the general election, which translates into a 2.8 percent decrease in Clinton's popular vote in the general election.[17] Compare this to 84 percent of primary Clinton voters who voted for Obama in 2008.[18] Fifteen percent of Sanders voters chose a minor party candidate, while 4.1 percent stayed home and 5.9 percent cast a vote for Trump.[19] Sanders voters with low levels of sexism overwhelmingly cast a vote for Clinton, while voters with higher rates of sexism voted for a minor party candidate. According to research from Angie Maxwell and Todd Shields at the Diane D. Blair Center of Southern Politics & Society, "Sanders' supporters with decidedly 'sexist' attitudes voted for Trump."[20] This indicates that sexism played a role in whether Sanders supporters voted for Clinton and ultimately played a role in determining the outcome of the election.

Economic Anxiety versus Prejudice

The 2016 election was also unique in its dramatic polarization of white vote choices based on educational level. This election had the largest gap between presidential vote choice for college-educated and non-college-educated whites since 1980.[21] Voters with a college degree preferred Trump to Clinton by a four-point margin, while those without a college degree gave Trump a nearly 40-point advantage.[22] This gap was "possibly the single most uniquely important divide documented in 2016."[23] Much of the postelection commentary focused on economic anxiety to explain Trump's upset, assisted by working-class voters, but the data show that the opposite is true. Shortly after the election, Sanders told a rally in Boston that "some people think that the people who voted for Trump are racists and sexists and homophobes and deplorable folks. I don't agree."[24] A few days later, Democratic senator Elizabeth Warren wrote a *New York Times* op-ed in which she claimed that Trump voters were "expressing their fierce opposition to an economic and political system that puts wealthy and corporate interests over their own."[25] Multiple studies indicate that these top Democrats are simply wrong. Trump voters were mostly driven by bias, not economic anxiety.

Brian Schaffner, Matthew MacWilliams, and Tatishe Nteta analyzed the relative influence of racism, sexism, and economic anxiety among Trump voters and found that economic dissatisfaction was only a small part of the story whereas racism and sexism accounted for two-thirds of the education gap among whites in the 2016 presidential election. The researchers find evidence that the 2016 election was unique in terms of racism and sexism driving the vote, and not part of a larger trend. Trump's explicit sexism and racism during the campaign tapped into higher rates of prejudice held by less educated whites. Sexism is generally acceptable in U.S. society to such an extent that it typically goes unnoticed, and racism has become more acceptable in public rhetoric in recent years. Nicholas Valentino et al. find that norms of what is considered appropriate racial rhetoric have shifted in the past few years as "whites now view themselves as an embattled racial group, and this has led to both strong ingroup identity and a greater tolerance for expressions of hostility toward outgroups."[26]

Another study conducted by Public Policy Research Institute delves into the question of why working-class white people voted for Trump over Clinton by a margin of roughly two to one.[27] They find that voter experiences of actual economic hardship increased the vote for Clinton and that working-class voters with economic concerns were 1.7 times more likely to vote for her than for Trump. The researchers also find that white working-class voters were driven to Trump by fears of cultural displacement. White voters who "feel like a stranger in their own land and who believe the U.S. needs protecting against foreign influence" made them 3.5 times more likely to vote for Trump.[28] Additionally, white working-class voters who want to deport undocumented immigrants were 3.3 times more likely to vote for Trump.

Several other studies also find that racial resentment and ethnocentrism (the belief that U.S. culture is inherently superior to other cultures), not economic concerns, predicted a vote for Trump, including analyses from Sean McElwee and Jason McDaniel,[29] Michael Tesler,[30] and Philip Klinkner.[31] A Reuters poll taken during the election found that Trump supporters are more likely to describe black Americans as "lazy and violent," "criminal," and "unintelligent" than other Republican voters and voters in general.[32] In Klinkner's study, he found that the biggest predictor of support for Trump was the answer "yes" to the question "Is Barack Obama a Muslim?"[33]

Sexism also played a significant role in vote choice. As shown in the figure below, nearly two-thirds of Trump voters hold sexist attitudes, compared to one-fifth of Clinton voters.[34]

Maxwell and Shields find that modern sexism, based on resentment or hostility toward working women (as opposed to classic sexism, marked by a belief in female inferiority), was a highly significant predictor of vote choice for Clinton.[35] They measure modern sexism as beliefs that women are too quick to complain about sexual harassment, that women want

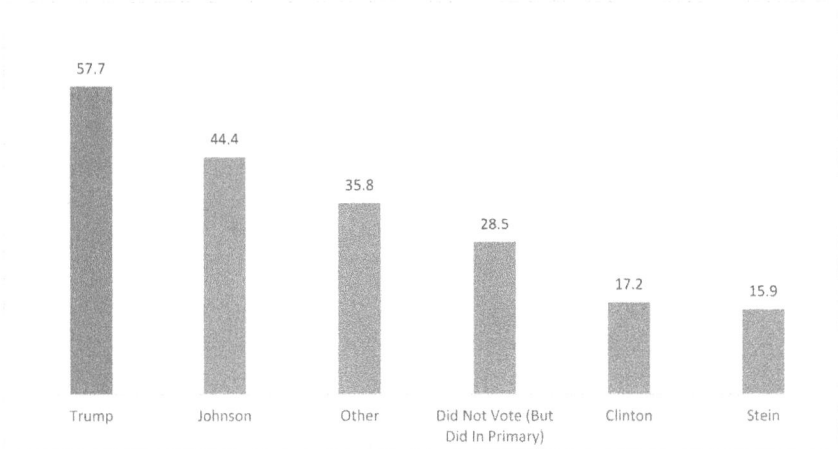

Figure 7.6 Percent of General Election Voters with "Sexist" Responses by Candidate

Source: Diane D. Blair Center of Southern Politics & Society.

special favors in the workplace, that feminists are fighting for dominance and not equality, and that gender discrimination is a thing of the past. The influence of modern sexist beliefs on vote choice holds true when other significant factors, such as party identification, race, and education, are held constant. Male and female voters with higher rates of modern sexism were significantly more likely to vote for Trump than Clinton.

Carly Wayne, Nicholas Valentino, and Marzia Oceno conducted a study that compares the significance of sexism to other significant factors in the election. They find that sexism was strongly correlated with support for Trump, even after controlling for ideology, party identification, ethnocentrism, and authoritarianism (support for obedience at the expense of personal freedom).[36] Comparing the various factors, they found that the impact of sexism was larger than the impact of authoritarianism and equivalent to the impact of ethnocentrism. Moreover, they found that sexism did not predict support for the Republican nominee in past elections; it was unique to 2016. They also found that Trump voters were driven, not by gender-based fear, but rather anger at recent societal advances in gender equality. This information fits with the modern sexism findings of the Maxwell and Shields study, that sexism today manifests as anger at women's advancements.

LOOKING FORWARD

The 2016 presidential race was the first time the United States advanced a woman to the general election, and given the long history of sexism and gender bias faced by nearly a dozen previous female contenders, it is no surprise that it played a role in the 2016 contest. After Clinton lost the Democratic primary in 2008, Rebecca Traister wrote: "To say that Hillary Clinton faced sexism is practically meaningless. She was the first woman in American history to get within spitting distance of a nomination for president; of course she faced sexism."[37] The same can be said for the 2016 race, but to an even a greater extent since Clinton faced an unapologetic misogynist in the general election.

The goal of our book was to analyze how sex and gender played out in the public and electoral spheres. With her extensive political pedigree, Clinton defied gender stereotypes about leadership and policy, but in the end, sex and gender bias presented barriers she could not scale. We conclude that sexism, racial resentment, ethnocentrism, and, to a lesser extent, authoritarianism were instrumental in a vote choice for Trump. His unambiguous displays of hypermasculinity, prejudice, and nationalism conjured biases to the surface for a portion of the American electorate who felt threatened or left behind by a shifting social order. Going beyond the data, it is possible that Trump's ascendency to the presidency on the right was made possible by his brand of unrestrained sexism against the first female presidential contender to advance to the general election. We question whether Republican voters would have voted for such a rhetorically extreme candidate sans eight years of a black president and the nomination of a female presidential candidate on the Democratic side. It is quite possible that, without a woman in the race to stoke fears of a shifting social order, Republicans would not have elevated Trump, the only Republican candidate who was overtly attacking Clinton in sexist terms during the Republican primary.

We approached our primary question from a democratic perspective with the idea that democracy is compromised when bias informally excludes 51 percent of the population from holding the highest political office. Electing female political leaders matters because male and female political leaders differ in their policy priorities and the processes they use to pass public policy. It is also important because the presence of female political leaders increases the political efficacy and participation of the girls and women they represent.

Electing a female president holds special symbolic importance given that the presidency is synonymous with who counts as the prototypical citizen. Barack Obama's blackness cut against the grain of the ideal citizen for some Americans, and he was therefore seen as an illegitimate president who violated a basic requirement for holding the office (whiteness). Clinton would have faced similar pushback had she been elected because she violates another basic requirement of ideal citizenship associated with the presidency (maleness). Obama's presidency challenged the confines of prejudice concerning the presidency, and while it was met with a swift backlash in the form of a president who played into and stirred racial resentment on the campaign trail, the election of the first black president was a sign of progress for democracy. Electing the first female president, regardless of party, will also be progress for descriptive representation in the United States. The effectiveness of Trump's misogyny on the campaign trail shows that the backlash against women's leadership is alive and well for millions of Americans, but her mere presence and perseverance in the face of sexist vitriol marks progress for gender justice.

One concern is that Clinton's ultimate failure to win the presidency, and the sexism and misogyny she faced along the way, may discourage women from seeking this office. After the 2008 presidential election, Anne Kornblut wrote that the race "set back the cause of equality in the political sphere by decades."[38] She argued that the blatant sexism directed at Clinton and vice presidential candidate Sarah Palin would discourage women from taking up the challenge and that political parties would be reluctant to run a female candidate given that sex and gender melt voter support. (Palin was the most pornified and ditzified female political candidate ever on the national stage, and she faced the same gendered scrutiny and comments about husbands, hair, and hemlines that Clinton faced in 2008.[39])

The events of the 2016 election may indeed dissuade some women from running for office, but it appears that, overall, Clinton's loss, or perhaps Trump's misogyny, are encouraging more women to run. In the first few months of Trump's presidency, women have signed up for candidate training at rates not seen since the early 1990s when Clarence Thomas was appointed to the Supreme Court despite allegations of repeated sexual harassment from Anita Hill.[40] That bump in interest produced a significant increase in female candidates running for and winning seats in Congress in 1992, what commentators have dubbed the Year of the Woman. EMILY's List, an organization that works to elect pro-choice, Democratic women to office, reported that just six months after the election, 11,000 women reached out to them expressing an interest in running for public office—many times greater than the usual interest.[41] According to Andrea Dew Steele, president of the campaign-training organization Emerge America, women's interest in running for public office after the 2016 election is "unlike anything we've ever seen."[42] Jean Sinzdak from the Center for American Women and Politics at Rutgers University attributes it to both Trump's positions and Clinton's loss: "Some of it is absolutely a reaction to President Trump and his policies. For others, it is Hillary Clinton's loss . . . sort of woke them up to the idea that maybe we haven't made as much progress as we thought." Carrie Almond, president of the National Federation of Republican Women, reports that her organization is seeing an uptick in interest in running for public office among Republican women, inspired by the high-profile women in Trump's campaign, namely Kellyanne Conway, the GOP's first female presidential campaign manager.[43] The sexism of the 2016 election did not depress women's interest in seeking political office and may in fact have spurred more women to run.

The way that Clinton lost the 2016 election (at the receiving end of sexism and misogyny) and the way Trump won the election (with appeals to sexism and misogyny) were a wake-up call for many Americans who underestimated the role that sex and gender continue to play in presidential politics. But we have had this "awakening" before. Back in the 2000 presidential election, political observers were surprised at the relentless press coverage that held Elizabeth Dole to a different standard during the Republican primary.[44] Many people again had this "awakening" after Clinton's 2008 loss, in which she was treated differently than male contenders in ways that sabotaged her viability.[45] The epiphany that women face unusually sexist barriers to the presidency is old news for anyone paying attention any time a woman gets within striking distance of the office. The fact that this is a lesson we keep learning every time a woman makes a serious bid for the presidency is part of the reason that the barriers are so persistent. As a nation, we have yet to have a common recognition that the presidency is a unique political office when it comes to excluding women and feminized male candidates. Recognizing anti-Democratic prejudice against power-seeking women, especially those seeking the presidency, is the first step in addressing this prejudice.

Notes

SERIES FOREWORD

1. Barbara Risman, "Gender as a Social Structure: Theory Wrestling with Activism," *Gender & Society* 18 (2004): 429–450.

2. See, for example, Leslie McCall, "The Complexity of Intersectionality," *Signs* 30 (2005): 1771–1800.

INTRODUCTION

1. Lynn Vavreck, *The Message Matters: The Economy and Presidential Campaigns* (Princeton, NJ: Princeton University Press, 2009).

2. For an excellent breakdown of presidents' previous public service experience, see Nelson Rosario, "Presidents Ranks by Public Service Experience." *Medium*, November 19, 2016, accessed February 6, 2018, https://medium.com/@nelsonm rosario/presidents-ranked-by-public-service-experience-d4c95d1ae55d.

3. Anne Fausto-Sterling complicates the male-female binary and its biological basis in *Sexing the Body: Gender Politics and the Construction of Sexuality* (New York: Basic Books, 2000).

4. Judith Butler, "Performance Acts and Gender Constitution: An Essay in Phenomenology and Feminist Theory," *Theater Journal* 40, no. 4 (1988): 519–531.

5. Henry J. Kaiser Family Foundation, "Population Distribution by Gender," 2015, accessed August 5, 2017, http://www.kff.org/other/state-/distribution-by -gender/?currentTimeframe=0&sortModel=%7B%22colId%22:%22Location%2 2,%22sort%22:%22asc%22%7D.

6. David Wasserman, "2016 Popular Vote Tracker," Cook Political Report, January 3, 2017, accessed July 25, 2017, http://cookpolitical.com/story/10174.

7. Karrin Vasby Anderson and Kristina Horn Sheeler, *Governing Codes: Gender, Metaphor, and Political Identity* (New York: Lexington Books, 2005), 19.

8. Jackson Katz, *Man Enough? Donald Trump, Hillary Clinton, and the Politics of Presidential Masculinity* (New York: Interlink Publishing Group, 2016).

9. Meredith Conroy, *Media, Masculinity, and the American Presidency* (New York: Palgrave, 2015).

10. Center for American Women and Politics (CAWP), "Fact Sheet: Women in the U.S. Congress 2015," accessed August 5, 2017, http://www.cawp.rutgers .edu/women-us-congress-2015.

11. Rebecca Beitsch, "Stalled Progress for Women in State Legislatures." *Pew Charitable Trusts*, December 8, 2015, accessed August 5, 2017, http:// www.pewtrusts.org/en/research-and-analysis/blogs/stateline/2015/12/08/stalled -progress-for-women-in-state-legislatures.

12. CAWP, "Fact Sheet."

13. Sue Thomas and Susan Welch, "The Impact of Women in State Legislatures: Numerical and Organizational Strength," in *The Impact of Women in Public Office*, ed. Susan J. Carroll (Bloomington: Indiana University Press, 2001).

14. John M. Carey, Richard G. Neimi, and Lynda W. Powell, *Term Limits in State Legislatures* (Ann Arbor: University of Michigan Press, 1994).

15. Lyn Kathlene, "In a Different Voice: Women and the Policy Process," in *Women and Elective Office: Past, Present, and Future*, ed. Sue Thomas and Clyde Wilcox (Cambridge: Oxford University Press, 2005).

16. Ibid.

17. Angela High-Pippert and John Comer, "Female Empowerment: The Influence of Women Representing Women," *Women and Politics* 19, no. 4 (1998): 53–65.

18. See Meredith Conroy, Sarah Oliver, Ian Breckenridge-Jackson, and Caroline Heldman, "From Ferraro to Palin: Sexism in Coverage of Vice Presidential Candidates in Old and New Media," *Politics, Groups, and Identities* 3, no. 4 (2015): 573–591; Kelly Dittmar, *Navigating Gendered Terrain: Stereotypes and Strategy in Political Campaigns* (Philadelphia: Temple University Press, 2015); and Danny Hayes and Jennifer L. Lawless, *Women on the Run: Gender, Media, and Political Campaigns in a Polarized Era* (New York: Cambridge University Press, 2016).

19. J. T. Havel, *U.S. Presidential Candidates and the Election: A Biographical and Historical Guide* (New York: Simon and Schuster, 1996).

20. Christopher S. Parker and Matt A. Barreto, *Change They Can't Believe In: The Tea Party and Reactionary Politics in America* (Princeton, NJ: Princeton University Press, 2013).

21. As quoted in Joseph P. Williams, "New Insurgents, Old Problems," *U.S. News and World Reports*, August 14, 2015, accessed February 6, 2018, https:// www.usnews.com/news/the-report/articles/2015/08/14/sanders-and-trump -are-a-new-breed-of-insurgent-candidates.

CHAPTER 1

1. Kelly DeVries, *Joan of Arc: A Military Leader* (Gloucestershire: Sutton Publishing, 1999).

2. Alice Eagly and Linda L. Carli, "Women and the Labyrinth of Leadership," *Harvard Business Review*, September 2007, accessed on December 20, 2016, https://hbr.org/2007/09/women-and-the-labyrinth-of-leadership.

3. Abigail Adams and John Adams, *My Dearest Friend: Letters of Abigail and John Adams*, ed. Margaret A. Hogan and C. James Taylor (New York: Belknap Press, 2010), 5.

4. Center for American Women and Politics, "Summary of Women Candidates for Elective Offices, 1970–2014," 2015, accessed December 20, 2016, http://www.cawp.rutgers.edu/sites/default/files/resources/can_histsum.pdf.

5. Ibid.

6. As quoted in Nancy Hatch Woodward, "Women in the Workplace: Still Fighting Stereotypes (Part One)," *West Human Resources Advisor*, 2007, accessed on December 31, 2016, https.west.advisor.thompson.com.

7. Danny Hayes and Jennifer Lawless, *Women on the Run: Gender, Media, and Political Campaigns in a Polarized Era* (New York: Cambridge University Press, 2016).

8. Jennifer L. Lawless and Richard L. Fox, "Girls Just Wanna Not Run: The Gender Gap in Young American's Political Ambition," American University School of Public Affairs, 2013, accessed on November 21, 2016, https://www.american.edu/spa/wpi/upload/Girls-Just-Wanna-Not-Run_Policy-Report.pdf.

9. Ibid., 2.

10. Jennifer L. Lawless and Richard L. Fox, *Running from Office: Why Young Americans Are Turned Off by Politics* (New York: Oxford University Press, 2015).

11. Eagly and Carli, "Women and the Labyrinth."

12. J. D. Nordell, "Positions of Power: How Female Ambition Is Shaped," *Slate.com*, November 21, 2006, accessed on December 20, 2016, http://www.slate.com/articles/news_and_politics/the_gist/2006/11/positions_of_power.html.

13. Lawless and Fox, "Running from Office."

14. Sophie von Stumm, Tomas Chamorro-Premuzic, and Adrian Furnham, "Decomposing Self-Estimates of Intelligence: Structure and Sex Differences Across 12 Nations," *British Journal of Psychology* 100, no. 2 (2009): 429–442.

15. Nordell, "Positions of Power."

16. Shelley Correll, "Constraints into Preferences: Gender, Status, and Emerging Career Aspirations," *American Sociological Review* 69, no. 1 (2004): 94–113.

17. Stumm, Chamorro-Premuzic, and Furnham, "Decomposing Self-Estimates of Intelligence."

18. Lawless and Fox, "Running from Office."

19. Jennifer L. Lawless and Richard L. Fox, *Men Rule: The Continued Under-Representation of Women in U.S. Politics*, Women and Politics Institute, American University, 2012, accessed on November 20, 2016, https://www.american.edu/spa/wpi/upload/2012-Men-Rule-Report-web.pdf.

20. Anna Fels, *Necessary Dreams: Ambition in Changing Women's Lives* (New York: Anchor, 2005).

21. Ibid.

22. Lawless and Fox, "Men Rule."

23. Ibid.

24. BallotReady, "Are Women Running for Senate More Qualified Than Men?" October 25, 2016, accessed December 27, 2016, https://blog.ballotready.org/state-by-state/election/are-women-running-for-congress-overqualified/.

25. Karen O'Connor, ed., *Gender and Women's Leadership: A Reference Handbook* (Thousand Oaks, CA: Sage Publications, 2010).

26. PolitiFact, "Congress Has 11% Approval Ratings but 96% Incumbent Reelection Rate, Meme Says," November 11, 2014, accessed December 20, 2016, http://www.politifact.com/truth-o-meter/statements/2014/nov/11/facebook-posts/congress-has-11-approval-ratings-96-incumbent-re-e/.

27. Alan S. Gerber and Eric Schickler, eds., *Governing in a Polarized Age: Elections, Parties, and Political Representation in America* (New York: Cambridge University Press, 2017).

28. Nelson Rosario, "Presidents Ranks by Public Service Experience," *Medium*, November 19, 2016, accessed February 6, 2018, https://medium.com/@nelsonmrosario/presidents-ranked-by-public-service-experience-d4c95d1ae55d.

29. W. Gardner Selby, "Ted Cruz Says about Half of Presidents Were Previously Governors, Half Were Senators," PolitiFact, April 27, 2015, accessed on February 6, 2018, http://www.politifact.com/texas/statements/2015/apr/27/ted-cruz/ted-cruz-says-half-presidents-were-previously-gove/.

30. Melody Crowder-Meyer, "Gendered Recruitment without Trying: How Local Party Recruiters Affect Women's Representation," *Politics & Gender* 9, no. 4 (2013): 390–413.

31. Susan J. Carroll and Kira Sanbonmatsu, *More Women Can Run: Gender and Pathways to the State Legislatures* (New York: Oxford University Press, 2013).

32. O'Connor, *Gender and Women's Leadership*.

33. Daniel M. Butler and Jessica Robinson Preece, "Recruitment and Perceptions of Gender Bias in Party Leadership Support," *Political Research Quarterly* 69, no. 4 (2016): 842–851.

34. J. M. Twenge, "Changes in Masculine and Feminine Traits over Time: A Meta Analysis," *Sex Roles* 36, no. 5–6 (1997): 305–325.

35. Janet T. Spence and Robert L. Helmreich, *Masculinity and Femininity: Their Psychological Dimensions, Correlates and Antecedents* (Austin: University of Texas Press, 1978).

36. Alice H. Eagly and Steven J. Karau, "Role Incongruity Theory of Prejudice toward Female Leaders," *Psychological Review* 109, no. 3 (2002): 573–98.

37. Kira Sanbonmatsu, "Political Parties and the Recruitment of Women to State Legislatures," *Journal of Politics* 64, no. 3 (2002): 791–809; Kira Sanbonmatsu and Kathleen A. Dolan, "Do Gender Stereotypes Transcend Party?" *Political Research Quarterly* 62, no. 3 (2009): 485–94; and Kathleen A. Dolan and Timothy Lynch, "It Takes a Survey: Understanding Gender Stereotypes, Abstract Attitudes, and Voting for Women Candidates," *American Politics Research* 42, no. 4 (2014): 656–676.

38. See Leonie Huddy and Nayda Terkildsen, "Gender Stereotypes and the Perception of Male and Female Candidates," *American Journal of Political Science* 37, no. 1 (1993): 119–47; Kim Kahn, *The Political Consequences of Being a Woman* (New York: Columbia University Press, 1996); Kathleen Dolan, "The Impact of Gender Stereotyped Evaluations on Support for Women Candidates," *Political*

Behavior 32, no. 1 (2010): 69–88; and Kathleen Dolan, "Gender Stereotypes, Candidate Evaluations, and Voting for Women Candidates: What Really Matters?" *Political Research Quarterly* 67, no. 1 (2014): 96–107.

39. Anne M. Koenig, Alice H. Eagly, Abigail A. Mitchell, and Tiina Ristikari, "Are Leader Stereotypes Masculine? A Meta-Analysis of Three Research Paradigms," *Psychological Bulletin* 137, no. 4 (2011): 616–42.

40. Kay Deaux, "Psychological Constructions of Masculinity and Femininity," in *Masculinity/Femininity: Basic Perspectives*, ed. J. M. Reinisch, L. A. Rosenblum, and S. A. Sanders (New York: Oxford University Press, 1987).

41. Koenig, et al., "Are Leader Stereotypes Masculine?"

42. Monica C. Schneider and Angela L. Bos, "Measuring Stereotypes of Female Politicians," *Political Psychology* 35, no. 2 (2014): 245–266.

43. Ibid., 249.

44. Ibid., 260.

45. See Huddy and Terkildsen, "Gender Stereotypes and the Perception of Male and Female Candidates"; and Susan J. Carroll and Kira Sanbonmatsu, *More Women Can Run: Gender and Pathways to the State Legislatures* (New York: Oxford University Press, 2013).

46. See Dolan, "The Impact of Gender Stereotyped Evaluations"; and Dolan, "Gender Stereotypes, Candidate Evaluations, and Voting for Women Candidates."

47. Michele Swers, "Building a Reputation on National Security: The Impact of Stereotypes Related to Gender and Military Experience," *Legislative Studies Quarterly* 32, no. 4 (2007): 559–95.

48. Ibid., 563.

49. Ann Gordon and Jerry Miller, "Gender, Race, and the Oval Office," in *Anticipating Madam President*, Robert P. Watson and Ann Gordon (Boulder, CO: Lynne Rienner, 2003).

50. See Georgia Duerst-Lahti, "Masculinity on the Campaign Trail," in *Rethinking Madame President: Are We Ready for a Woman in the White House?* ed. Lori Cox Han and Caroline Heldman (Boulder, CO: Lynne Rienner, 2007); and Georgia Duerst-Lahti and Rita Mae Kelly, eds., "Gender, Power, and Leadership," in *Gender, Power, Leadership, and Governance* (Ann Arbor: University of Michigan Press, 1995).

51. Jennifer L Lawless, "Women, War, and Winning Elections: Gender Stereotyping in the Post–September 11th Era," *Political Research Quarterly* 57, no. 3 (2004): 479–90.

52. Ibid., 480.

53. David S. Bernstein, "Where Are All the Republican Women?" Politico, August 7, 2016, accessed August 16, 2017, http://www.politico.com/magazine/story/2016/08/gop-republican-women-politics-disparity-feminism-214140.

54. John R. Petrocik, "Issue Ownership in Presidential Elections, with a 1980 Case Study," *American Journal of Political Science* 40, no. 3 (1996): 825–59.

55. Dolan and Lynch, "It Takes a Survey."

56. See Mirya Holman, Jennifer L. Merolla, and Elizabeth J. Zechmeister, "Terrorist Threat, Male Stereotypes, and Candidate Evaluations," *Political*

Research Quarterly 69, no. 1 (2016): 134–47; Erica Falk and Kate Kenski, "Issue Saliency and Gender Stereotypes: Support for Women as Presidents in Times of War and Terrorism," Social Science Quarterly 87, no. 1 (2006): 1–18; and Kira Sanbonmatsu and Kathleen A. Dolan, "Do Gender Stereotypes Transcend Party?" Political Research Quarterly 62, no. 3 (2009): 485–494.

57. Susan Nierenberg and Serena Fong, "Damned or Doomed: Catalyst Study on Gender Stereotyping at Work Uncovers Double-Bind Dilemmas for Women," Catalyst, July 15, 2007, accessed December 31, 2016, http://www.catalyst.org/knowledge/double-bind.

58. Linda Borrelli, "Gender, Credibility, and Politics: The Senate Nomination Hearings of Cabinet Secretaries-Designate, 1975 to 1993," Political Research Quarterly 50, no. 1, (1997): 171–197.

59. Lawless and Fox, "Girls Just Wanna Not."

60. Eagly and Carli, "Women and the Labyrinth."

61. Catalyst, Inc., The Bottom Line: Connecting Corporate Performance and Gender Diversity, 2004, accessed on December 31, 2016, http://www.catalyst.org/system/files/The_Bottom_Line_Connecting_Corporate_Performance_and_Gender_Diversity.pdf.

62. Marcus Noland, Tyler Moran, and Barbara Kotschwar, Is Gender Diversity Profitable? Evidence from a Global Study, Peterson Institute for International Economics, 2016, accessed December 28, 2016, https://piie.com/publications/wp/wp16-3.pdf.

63. Rebecca Riffkin, "Americans Still Prefer a Male Boss to a Female Boss," Gallup, October 14, 2014, accessed December 28, 2016, http://www.gallup.com/poll/178484/americans-prefer-male-boss-female-boss.aspx; and Alice Eagly, "Female Leadership Advantage and Disadvantage: Resolving the Contradictions," Psychology of Women Quarterly 31, no. 1 (2007): 1.

64. Alice Eagly and Steven J. Karau, "Role Congruity Theory of Prejudice Toward Female Leaders," Psychological Review 109, no. 3 (2002): 573–598.

65. Nierenberg and Fong, "Damned or Doomed."

66. Robert W. Rice, Lisa Richer Bender, and Alan G. Vitters, "Leader Sex, Follower Attitudes Toward Women, and Leadership Effectiveness: A Laboratory Experiment," Organizational Behavior and Human Performance 25, no. 1 (1980).

67. Kathleen Hall Jamieson, Beyond the Double Bind: Women and Leadership (New York: Oxford University Press, 1997).

68. Georgia Duerst-Lahti, "Reconceiving Theories of Power: Consequences of Masculinism in the Executive Branch," in The Other Elites: Women, Politics, and Power in the Executive Branch, ed. MaryAnne Borrelli and Janet M. Martin (Boulder, CO: Lynne Rienner, 1997).

69. Georgia Duerst-Lahti, "Masculinity on the Campaign Trail," in Rethinking Madame President: Are We Ready for a Woman in the White House? ed. Lori Han and Caroline Heldman (Boulder, CO: Lynne Rienner, 2007).

70. Jennifer L. Lawless, "Women, War, and Winning Elections: Gender Stereotyping in the Post–September 11th Era," Political Research Quarterly 57, no. 3 (2004): 479–490.

71. Jamieson, *Beyond the Double Bind*.

72. Ibid., 6.

73. Nierenberg and Fong, *Damned or Doomed*.

74. Victoria Brescoll, "How to Walk the Tightrope of 'Nice and Able': Overcoming Workplace Challenges for Female Bosses," *Psychology of Women Quarterly* 31, no. 2 (2007): 217–218.

75. Caroline Heldman and Lisa Wade, "Sexualizing Sarah Palin: The Social and Political Context of the Sexual Objectification of Female Candidates," *Sex Roles* 65, no. 3 (2011): 156–164; and Nathan A. Heflick and Jamie L. Goldenberg, "Objectifying Sarah Palin: Evidence that Objectification Causes Women to be Perceived as Less Competent and Less Fully Human," *Journal of Experimental Social Psychology* 45, no. 3 (2009): 598–601.

76. Caroline Heldman, *The Sexy Lie: The War on Women's Bodies and How to Fight Back* (New Orleans: Feminist Fight Club, 2017).

77. Celinda Lake, *Name It. Change It*, Women's Media Center, September 2010, accessed December 28, 2016, http://www.lakeresearch.com/news/NameItChangeIt/NameItChangeIt.pres.pdf; and Heflick and Goldenberg, "Objectifying Sarah Palin."

78. Ibid.

79. Heflick and Goldenberg, "Objectifying Sarah Palin."

80. Peter S. Glick, Sadie E. Larsen, Cathryn Johnson, and Heather Branstiter, "Evaluations of Sexy Women in Low- and High-Status Jobs," *Psychology of Women Quarterly* 29, no. 4 (2005): 389–395.

81. Heldman, *The Sexy Lie*.

82. Hayes and Lawless, "Women on the Run."

83. Gina Serignere Woodall and Kim L. Fridkin, "Shaping Women's Chances: Stereotypes and the Media," *Rethinking Madame President: Are We Ready for a Woman in the White House?*, ed. Lori Han and Caroline Heldman (Boulder, CO: Lynne Rienner, 2007); and Meredith Conroy, Sarah Oliver, Ian Breckenridge-Jackson, and Caroline Heldman, "From Ferraro to Palin: Sexism in Coverage of Vice Presidential Candidates in Old and New Media," *Politics, Groups, and Identities* 3, no. 4 (2015): 573–591.

84. Shanto Iyengar and Donald R. Kinder, *News That Matters: Television and Public Opinion* (Chicago: University of Chicago Press, 1987).

85. Dennis Chong and James N. Druckman, "Framing Theory," *Annual Review of Political Science* 10 (2007): 103–126; and Thomas E. Nelson, Rosalee A. Clawson, and Zoe M. Oxley, "Media Framing of a Civil Liberties Conflict and Its Effect on Tolerance," *American Political Science Review* 91, no. 3 (1997): 567–584.

86. Kim Kahn, *The Political Consequences of Being a Woman* (New York: Columbia University Press, 1996); Kim Kahn, "Does Gender Make a Difference? An Experimental Examination of Sex Stereotypes and Press Patterns in Statewide Campaigns," *American Journal of Political Science* 38, no. 1 (1994): 162–195; Kim Kahn, "Does Being Male Help? An Investigation of the Effects of Candidate

Gender and Campaign Coverage on Evaluations of U.S. Senate Candidates," *Journal of Politics* 54, no. 2 (1992): 497–517.

87. Woodall and Fridkin, "Shaping Women's Chances: Stereotypes and the Media"; and Caroline Heldman, Susan J. Carroll, and Stephanie Olson, "'She Brought Only a Skirt': Print Media Coverage of Elizabeth Dole's Bid for the Republican Nomination," *Political Communication* 22, no. 3 (2005): 315–335.

88. Regina G. Lawrence and Melody Rose, *Hillary Clinton's Race for the White House: Gender Politics and Media on the Campaign Trail* (Boulder CO: Lynne Rienner, 2009); Heldman et al., "She Brought Only a Skirt"; Kahn, "Does Being Male Help..."

89. Shawn J. Parry-Giles, *Hillary Clinton in the News: Gender and Authenticity in American Politics* (Urbana: University of Illinois Press, 2014).

90. Erika Falk, *Women for President: Media Bias in Nine Campaigns*, 2nd ed. (Urbana: University of Illinois Press, 2010), 56.

91. Falk, *Women for President*, 60.

92. Hayes and Lawless, "Women on the Run."

93. Conroy et al., "From Ferraro to Palin..."; Mark Halperin and John Harris, *The Way to Win: Taking the White House in 2008* (New York: Random House, 2008); and Matthew A. Baum and Tim Groeling, "New Media and the Polarization of American Political Discourse," *Political Communication* 25, no. 4 (2008): 245–265.

94. Benjamin R. Barber, "Which Technology and Which Democracy?" *Democracy and New Media*, ed. Henry Jenkins and David Thorburn (Cambridge, MA: MIT Press, 2003); and Arthur D. Santana, "Virtuous or Vitriolic: The Effect of Anonymity on Civility in Online Newspaper Reader Comment Boards," *Journalism Practice* 8, no. 1 (2013): 18–33.

95. Conroy et al., "From Ferraro to Palin."

96. Santana, "Virtuous or Vitriolic."

97. Conroy et al., "From Ferraro to Palin."

98. Hayes and Lawless, "Women on the Run"; and Richard A. Seltzer, Jody Newman, and Melissa Voorhees Leighton, *Sex as a Political Variable: Women as Candidates and Voters in U.S. Elections* (Boulder, CO: Lynne Rienner, 1997).

99. BallotReady, "Are Women Running."

100. Rogers M. Smith, *Civic Ideals: Conflicting Visions of Citizenship in US History* (New Haven, CT: Yale University Press, 1999).

101. Evelyn Glenn, "Race, Gender, and Unequal Citizenship in the United States," *The Changing Terrain of Race and Ethnicity*, ed. Maria Krysan and Amanda Lewis (New York: Russell Sage Foundation, 2004), 187–202, 199.

102. Vincent N. Pham, "Our Foreign President Barack Obama: The Racial Logics of Birther Discourse," *Journal of International and Intercultural Communications* 8, no. 2 (2015): 86–107.

103. Jaclyn Howell, "Not Just Crazy: An Explanation for the Resonance of the Birther Narrative," *Communication Monographs* 79, no. 4 (2012): 428–447.

104. John Clinton and Carrie Roush, "Poll: Persistent Partisan Divide Over 'Birther' Question," NBC News, August 10, 2016, accessed December 30, 2016,

http://www.nbcnews.com/politics/2016-election/poll-persistent-partisan-divide
-over-birther-question-n627446?cid=sm_tw.

105. Matthew W. Hughey, "Show Me Your Papers! Obama's Birth and the
Whiteness of Belonging," *Qualitative Sociology* 35, no. 2 (2012): 1–19.

106. Judith N. Shklar, *American Citizenship: The Quest for Inclusion* (Cambridge,
MA: Harvard University Press, 1991).

107. Glenn, "Race, Gender," 20.

108. Carole Pateman, "Equality, Difference and Subordination: The Politics of
Motherhood and Women's Citizenship," *Beyond Equality and Difference: Citizen-
ship, Feminist Politics, and Female Subjectivity*, ed. Gisela Bock and Susan James
(New York: Routledge, 1992); Susan Moller Okin, *Justice, Gender, and the Family*
(New York: Basic Books, 1991); Iris Marion Young, *Justice and the Politics of Dif-
ference* (Princeton, NJ: Princeton University Press, 1990).

109. Ruth Lister, "Dialectics of Citizenship," *Hypatia* 12, no. 4 (1997): 6–26, 6.

110. Georgia Duerst-Lahti and Rita Mae Kelly, *Gender Power, Leadership, and
Governance* (Ann Arbor: University of Michigan Press, 1996).

111. Lawless, "Women, War," 480.

112. Falk, *Women for President*.

113. Susan J. Carroll, "Reflections on Gender and Hillary Clinton's Presidential
Campaign: The Good, the Bad, and the Misogynic," *Politics & Gender* 5 (2009):
1–20, 12.

CHAPTER 2

1. Jackson Katz, *Man Enough? Donald Trump, Hillary Clinton, and the Politics of
Presidential Masculinity* (New York: Interlink Publishing Group, 2016).

2. Meredith Conroy, *Media, Masculinity, and the American Presidency* (New York:
Palgrave, 2015).

3. Philip Norton and Pippa Norris, "Feminist Organizational Structure in the
White House: The Office of the Women's Initiative and Outreach," *Political
Research Quarterly* 56, no. 4 (2003): 477–87.

4. King, "Sex Role Identity and Decision Styles: How Gender Helps Explain
the Paucity of Women at the Top," *Gender, Power, Leadership, and Governance*, ed.
Georgia Duerst-Lahti and Rita Mae Kelly (Ann Arbor: University of Michigan
Press, 1997).

5. Ibid., 191.

6. Borrelli, "Gender, Credibility, and Politics," 182.

7. For an extended discussion of woman in positions of power, see Duerst-Lahti
and Kelly, "Gender, Power, Leadership, and Governance"; and Winsky Mattei,
"Gender and Power in American Legislative Discourse," *Journal of Politics* 60, no.
2 (1998), 440–461.

8. Duerst-Lahti, "Reconceiving Theories of Power," 11.

9. Conroy, "Are You Man Enough? The Gender of Presidential Candidates by
Print Media." Presented at the American Political Science Association Conference, Philadelphia, PA, August 31–September 3, 2006.

10. Conroy conducted two analyses, one involving the 1992 and 1996 elections, and a second analysis involving the 2000 to 2012 elections. These figures are based on her analysis from 2000 to 2012.

11. Alex Williams, "Live from Miami, a Style Showdown," *New York Times*, September 26, 2004.

12. Sarah Watts, *Rough Rider in the White House: Theodore Roosevelt and the Politics of Desire* (Chicago: University of Chicago Press, 2003).

13. Eric Garland, "The Crisis of American Masculinity," December 20, 2012, accessed August 18, 2017, http://www.ericgarland.co/2012/12/20/the-crisis-of -american-masculinity/.

14. Brad Neely, "Washington," YouTube, March 13, 2009, accessed on August 18, 2017, https://www.youtube.com/watch?v=l7iVsdRbhnc.

15. Watts, *Rough Rider in the White House*, 123.

16. James Bradley, *The Imperial Cruise: A Secret History of Empire and War* (New York: Little Brown and Company, 2009), 50.

17. Ibid., 51.

18. Ibid.

19. Harvey Mansfield, "The Manliness of Theodore Roosevelt," *The New Criterion* 23, no. 7 (March 2005): 4.

20. Jackson Katz, "Tough Guise 2: Violence, Manhood & American Culture," transcript, accessed August 20, 2017, http://www.mediaed.org/transcripts/Tough -Guise-2-Transcript.pdf.

21. Ibid.

22. Victoria Bekiempis, "The Cowboy in Crisis, or Male Anxiety in American Politics," *The Guardian*, October 25, 2011, accessed August 20, 2017, https:// www.theguardian.com/commentisfree/cifamerica/2011/oct/25/cowboy -crisis-male-anxiety.

23. Amanda Marcotte, "The Party of Anxious Masculinity," Slate, November 9, 2009, accessed August 20, 2017, http://www.slate.com/blogs/xx_factor/2009/11/09 /republicans_have_to_choose_between_sexism_and_women.html.

24. Katz, *Man Enough?*

25. Katz, *Man Enough?*

26. The American Presidency Project, "Election of 1988," accessed August 20, 2017, http://www.presidency.ucsb.edu/showelection.php?year=1988.

27. Margaret G. Warner, "Bush Battles the 'Wimp Factor,'" *Newsweek*, October 19, 1987.

28. Roger Simon, "Questions that Kill Candidates' Careers," Politico, April 20, 2007, accessed August 20, 2017, http://www.politico.com/story/2007/04 /questions-that-kill-candidates-careers-003617.

29. Adam Nagourney and Janet Elder, "The 2004 Campaign: Public Opinion; Bush's Rating Falls to Its Lowest Point, New Survey Finds," *New York Times*, June 29, 2004, accessed on August 20, 2017, http://www.nytimes.com/2004/06/29/us/2004-campaign-public-opinion-bush-s-rating-falls-its-lowest-point-new-survey.html.

30. Atlas, "2004 Presidential General Election Results," accessed August 20, 2017, http://uselectionatlas.org/RESULTS/national.php?year=2004.

31. Kevin Coe et al., "Masculinity as Political Strategy: George W. Bush, the 'War on Terrorism,' and an Echoing Press," *Journal of Women, Politics & Policy* 29, no. 1 (2007): 31–55.

32. Pew Research Center for the People and the Press, "Race Tightens Again, Kerry's Image Improves: Democrats, Blacks Less Confident in Accurate Vote Count," October 20, 2004, accessed May 3, 2018, http://www.people-press.org/2004/10/20/race-tightens-again-kerrys-image-improves/.

33. Howard Kurtz, "Jeff Gannon Admits Past 'Mistakes,' Berates Critics," *Washington Post*, February 19, 2005, accessed May 3, 2018, http://www.washingtonpost.com/wp-dyn/articles/A36733-2005Feb18.html.

34. Jeremy Cluchey, "Cameron's Fake Kerry Story Capped FOX Commentators' Manicure Fixation," Media Matters for America, October 4, 2004, accessed May 3, 2018, https://www.mediamatters.org/research/2004/10/04/camerons-fake-kerry-story-capped-fox-commentato/132001.

35. Ibid.

36. Michael Tomasky, "Mitt Romney: A Candidate with a Serious Wimp Problem," *Newsweek*, July 29, 2012.

37. Chris Cillizza and Aaron Blake, "Mitt Romney and the Wimp Factor," *Washington Post*, July 30, 2012, accessed August 20, 2017, https://www.washingtonpost.com/blogs/the-fix/post/mitt-romney-and-the-wimp-factor/2012/07/30/gJQA4Dd5JX_blog.html?utm_term=.d717afb8fed9.

38. Elspeth Reeve, "Growing Concern that Romney's a Wimp," *Atlantic*, February 9, 2012, accessed on August 20, 2017, https://www.theatlantic.com/politics/archive/2012/02/growing-concern-romneys-wimp/332026/.

39. Dana Milbank, "Barack Obama, The First Female President," *Washington Post*, May 14, 2012, accessed August 20, 2017, https://www.washingtonpost.com/opinions/barack-obama-the-first-female-president/2012/05/14/gIQAViBlPU_story.html?utm_term=.2e183bd9e564.

40. Frank R. Cooper, "Our First Unisex President?: Black Masculinity and Obama's Feminine Side," Suffolk University Law School Faculty Publications, Paper 52 (2009), http://lsr.nellco.org/suffolk_fp/52.

41. Katz, *Man Enough?*

42. Abbey Coholic, "Obama vs. Romney Heteronormative Masculinity Paper," academic.edu, accessed August 20, 2017, http://www.academia.edu/29965765/Obama_vs_Romney_Heteronormative_Masculinity_Paper.

43. Atlas, "2012 Presidential General Election Results," accessed August 20, 2017, http://uselectionatlas.org/RESULTS/national.php?year=2012.

44. Philip Bump, "Trump Got the Most GOP Votes Ever—Both for and against Him—and Other Fun Facts," *Washington Post*, June 8, 2016, accessed August 20, 2017, http://uselectionatlas.org/RESULTS/national.php?year=2012.

45. Eliza Collins, "Cruz Camp Mocks Rubio's 'High-Heeled Booties,'" Politico, January 5, 2016, accessed August 21, 2017, http://www.politico.com/story/2016/01/ted-cruz-marco-rubio-boots-tweet-217388.

46. Scott Bixby, "Marco Rubio's 'High-Heeled Booties' Mocked by Republican Rivals," *The Guardian*, January 6, 2012, accessed August 21, 2017, http://www.slate.com/blogs/the_slatest/2016/01/06/republicans_make_fun_of_marco_rubio_s_fancy_heeled_boots.html.

47. Jim Newell, "Serious Adult Presidential Candidates Make Fun of Marco Rubio's Fancy Shoes," Slate, January 6, 2016, accessed August 21, 2017, http://www.slate.com/blogs/the_slatest/2016/01/06/republicans_make_fun_of_marco_rubio_s_fancy_heeled_boots.html.

48. Bixby, "Marco Rubio's 'High-Heeled Booties.'"

49. Gary Legum, "The Raging Idiocy of the GOP's Masculinity Brigade," Salon, January 20, 2016, accessed August 21, 2017, http://www.salon.com/2016/01/20/the_raging_idiocy_of_the_gops_masculinity_brigade/.

50. Theodore Schleifer, "Rick Perry's Tough Guy Challenge for Donald Trump," CNN.com, July 30, 2015, http://www.cnn.com/2015/07/29/politics/rick-perry-donald-trump-pull-up-contest/.

51. Theodore Schleifer, "Rick Perry's Tough Guy Challenge for Donald Trump," CNN, July 30, 2015, accessed August 20, 2017, http://www.cnn.com/2015/07/29/politics/rick-perry-donald-trump-pull-up-contest/index.html.

52. Jess Byrnes, "Trump Calls Cruz a 'Pussy,'" thehill.com, February 8, 2016, http://thehill.com/blogs/blog-briefing-room/news/268714-trump-calls-cruz-a-puy.

53. Jeremy Diamond, "Trump: Cruz Is 'Like a Little Baby,'" CNN, February 23, 2016, accessed August 21, 2017, http://www.cnn.com/2016/02/23/politics/donald-trump-ted-cruz-nevada-baby/.

54. Legum, "The Raging Idiocy."

55. Alexandra Jaffe, "Donald Trump Has 'Small Hands,' Marco Rubio Says," NBCNews.com, February 29, 2016, http://www.nbcnews.com/politics/2016-election/donald-trump-has-small-hands-marco-rubio-says-n527791.

56. Daniel White, "Watch Trump Talk about His Private Parts at the Debate," CNN, March 3, 2016, accessed August 21, 2017, http://time.com/4247366/republican-debate-donald-trump-small-hands-penis/.

57. Emily Shapiro, "The History behind the Donald Trump 'Small Hands' Insult," ABC News, March 4, 2016, accessed August 21, 2017, http://abcnews.go.com/Politics/history-donald-trump-small-hands-insult/story?id=37395515.

58. Gary Legum, "The Raging Idiocy."

59. David Frum, "Could Trump Be the 'Man's Man' America Wants?" *Atlantic*, August 2, 2016, accessed August 21, 2017, https://www.theatlantic.com/politics/archive/2016/08/trump-may-be-the-man-america-wants/494009/.

60. Elizabeth Debold, "Is the Current Leadership Crisis a Crisis of Masculinity?" February 15, 2017, accessed August 21, 2017, http://elizabethdebold.com/is-the-current-leadership-crisis-a-crisis-of-masculinity/.

61. Daniel Goleman, "Leadership That Gets Results," *Harvard Business Review* (March–April 2000), accessed August 21, 2017, https://hbr.org/2000/03/leadership-that-gets-results.

62. Jack Zenger and Joe Folkman, "A Study in Leadership: Women Do It Better Than Men," Zenger Folkman, 2012, accessed August 21, 2017, http://zengerfolkman.com/media/articles/ZFCo.WP.WomenBetterThanMen.033012.pdf.

CHAPTER 3

1. Meredith Conroy, Sarah Oliver, Ian Breckenridge-Jackson, and Caroline Heldman, "From Ferraro to Palin: Sexism in Coverage of Vice Presidential Candidates in Old and New Media," *Politics, Groups, and Identities* 3, no. 4 (2015): 573–591.

2. J. T. Havel, *U.S. Presidential Candidates and the Election: A Biographical and Historical Guide* (New York: Simon and Schuster, 1996).

3. We define "major bids" as candidacies that received formal nominations from a national party, or raised sufficient money to be considered a competitor, had a national political profile prior to running for the presidency, or were placed on multiple primary state ballots.

4. Maria Braden, *Women Politicians and the Media* (Lexington: University of Kentucky Press, 1996), 2.

5. We do not analyze Clinton's 2016 bid in this chapter since the remainder of the book revolves around aspects of her campaign.

6. Erika Falk, *Women for President: Media Bias in Nine Campaigns*, 2nd ed. (Chicago: University of Chicago Press, 2010).

7. Regina G. Lawrence and Melody Rose, *Hillary Clinton's Race for the White House: Gender Politics and Media on the Campaign Trail* (Boulder, CO: Lynne Rienner, 2009); and Melissa K. Miller, Jeffrey S. Peake, and Brittany Anne Boulton, "Testing the Saturday Night Live Hypothesis: Fairness and Bias in Newspaper Coverage of Hillary Clinton's Presidential Campaign," *Politics & Gender* 6, no. 2 (2010): 169–198.

8. Falk, *Women for President*, 101.

9. Ibid., 61.

10. Ibid., 119.

11. Kim Kahn, *The Political Consequences of Being a Woman* (New York: Columbia University Press, 1996).

12. Lawrence and Rose, *Hillary Clinton's Race*.

13. Falk, *Women for President*, 57.

14. Ibid., 60.

15. Ibid., 87.

16. Conroy et al., "From Ferraro to Palin."

17. Nathan A. Heflick and Jamie L. Goldenberg, "Objectifying Sarah Palin: Evidence That Objectification Causes Women to Be Perceived as Less Competent

and Less Fully Human," *Journal of Experimental Social Psychology* 45, no. 3 (2009): 598–601.

18. Falk, *Women for President*, 86.

19. Ibid., 67.

20. Michael Lipka, "U.S. Religious Groups and Their Political Leanings," Pew Research Center, February 20, 2016, accessed on January 2, 2017, http://www .pewresearch.org/fact-tank/2016/02/23/u-s-religious-groups-and-their-political -leanings/.

21. Conroy et al., "From Ferraro to Palin."

22. Jeffrey Gottfried and Elisha Shearer, "News Use across Social Media Platforms 2016," Pew Research Center, May 26, 2016, accessed January 4, 2017, http://www .journalism.org/2016/05/26/news-use-across-social-media-platforms-2016/.

23. Women's Media Center, "Where Voters Saw Most Sexist Treatment of Women Candidates in Media," November 18, 2016, accessed on January 4, 2017, http://www.womensmediacenter.com/press/entry/voters-say-social-media-most -sexist-in-treatment-of-women-candidates.

24. This chapter draws heavily from Erika Falk's *Women for President: Media Bias in Nine Campaigns* (Chicago, University of Chicago Press, 2010). We especially rely on Falk's analysis of 19th-century candidates and her identification of the major candidates throughout U.S. history. Falk identified key female contenders based on the amount of money they raised, the number of states where they got on the ballot, and their previous political experience.

25. Falk, *Women for President*, 41.

26. Ibid.

27. Ibid., 60.

28. Ibid., 83.

29. Ibid., 57.

30. Ibid., 68.

31. Ibid., 67.

32. Ibid., 39.

33. Ibid., 39.

34. Ibid.

35. Frank Leslie, *Frank Leslie's Illustrated Newspaper*, November 1, 1884, accessed on January 8, 2017, https://www.google.com/culturalinstitute/beta/u/0 /asset/mock-belva-lockwood-mother-hubbard-parade/bgGiFPr0NMFtyA.

36. Ibid., 88.

37. Falk, *Women for President*, 69.

38. Sara Nachlis, "Before Hillary, There Was Victoria, Belva and 200+ More," Spring Street, June 9, 2016, accessed on January 8, 2017, http://www.spring.st /women-besides-hillary-ran-president.

39. Falk, *Women for President*.

40. Ibid., 33.

41. Ibid.

42. Ibid., 41.

43. Ibid., 43.

44. Ibid.

45. Ibid., 65.

46. Ibid., 64.

47. Ibid., 108.

48. Ibid., 119.

49. Ibid., 87.

50. Ibid.

51. Ibid., 70.

52. Ibid., 34.

53. Ibid.

54. Ibid.

55. Ibid., 37.

56. Ibid., 37.

57. Ibid., 110.

58. Ibid., 119.

59. Ibid., 62.

60. Ibid., 89.

61. Ibid.

62. Ibid., 58.

63. Patricia Schroeder, *Champion of the Great American Family* (New York: Random House, 1989), 43.

64. Ibid., 368.

65. Falk, *Women for President*, 9.

66. Ibid., 41.

67. Ibid., 42.

68. Ibid.

69. Ibid., 65.

70. Ibid., 119.

71. Ibid.

72. Lisa Belkin, "In Politics, Women Run by a Different Set of Rules," *New York Times*, September 9, 1984, accessed on January 8, 2017, http://www.nytimes.com/1984/09/09/weekinreview/in-politics-women-run-by-a-different-set-of-rules.html.

73. Falk, *Women for President*, 71.

74. Ibid., 58.

75. Dave Perry, "PERRY: Hillary's Push through Glass Ceiling May Transcend Pat Schroeder's Sexist Crying Shame," *Aurora Sentinel*, June 8, 2016, accessed January 8, 2017, https://www.sentinelcolorado.com/opinion/perry-hillary-may-transcend-pat-schroeders-sexist-crying-shame/.

76. Falk, *Women for President*.

77. Lenora Fulani, *The Making of a Fringe Candidate* (New York: Castillo International, 1992).

78. Stephanie Greco Larson, *Media & Minorities: The Politics of Race in News and Entertainment* (New York: Rowman & Littlefield, 2006).

79. Falk, *Women for President*.

80. Ibid.

81. Ibid., 44.

82. Caroline Heldman, Susan J. Carroll, and Stephanie Olson, "'She Brought Only a Skirt': Print Media Coverage of Elizabeth Dole's Bid for the Republican Nomination," *Political Communication* 22, no. 3 (2005): 315–335.

83. Karen F. Stein, "The Cleavage Commotion: How the Press Covered Senator Clinton's Campaign," *Cracked but Not Shattered: Hillary Rodham Clinton's Unsuccessful Campaign for the Presidency*, ed. Theodore F. Sheckels (Lanham, MD: Lexington Books, 2009); and Heldman et al., "'She Brought Only a Skirt.'"

84. Falk, *Women for President*, 66.

85. Heldman, "She Brought Only"; and Karrin Vasby Anderson, "From Spouses to Candidates: Hillary Rodham Clinton, Elizabeth Dole, and the Gendered Office of the U.S. President," *Rhetoric and Public Affairs* 5, no. 1 (2002): 105–132.

86. Heldman, "She Brought Only a Skirt…"

87. Lawrence and Rose, *Hillary Clinton's Race*; Heldman et al., "'She Brought Only a Skirt'"; Kim Kahn, "Does Being Male Help? An Investigation of the Effects of Candidate Gender and Campaign Coverage on Evaluations of U.S. Senate Candidates," *Journal of Politics* 54, no. 2, (1992): 497–517.

88. Heldman et al., "She Brought Only a Skirt…"

89. Diane J. Heith, "The Lipstick Watch: Media Coverage, Gender, and the Presidential Campaigns," *Anticipating Madame President*, ed. Robert P. Watson and Ann Gordon (Boulder, CO: Lynne Rienner, 2003).

90. Falk, *Women for President*, 83.

91. Heldman et al., "She Brought Only a Skirt…"

92. Patricia Gilmartin, "Still the Angel in the Household: Political Cartoons of Elizabeth Dole's Presidential Campaign," *Journal of Women in Politics and Public Policy* 22, no. 4 (2001): 51–67.

93. Falk, *Women for President*, 85.

94. Ibid., 72.

95. Carole Kennedy, "Is America Ready for a Woman President? Is the Pope Protestant? Does a Bear Live in the City?" *White House Studies Compendium*, vol. 1, ed. Robert Watson (New York: Nova Publishers, 2007), 243–256.

96. As quoted in Falk, *Women for President*, 34.

97. Dianne Bystrom, "Advertising, Web Sites, and Media Coverage: Gender and Communication along the Campaign Trail," *Gender and Elections: Shaping the Future of American Politics*, ed. Susan J. Carroll and Richard Logan Fox (New York: Cambridge University Press, 2010), 239–262.

98. Falk, *Women for President*, 114.

99. Ibid., 42.

100. See Warren Weaver Jr., "Schroeder, Assailing 'The System,' Decides Not to Run for President," *New York Times*, September 27, 1987, accessed January 8, 2017, http://www.nytimes.com/1987/09/29/us/schroeder-assailing-the-system-decides-not-to-run-for-president.html.

101. Ibid., 67.

102. Quoted in Falk, *Women for President*, 41.

103. Lawrence and Rose, *Hillary Clinton's Race*.

104. Stein, "The Cleavage Commotion."

105. Joseph E. Uscinski and Lily J. Goren, "What's in a Name? Coverage of Hillary Clinton during the 2008 Democratic Primary," *Political Research Quarterly* 64, no. 4 (2010): 884–896.

106. Falk, *Women for President*, 160.

107. Miller et al., "Testing the Saturday Night."

108. Lawrence and Rose, *Hillary Clinton's Race*; and Miller et al., "Testing the Saturday Night."

109. Ibid.

110. Falk, *Women for President*, 157.

111. Stein, "The Cleavage Commotion."

112. Ibid., 158.

113. Falk, *Women for President*, 158.

114. Ibid., 159.

115. Diana B. Carlin and Kelly L. Winfrey, "Have You Come a Long Way, Baby? Hillary Clinton, Sarah Palin, and Sexism in 2008 Campaign Coverage," *Communication Studies* 60, no. 4, (2009): 326–343.

116. Samantha Sault, "My Fair Lady? Hillary Tries to Embrace Her Feminine Side," *Weekly Standard*, January 7, 2008, accessed January 1, 2017, http://www .weeklystandard.com/my-fair-lady/article/15661.

117. Lawrence and Rose, *Hillary Clinton's Race*.

118. Falk, *Women for President*, 161.

119. Ibid., 162.

120. Ibid., 163.

121. Karrin Vasby Anderson, "Rhymes with Rich: 'Bitch' as a Tool of Containment in Contemporary American Politics," *Rhetoric and Public Affairs* 22, no. 4 (1999): 599–623.

122. Ibid.

123. Falk, *Women for President*, 164.

124. Russell Goldman, "Michele Bachmann Drops Out of Presidential Race," ABC News, January 4, 2012, accessed January 8, 2017, http://abcnews.go.com /blogs/politics/2012/01/bachmann-drops-out-of-presidential-race/.

125. Michelle Goldberg, "Did Sexism Do Michele Bachmann In?" *Daily Beast*, January 4, 2012, accessed December 22, 2016, http://www.thedailybeast.com /articles/2012/01/04/how-michele-bachmann-scared-off-iowa-caucus-voters.html.

126. Maggie Haberman, "Michele Bachmann's Hard Fall," Politico, December 29, 2011, accessed December 23, 2016, http://www.politico.com/story/2011/12 /michele-bachmanns-hard-fall-070950.

127. Goldberg, "Did Sexism Do."

128. Brent Lang, "The Media's Michele Bachmann Obsession: Tough Reporting or Sexism?" The Wrap, August 16, 2011, accessed December 23, 2016, http:// www.thewrap.com/michele-bachmann-sexist-coverage-newsweek-30164/.

129. Elizabeth Dias, "Submission," *Time*, August 19, 2011, accessed January 2, 2017, http://swampland.time.com/2011/08/19/understanding-michele-bach-manns-submission/.

130. As quoted in Sam Stein, "Michele Bachmann Empathizes with the Sexist Crap Hillary Clinton Has to Endure," *Huffington Post*, January 18, 2016, accessed December 23, 2016, http://www.huffingtonpost.com/entry/michele-bachmann-hillary-clinton-campaign-sexism_us_5699385ee4b0b4eb759e3dad.

131. Our Campaigns, "MA Governor," accessed on January 9, 2017, http://www.ourcampaigns.com/RaceDetail.html?RaceID=409676.

132. Erin Blakemore, "5 Other Women Who Ran for President," *Time Magazine*, April 12, 2015, accessed on January 9, 2017, http://time.com/3771209/hillary-clinton-female-candidates/.

133. Matthew Rozsa, "Jill Stein Spoiled the 2016 Election for Hillary Clinton," December 2, 2016, accessed on January 9, 2017, http://www.salon.com/2016/12/02/jill-stein-spoiled-the-2016-election-for-hillary-clinton/.

134. We used Lexis-Nexis to calculate the number of articles that mention Stein and Johnson for the six-month period examined. We searched for articles in major papers and found that Stein was mentioned in 2,464 articles compared to Johnson's 5,090 mentions.

135. Rahel Gebreyes, "Jill Stein: Women in Politics Are Regularly 'Dismissed' and 'Sidelined,'" *Huffington Post*, August 29, 2016, accessed December 26, 2016, http://www.huffingtonpost.com/entry/jill-stein-women-politics_us_57ec2dabe4b024a52d2ca20a.

136. Patricia Sellers, "Behind Fortune's Most Powerful Woman," *Fortune*, March 23, 2009, accessed December 22, 2016, http://fortune.com/2009/03/23/behind-fortunes-most-powerful-women/.

137. Shawna Thomas and John Lapinski, "Donald Trump Still in the Lead after Debates: New NBC News Survey Monkey Poll," NBC News, August 10, 2015, accessed December 22, 2016, http://www.nbcnews.com/meet-the-press/new-nbc-news-survey-monkey-poll-donald-trump-still-lead-n406766.

138. Ala Rappaport, "Carly Fiorina's Numbers Plunge in Latest CNN Poll," *New York Times*, October 20, 2015, accessed December 22, 2016, http://www.nytimes.com/politics/first-draft/2015/10/20/carly-fiorinas-numbers-plunge-in-latest-cnn-poll/.

139. Katie Glueck, "Carly Fiorina Steps into White House Race, Swinging at Hillary," *Politico*, May 4, 2016, accessed December 22, 2016, http://www.politico.com/story/2015/05/carly-fiorina-2016-presidential-bid-launch-117605.

140. Liz Mair, "Carly Fiorina Is Not Running for Vice President," The Daily Beast, June 4, 2015, accessed on May 4, 2018, https://www.thedailybeast.com/carly-fiorina-is-not-running-for-vice-president.

141. Mark Hensch, "Fiorina: 'Sexist' to Treat Me as Only VP Material," The Hill, September 2, 2015, accessed on January 9, 2017, http://thehill.com/blogs/ballot-box/252520-fiorina-its-sexist-to-only-treat-me-as-vp-material.

142. Jonathan Capehart, "Carly Fiorina, Pink Nail Polish, and Sexism," April 16, 2015, accessed on January 9, 2017, http://thehill.com/blogs/ballot-box/252520-fiorina-its-sexist-to-only-treat-me-as-vp-material.

143. Andrew Kirell, "*Fox & Friends* Asks Carly Fiorina about 'Hormones,' She Says She's Going to Announce Soon," Mediate, April 18, 2015, accessed January 9, 2017, http://www.mediaite.com/tv/fox-friends-asks-carly-fiorina-about-hormones-she-says-shes-going-to-announce-soon/.

144. Neetzan Zimmerman, "Trump Mocks Fiorina's Physical Appearance: 'Look at That Face!'" The Hill, September 9, 2015, accessed on January 9, 2017, http://thehill.com/blogs/blog-briefing-room/253178-trump-insults-fiorinas-physical-appearance-look-at-that-face.

145. Lauren Gambino, "Carly Fiorina Expertly Defuses Trump on 'Beautiful Face' Retort and Foreign Policy," *Guardian*, September 17, 2015, accessed on January 9, 2017, https://www.theguardian.com/us-news/2015/sep/17/carly-fiorina-republican-debate-donald-trump-sexism-foreign-policy-women.

146. Alex Griswold, "*The View* Hosts: Carly Fiorina's Face 'Looked Demented,' Like a Halloween Mask," Mediate, October 29, 2015, accessed on January 9, 2017, http://www.mediaite.com/tv/the-view-hosts-carly-fiorinas-face-looked-demented-like-a-halloween-mask/.

147. Ibid.

CHAPTER 4

1. Nate Silver, "Was the Democratic Primary a Close Call or a Landslide?" FiveThirtyEight, July 27, 2016, accessed July 6, 2017, http://fivethirtyeight.com/features/was-the-democratic-primary-a-close-call-or-a-landslide/.

2. Ibid.

3. Karrin Vasby Anderson and Kristina Horn Sheeler, *Governing Codes: Gender, Metaphor, and Politics Identity* (New York: Rowman & Littlefield, 2005).

4. See Vasby Anderson and Horn Sheeler, *Governing Codes*, 117–149. Although the authors do not explicitly analyze Clinton's strategies in terms of "masculine" and "feminine" shifts, the narratives they provide neatly fit these categories.

5. Amber Jamieson and Adam Gabbatt, "'You Don't Fit the Image': Hillary Clinton's Decades-Long Push Against a Sexist Press," *Guardian*, September 15, 2016, accessed July 25, 2017, https://www.theguardian.com/us-news/2016/sep/15/hillary-clinton-press-sexism-media-interviews.

6. Henry Louis Gates, "Hating Hillary," *New Yorker*, February 26, 1996, accessed August 3, 2017, http://www.newyorker.com/magazine/1996/02/26/hating-hillary.

7. Martin Amis, "First Lady on Trial," *Sunday Times* (London), March 17, 1996, accessed August 3, 2017, http://www.martinamisweb.com/pre_2006/hillary.htm.

8. Jessica Valenti, "Sexism for the Win! Could Prejudice Bring It Home for Hillary Clinton in 2016?" *Washington Post*, January 24, 2014, accessed July 28, 2017, https://www.washingtonpost.com/opinions/sexism-for-the-win-could-prejudice-bring-it-home-for-hillary-clinton-in-2016/2014/01/24/ee61eb00-8450-11e3-bbe5-6a2a3141e3a9_story.html?utm_term=.70391916b862.

9. Jeffrey M. Jones, "Obama Bests Trump as Most Admired Man in 2016," Gallup, December 28, 2016, accessed June 26, 2017, http://www.gallup.com/poll/200771/obama-bests-trump-admired-man-2016.aspx.

10. Sady Doyle, "America Loves Women Like Hillary Clinton—As Long as They're Not Asking for a Promotion," Quartz, February 25, 2016, accessed June 26, 2017, https://qz.com/624346/america-loves-women-like-hillary-clinton-as-long-as-theyre-not-asking-for-a-promotion/.

11. Patrick O'Connor, "Hillary Clinton Exits with 69% Approval Rating," Wall Street Journal, January 17, 2013, accessed June 26, 2017, https://blogs.wsj.com/washwire/2013/01/17/wsjnbc-poll-hillary-clinton-exits-with-69-approval-rating/.

12. Nate Silver, "Why Hillary Clinton Would Be Strong in 2016 (It's Not Her Favorability Ratings)," New York Times, December 11, 2012, accessed June 26, 2017, https://fivethirtyeight.blogs.nytimes.com/2012/12/11/why-hillary-clinton-would-be-strong-in-2016-its-not-her-favorability-ratings/?hp&_r=0&mtrref=u ndefined&gwh=B446620470F94B291DEDF834C5D3F6C7&gwt=pay.

13. Ibid.

14. Tyler G. Okimoto, and Victoria L. Brescoll, "The Price of Power: Power Seeking and Backlash against Female Politicians," Personality and Social Psychology Bulletin 36, no. 7 (2010): 923–936.

15. See Meredith Conroy, Sarah Oliver, Ian Breckenridge-Jackson, and Caroline Heldman, "From Ferraro to Palin: Sexism in Coverage of Vice Presidential Candidates in Old and New Media," Politics, Groups, and Identities 3, no. 4 (2015): 573–591. Sarah Palin received an abundance of sexist media coverage and misogynistic public discourse during her 2008 vice presidential run.

16. Joseph Carroll, "Clinton Maintains Large Lead over Obama Nationally," Gallup, December 18, 2007, accessed June 27, 2017, http://www.gallup.com/poll/103351/clinton-maintains-large-lead-over-obama-nationally.aspx.

17. Diana B. Carlin and Kelly L. Winfrey, "Have You Come a Long Way, Baby? Hillary Clinton, Sarah Palin, and Sexism in 2008 Campaign Coverage," Communication Studies 60, no. 4 (2009): 326–343.

18. Thomas E. Patterson, "Pre-Primary News Coverage of the 2016 Presidential Race: Trump's Rise, Sanders' Emergence, Clinton's Struggle," Harvard Kennedy School, Shorenstein Center on Media, Politics and Public Policy, June 13, 2016, accessed June 27, 2017, https://shorensteincenter.org/pre-primary-news-coverage-2016-trump-clinton-sanders/.

19. Regina G. Lawrence and Melody Rose, Hillary Clinton's Race for the White House: Gender Politics and the Media on the Campaign Trail (Boulder, CO: Lynne Rienner, 2010), 157.

20. Eileen L. Zurbriggen and Aurora M. Sherman, "Race and Gender in the 2008 Presidential Election: A Content Analysis of Editorial Cartoons," Analyses of Social Issues and Public Policy 10, no. 1 (2010): 223–247.

21. Joseph E. Uscinski and Lilly J. Goren, "What's in a Name? Coverage of Senator Hillary Clinton during the 2008 Democratic Primary," Political Research Quarterly 64, no. 4 (2010): 1–13.

22. Regina G. Lawrence and Melody Rose, "Bringing Out the Hook: Exit Talk in Media Coverage of Hillary Clinton and Past Presidential Campaigns," Political Research Quarterly 64 (2011): 870–883.

23. Carlin and Winfrey, "Have You Come," 331.

24. Ashleigh Crowther, "Sexist Language in Media Coverage of Hillary Clinton," December 12, 2007, accessed June 27, 2017, http://mediacrit.wetpaint .com/page/Sexist+Language+in+Media+Coverage+of+Hillary+Clinton.

25. Ellen Wulfhorst, "Clinton Candidacy Sparks Women's Interest: Poll," Reuters, November 8, 2007, accessed June 27, 2017, http://www.reuters.com /article/us-usa-politics-women-idUSN0752909220071108?feedType=RSS&feed Name=topNews&sp=true.

26. Ibid.

27. CBS Poll, "Race, Gender, and Politics," fielded March 15–18, 2008, http:// www.cbsnews.com/htdocs/pdf/RACE_AND_SEX-mar08a.pdf.

28. Erika Falk, "Clinton and the Playing-the-Gender-Card Metaphor in Campaign News," *Feminist Media Studies* 13, no. 2 (2013): 192–207.

29. Tom Curry, "Clinton versus Obama: Is There Any Difference?" NBCNews .com, November 29, 2006, accessed June 28, 2017, http://www.nbcnews.com/id /15920730/ns/politics-tom_curry/t/clinton-versus-obama-there-any-difference/#. WVPILIjyvIU.

30. Patterson, "Pre-Primary News Coverage."

31. Ibid.

32. *USA Today*, "Congress Spent More Time Investigating Benghazi Than It Did 9/11," June 28, 2016, accessed June 26, 2017, https://www.usatoday.com /media/cinematic/video/86493442/congress-spent-more-time-investigating -benghazi-than-it-did-911/.

33. Quoted in E. J. Dionne Jr., "Kevin McCarthy's Truthful Gaffe on Benghazi," *Washington Post*, September 20, 2015, https://www.washingtonpost.com/opin-ions/kevin-mccarthys-truthful-gaffe/2015/09/30/f12a9fac-67a8-11e5-8325 -a42b5a459b1e_story.html?utm_term=.c0f26279fb54.

34. Cindy Burke and Sharon R. Mazzarella, "'A Slightly New Shade of Lipstick': Gendered Mediation in Internet News Stories," *Women's Studies in Communication* 31, no. 3 (2008): 395–418.

35. Leonie Huddy and Nayda Terkildsen, "The Consequences of Gender Stereotypes for Women Candidates at Different Levels and Types of Offices," *Political Research Quarterly* 46, no. 3 (1993): 503–525.

36. Kurt Eichenwald, "The Scandal Over Clinton's Emails Still Isn't a Scandal," *Newsweek*, May 27, 2016, accessed August 4, 2017, http://www.newsweek.com /hillary-clinton-email-scandal-not-scandal-464414.

37. Lauren Carroll, "FBI Findings Tear Holes in Hillary Clinton's Email Defense," PolitiFact, July 6, 2016, http://www.politifact.com/truth-o-meter/statements/2016 /jul/06/hillary-clinton/fbi-findings-tear-holes-hillary-clintons-email-def/.

38. Federal Bureau of Investigation, "Statement by FBI Director James B. Comey on the Investigation of Secretary Hillary Clinton's Use of a Personal E-Mail System," July 5, 2016, accessed on August 4, 2017, https://www.fbi.gov/news/pressrel /press-releases/statement-by-fbi-director-james-b-comey-on-the-investigation-of -secretary-hillary-clinton2019s-use-of-a-personal-e-mail-system.

39. Matthew Miller, "James Comey's Abuse of Power," *Washington Post*, July 6, 2016, accessed August 4, 2017, https://www.washingtonpost.com/opinions/james -comeys-abuse-of-power/2016/07/06/7799d39e-4392-11e6-8856-f26de2537a9d_ story.html?utm_term=.56f17940095c.

40. Janet Reitman, "Hillary v. the Hate Machine: How Clinton Became a Vessel for America's Fury," *Rolling Stone*, September 20, 2016, accessed August 4, 2017, http://www.rollingstone.com/politics/features/how-hillary-clinton-became -a-vessel-for-americas-fury-w440914.

41. Rosie Gray, "What Does the Billionaire Family Backing Donald Trump Really Want?" *Atlantic*, January 27, 2017, accessed August 4, 2017, https://www .theatlantic.com/politics/archive/2017/01/no-one-knows-what-the-powerful -mercers-really-want/514529/.

42. Eric Wemple, "Fox News, Washington Post, NYT Pursuing 'Exclusive' Threads from New Anti-Hillary Clinton Book," April 20, 2015, accessed August 4, 2017, https://www.washingtonpost.com/blogs/erik-wemple/wp/2015/04/20 /fox-news-washington-post-nyt-pursuing-exclusive-threads-from-new-anti -hillary-clinton-book/?utm_term=.80043cabf6c3.

43. Jo Becker and Mike McIntire, "Cash Flowed to Clinton Foundation Amid Russian Uranium Deal," *New York Times*, April 23, 2015, accessed August 4, 2017, https://www.nytimes.com/2015/04/24/us/cash-flowed-to-clinton-foundation-as -russians-pressed-for-control-of-uranium-company.html.

44. Linda Qiu, "Donald Trump Inaccurately Suggests Clinton Got Paid to Approve Russia Uranium Deal," PolitiFact, June 30, 2016, accessed August 4, 20167, http://www.politifact.com/truth-o-meter/statements/2016/jun/30/donald -trump/donald-trump-inaccurately-suggests-clinton-got-pai/.

45. Reitman, "Hillary v. The Hate Machine."

46. Ibid.

47. Patterson, "Pre-Primary News Coverage."

48. PolitiFact, "Fact Checking the 2016 Presidential Candidates," May 2016, accessed July 23, 2017, http://www.politifact.com/truth-o-meter/lists/people/fact -checking-2016-democratic-presidential-candida/.

49. Jill Abramson, "This May Shock You: Hillary Clinton Is Fundamen- tally Honest," *The Guardian*, March 28, 2016, accessed July 23, 2017, https:// www.theguardian.com/commentisfree/2016/mar/28/hillary-clinton-honest -transparency-jill-abramson.

50. William Cheng, "The Long, Sexist History of 'Shrill' Women," *Time*, March 23, 2016, accessed July 12, 2017, http://time.com/4268325/history-calling -women-shrill/.

51. Jay Newton-Small, *Broad Influence: How Women Are Changing the Way America Works* (New York: Time, 2016).

52. Barbara Lee Family Foundation, "Pitch Perfect: Winning Strategies for Women," November 8, 2012, accessed June 29, 2017, http://www.barbaraleefoundation.org /wp-content/uploads/BLFF-Lake-Pitch-Perfect-Wining-Strategies-for-Women -Candidates-11.08.12.pdf.

53. Ibid.

54. Hillary Clinton, Humans of New York, 2016, accessed June 29, 2017, http://www.humansofnewyork.com/post/150127870371/i-was-taking-a-law -school-admissions-test-in-a.

55. Marc Fisher, "Is She 'Likable Enough?'" *Washington Post*, September 23, 2016, accessed June 29, 2017, https://www.washingtonpost.com/politics/is-she -likable-enough/2016/09/23/5c8fd252-80e0-11e6-a52d-9a865a0ed0d4_story .html?utm_term=.2d294a552c72.

56. Charles Blow, "Hillary Clinton's Crucible," *New York Times*, January 28, 2016, accessed June 30, 2017, https://www.nytimes.com/2016/01/28/opinion /campaign-stops/hillary-clintons-crucible.html.

57. Dasha Burns, "For Millennials, Sanders Is a Grandpa Who Gets Them," CNN, January 18, 2016, accessed June 30, 2017, http://www.cnn.com/2016/01/17 /opinions/burns-millennials-bernie-sanders/index.html.

58. Jean Drevenstedt, "Perceptions of Onset of Young Adulthood, Middle Age, and Old Age," *Journal of Gerontology* 31, no. 1 (1976): 53–37.

59. Dario Maestripieri et al., "A Greater Decline in Female Facial Attractive-ness during Middle Age Reflects Women's Loss of Reproductive Value," *Frontiers in Psychology* 5 (2014): 179.

60. Burns, "For Millennials."

61. Josh Voorhees, "Hillary Clinton Says She's Not an 'Establishment' Candidate—Because She's a Woman," Slate, February 4, 2016, accessed July 5, 2017, http://www.slate.com/blogs/the_slatest/2016/02/04/hillary_says_she_s_not_ an_establishment_candidate_because_she_s_a_woman.html.

62. Derek Willis, "The Senate Votes That Divided Hillary Clinton and Bernie Sanders," *New York Times*, May 27, 2015, accessed June 28, 2017, https://www .nytimes.com/2015/05/28/upshot/the-senate-votes-that-divided-hillary-clinton -and-bernie-sanders.html.

63. Jeffrey Lazarus, "Hillary Clinton Was a More Effective Lawmaker Than Bernie Sanders," *Washington Post*, April 7, 2016, accessed July 5, 2017, https:// www.washingtonpost.com/news/monkey-cage/wp/2016/04/07/hillary-clinton -was-a-more-effective-lawmaker-than-bernie-sanders/?utm_term=.1350ff4b6031.

64. Eliza Collins, "Planned Parenthood Pushes Back against Sanders for 'Estab-lishment' Comment," Politico, January 20, 2016, accessed July 5, 2017, http:// www.politico.com/story/2016/01/planned-parenthood-bernie-sanders-218026.

65. Blow, "Hillary Clinton's Crucible."

66. Susan Bordo, *The Destruction of Hillary Clinton: Sexism, Sanders, and the Millennial Feminists*" (London: Melville House), 77.

67. Christopher J. Clark, "Collective Descriptive Representation and Black Voter Mobilization in 2008," *Political Behavior* 36, no. 2 (2014): 315–333.

68. Craig Leonard Brians, "Women for Women? Gender and Party Bias in Voting for Female Candidates," *American Politics Research* 33, no. 3 (2005): 357–375.

69. Danielle Kurtzleben, "Is It OK to Vote for Hillary Clinton Because She's a Woman?" NPR, April 11, 2016, http://www.npr.org/2016/04/11/473792646/is -it-ok-to-vote-for-clinton-because-she-s-a-woman-an-8-year-old-weighs-in.

70. Ibid.

71. Taryn Hilln, "Here's Every Wildly Sexist Moment from the 2016 Presidential Election," Business Insider, November 6, 2016, accessed June 28, 2017, http://www.businessinsider.com/heres-every-wildly-sexist-moment-from-the-2016-presidential-election-2016-11.

72. Ibid.

73. Ibid.

74. Ibid.

75. Blow, "Hillary Clinton's Crucible."

76. Susan J. Douglas, "You Don't Have to Like Hillary Clinton—But Sexist Attacks on Her Supporters Are Shameful," In These Times, June 20, 2016, accessed July 5, 2017, http://inthesetimes.com/article/19191/out-damn-misogyny.

77. Andrew Husband, "Sanders Campaign Manager: Clinton Would Make a 'Great Vice President,'" October 28, 2015, accessed June 29, 2017, http://www.mediaite.com/online/sanders-campaign-manager-clinton-would-make-a-great-vice-president/.

78. Robinson Meyer, "Here Come the Berniebro," Atlantic, October 17, 2015, accessed June 29, 2017, https://www.theatlantic.com/politics/archive/2015/10/here-comes-the-berniebro-bernie-sanders/411070/.

79. Esther Zuckerman, "'Why Is Reddit So Anti-Woman?' An Epic Thread Counts the Ways," Atlantic, July 26, 2012, accessed June 29, 2017, https://www.theatlantic.com/entertainment/archive/2012/07/why-reddit-so-anti-women-epic-reddit-thread-counts-ways/325357/.

80. Amanda Hess, "Everyone Is Wrong about the Bernie Bros," Slate, February 3, 2016, accessed June 29, 2017, http://www.slate.com/articles/technology/users/2016/02/bernie_bros_are_bad_the_conversation_around_them_is_worse.html.

81. Glenn Greenwald, "The 'Bernie Bros' Narrative: A Cheap Campaign Tactic Masquerading as Journalism and Social Activism," The Intercept, January 31, 2016, accessed June 28, 2017, https://theintercept.com/2016/01/31/the-bernie-bros-narrative-a-cheap-false-campaign-tactic-masquerading-as-journalism-and-social-activism/.

82. Quoted in Jamilah Lemieux, "Sen. Bernie Sanders Speaks to the Issues," Ebony, January 21, 2016, accessed June 29, 2017, http://www.ebony.com/news-views/sen-bernie-sanders-interview-jamilah-lemieux#axzz3yeJNiGsx.

83. Riley Snyder, "Allegations of Fraud and Misconduct at Nevada Democratic Convention Unfounded," PolitiFact, May 18, 2016, accessed June 28, 2017, http://www.politifact.com/nevada/statements/2016/may/18/jeff-weaver/allegations-fraud-and-misconduct-nevada-democratic/.

84. Hilln, "Here's Every Wildly Sexist."

CHAPTER 5

1. Quoted in "President Obama's Speech at the Democratic Convention," Washington Post, July 28, 2016, accessed July 27, 2017, https://www.washingtonpost

.com/news/the-fix/wp/2016/07/27/president-obamas-speech-at-the-democratic
-convention/?utm_term=.0908617b176f.

2. Thomas E. Patterson, "News Coverage of the 2016 Election: How the Press Failed the Voters," Harvard Kennedy School, Shorenstein Center on Media, Politics, and Public Policy, December 7, 2016, accessed July 8, 2017, https:// shorensteincenter.org/news-coverage-2016-general-election/.

3. Thomas E. Patterson, "Pre-Primary News Coverage of the 2016 Presidential Race: Trump's Rise, Sanders' Emergence, Clinton's Struggle," Harvard Kennedy School, Shorenstein Center on Media, Politics, and Public Policy, June 13, 2016, accessed July 27, 2017, https://shorensteincenter.org/pre-primary-news-coverage -2016-trump-clinton-sanders/.

4. Kim Kahn, *The Political Consequences of Being a Woman* (New York: Columbia University Press, 1996).

5. Alice Eagly and Steven J. Karau, "Role Congruity Theory of Prejudice toward Female Leaders," *Psychological Review* 109, no. 3 (2002): 573–598.

6. Cindy Burke and Sharon R. Mazzarella, "A Slightly New Shade of Lipstick: Gendered Mediation in Internet News Stories," *Women's Studies in Communication* 31, no. 3 (2008): 395–418.

7. Daniella Diaz, "RNC Chief Critique: Clinton Didn't Smile during National Security Forum," CNN, September 8, 2016, accessed July 9, 2017, http://www .cnn.com/2016/09/07/politics/reince-priebus-donald-trump-2016-election /index.html.

8. Lucy Clarke-Billings, "How Facial Expressions Could Hurt Hillary Clinton's Election Results," *Newsweek*, October 19, 2016, accessed July 7, 2017, http:// www.newsweek.com/body-language-analysts-reveal-why-hillary-clintons -face-could-lose-her-511342.

9. Quoted in ibid.

10. Yochai Benkler et al., "Study: Breitbart-Led Right-Wing Media Ecosystem Altered Broader Media Agenda," *Columbia Journalism Review*, March 3, 2017, accessed July 25, 2017, https://www.cjr.org/analysis/breitbart-media-trump -harvard-study.php.

11. Ibid.

12. Jesse Byrnes, "Trump Involved in 3,500 Lawsuits," The Hill, June 1, 2016, accessed June 28, 2016, http://thehill.com/blogs/blog-briefing-room/news /281908-report-trump-involved-in-3500-lawsuits.

13. Patterson, "News Coverage of the 2016 Election."

14. Nate Silver, "How Much Did Comey Hurt Clinton's Chances?" FiveThirtyEight, November 6, 2016, accessed June 26, 2017, https://fivethirtyeight.com /features/how-much-did-comey-hurt-clintons-chances/.

15. Patterson, "News Coverage of the 2016 Election."

16. Nate Silver, "The Comey Letter Probably Cost Clinton the Election: So Why Won't the Media Admit as Much?" FiveThirtyEight, May 3, 2017, accessed July 8, 2017, https://fivethirtyeight.com/features/the-comey-letter -probably-cost-clinton-the-election/.

17. Harry Enten, "How Much Did WikiLeaks Hurt Hillary Clinton?" FiveThirtyEight, December 23, 2016, accessed July 10, 2017, https://fivethirtyeight.com/features/wikileaks-hillary-clinton/.

18. Chas Dannar, "Clinton Maintains Lead in Two New Polls, but Trump Tape Impact Is Mixed," *New York Magazine*, October 16, 2016, accessed July 10, 2017, http://nymag.com/daily/intelligencer/2016/10/clinton-holds-lead-in-new-polls -but-trump-tape-impact-mixed.html.

19. Brandy Zadrozny and Tim Mak, "Ex-Wife: Donald Trump Made Me Feel 'Violated' during Sex," Daily Beast, July 27, 2015, accessed July 10, 2017, http://www.thedailybeast.com/ex-wife-donald-trump-made-me-feel-violated -during-sex.

20. Brandy Zadrozny, "The Billionaire Pedophile Who Could Bring Down Donald Trump and Hillary Clinton," The Daily Beast, June 30, 2016, accessed July 10, 2017, http://www.thedailybeast.com/the-billionaire-pedophile-who -could-bring-down-donald-trump-and-hillary-clinton.

21. Jill Abramson, "This May Shock You: Hillary Clinton Is Fundamentally Honest," *Guardian*, March 28, 2016, accessed July 23, 2017, https://www .theguardian.com/commentisfree/2016/mar/28/hillary-clinton-honest -transparency-jill-abramson.

22. Jonathan Martin, "Republicans Paint Clinton as Old News," *New York Times*, June 29, 2016, accessed July 11, 2017, http://www.nytimes.com/2013/06/30 /us/politics/republicans-paint-clinton-as-old-news-for-2016-presidential-election.html?pagewanted=all&_r=0&mtrref=undefined&gwh=91C86F56690 A036D421565BE207C43EF&gwt=pay.

23. Corrine Cathcart, "A Look Back at Hillary Clinton's Health," ABC News, September 11, 2016, accessed July 11, 2017, http://abcnews.go.com/Politics /back-hillary-clintons-health/story?id=42019034.

24. Annie Karni, "Hillary's Health 'Excellent,' Doctor Says," Politico, July 31, 2015, accessed July 11, 2017, http://www.politico.com/story/2015/07 /hillary-clinton-health-excellent-doctor-letter-2016-campaign-120861.

25. Jessica Taylor, "Trump Releases Weight, Cholesterol, Blood Sugar, and Other Medical Information," NPR, September 15, 2016, accessed July 11, 2017, http://www.npr.org/2016/09/15/494081537/trump-releases-weight-cholesterol -blood-sugar-and-other-medical-information.

26. David A. Graham, "Questions about Hillary's Health: The Birtherism of 2016," *Atlantic*, August 22, 2016, accessed May 8, 2018, https://www.theatlantic .com/politics/archive/2016/08/hillarys-health-the-birtherism-of-2016/496847/.

27. Nick Gass, "Trump Co-Chair: Clinton Seems 'Wobbly and a Little Frail,'" Politico, September 2, 2016, accessed July 11, 2017, http://www.politico.com /story/2016/09/clinton-health-sam-clovis-227678.

28. Cathcart, "A Look Back."

29. Eric Bradner, Shimon Prokupecz, and Dan Merica, "Hillary Clinton Has Pneumonia, Doctors Say, after Early 9/11 Event Exit," CNN, September 12, 2016, accessed July 11, 2017, http://www.cnn.com/2016/09/11/politics/hillary -clinton-health/index.html.

30. Cathcart, "A Look Back."

31. MSNBC, "Trump Ad Depicts Clinton as Physically Frail," October 12, 2016, accessed July 11, 2017, http://www.msnbc.com/msnbc-news/watch/trump-ad-depicts-clinton-as-physically-frail-784090691645.

32. Sophie Tatum, "Trump: Clinton 'Doesn't Have the Stamina' to Be President," CNN, September 27, 2016, accessed July 11, 2017, http://www.cnn.com/2016/09/27/politics/donald-trump-hillary-clinton-stamina/index.html.

33. Quoted in ibid.

34. Quoted in Amanda Hess, "What's Really Behind Trump's Obsession with Clinton's 'Stamina'?" *New York Times Magazine*, October 11, 2016, accessed July 11, 2017, https://www.nytimes.com/2016/10/16/magazine/whats-really-behind-trumps-obsession-with-clintons-stamina.html.

35. Judy Stone, "The Surprises in Hillary Clinton's Newly Released Medical Records," *Forbes*, September 14, 2016, accessed July 11, 2017, https://www.forbes.com/sites/judystone/2016/09/14/the-surprises-in-hillary-clintons-newly-released-medical-records/#68fe19b55023.

36. James Hamblin, "When Hillary Clinton Coughs," *Atlantic*, September 6, 2016, accessed July 11, 2017, https://www.theatlantic.com/health/archive/2016/09/should-a-president-cough/498734/.

37. Ibid.

38. Graham, "Questions about Hillary's Health."

39. Hess, "What's Really Behind."

40. Quoted in ibid.

41. Sean Cockerham and Leslie Clark, "Clinton Has Lead, but Is Vulnerable on Trust, Connection with Voters," McClatchy DC Bureau, September 23, 2017, accessed July 11, 2017, http://www.mcclatchydc.com/news/politics-government/election/article103597247.html.

42. Maxwell Tani, "Bernie Sanders Is Escalating His Attacks on Hillary Clinton—and Trump Is Taking Notes," *Business Insider*, May 2, 2016, accessed July 5, 2017, http://www.businessinsider.com/bernie-sanders-hillary-clinton-indiana-polls-attacks-2016-5.

43. Lisa Hagen and Jonathan Swan, "Trump on Hillary: 'The Only Thing She's Got Is the Woman Card,'" The Hill, March 26, 2016, accessed July 12, 2017, http://thehill.com/blogs/ballot-box/presidential-races/277795-trump-if-hillary-were-a-man-she-wouldnt-get-5-percent-of.

44. Bill Allison et al., "Tracking the 2016 Presidential Money Race," Bloomberg, December 9, 2016, accessed July 12, 2017, https://www.bloomberg.com/politics/graphics/2016-presidential-campaign-fundraising/.

45. Alan Rappeport, "Donald Trump Keeps Playing 'Woman's Card' against Hillary Clinton," *New York Times*, April 27, 2016, accessed July 12, 2017, https://www.nytimes.com/politics/first-draft/2016/04/27/donald-trump-keeps-playing-womans-card-against-hillary-clinton/.

46. Nick Gass, "Trump Escalates 'Woman Card' Attack on Clinton," Politico, April 29, 2016, accessed July 12, 2017, http://www.politico.com/blogs/2016-gop-primary-live-updates-and-results/2016/04/trump-hillary-clinton-women-card-222564.

47. David French, "Progressive Orthodoxy Narrows Choices and Minds," *New York Times*, November 25, 2015, accessed July 12, 2017, https://www.nytimes.com/roomfordebate/2016/11/23/is-criticism-of-identity-politics-racist-or-long-overdue/progressive-orthodoxy-narrows-choices-and-minds.

48. Abigail Tracy, "Brit Hume Can't Stop Making Sexist Comments about Clinton," *Vanity Fair*, September 27, 2016, accessed July 23, 2017, http://www.vanityfair.com/news/2016/09/brit-hume-hillary-clinton-debate.

49. Cydney Hargis, "Trump's 'Women's Card' Attack against Hillary Clinton Comes from the Right-Wing Media Playbook," Media Matters for America, April 27, 2016, accessed July 25, 2017, https://www.mediamatters.org/research/2016/04/27/trump-s-women-s-card-attack-against-hillary-clinton-comes-right-wing-media-s-playbook/210110.

50. Ibid.

51. "Hating Hillary," *Economist*, October 22, 2016, accessed July 28, 2017, https://www.economist.com/news/united-states/21709053-americas-probable-next-president-deeply-reviled-why-hating-hillary.

52. Benkler et al., "Study: Breitbart-Led Right-Wing Media Ecosystem."

53. Elizabeth Strassner, "4 Sexist Headlines about Hillary Clinton That Show More Cracks Are Needed in That Glass Ceiling," Bustle, December 16, 2016, accessed July 28, 2017, https://www.bustle.com/articles/200232-4-sexist-headlines-about-hillary-clinton-that-show-more-cracks-are-needed-in-that-glass-ceiling.

54. Ibid.

55. Anne Gearan and Katie Zezima, "Trump's 'Woman Card' Comment Escalates the Campaign's Gender Wars," *Washington Post*, April 27, 2016, accessed July 12, 2017, https://www.washingtonpost.com/politics/trumps-womans-card-comment-escalates-gender-wars-of-2016-campaign/2016/04/27/fbe4c67a-0c2b-11e6-8ab8-9ad050f76d7d_story.html?utm_term=.8b66af6ada6a.

56. Max J. Rosenthal, "Yet Another Sexist Joke from a Trump Surrogate," *Mother Jones*, November 4, 2016, accessed July 25, 2017, http://www.motherjones.com/politics/2016/11/trump-surrogate-john-sununu-hillary-clinton/.

57. Rex Huppke, "The Sexism Undergirding Trump's Campaign," *Chicago Tribune*, October 3, 2016, accessed July 24, 2017, http://www.chicagotribune.com/news/opinion/huppke/ct-trump-giuliani-woman-sexism-huppke-20161003-story.html.

58. Jeremy Diamond, "Donald Trump: Hillary Clinton 'Got Schlonged' in 2008," CNN, December 22, 2015, accessed July 28, 2017, http://www.cnn.com/2015/12/21/politics/donald-trump-hillary-clinton-disgusting/index.html.

59. Ashley Parker, "Donald Trump Says Hillary Clinton Doesn't Have 'a Presidential Look,'" *New York Times*, September 6, 2016, accessed July 20, 2017, https://www.nytimes.com/2016/09/07/us/politics/donald-trump-says-hillary-clinton-doesnt-have-a-presidential-look.html.

60. Nolan McCaskill, "Trump: Clinton Walked in Front of Me and 'I Wasn't Impressed,'" Politico, October 14, 2016, accessed July 20, 2017, http://www.politico.com/story/2016/10/trump-clinton-debate-walk-not-impressed-229810.

61. Tina Nguyen, "Trump Accuses Hillary of Cheating on Bill in Bizarre Sexist Rant," *Vanity Fair*, October 3, 2016, accessed July 25, 2017, http://www.vanity-fair.com/news/2016/10/donald-trump-clinton-sexism.

62. Amy Chozick and Ashley Parker, "Donald Trump's Gender-Based Attacks on Hillary Clinton Have Calculated Risks," *New York Times*, April 28, 2016, accessed July 25, 2017, https://www.nytimes.com/2016/04/29/us/politics/hillary-clinton-donald-trump-women.html.

63. Gearan and Zezima, "Trump's 'Woman Card.'"

64. Jenna Johnson, "Donald Trump Calls Hillary Clinton 'Shrill,'" *Washington Post*, September 23, 2015, accessed July 12, 2017, https://www.washingtonpost.com/politics/donald-trump-calls-hillary-clinton-shrill/2015/09/23/63c6d5be-6216-11e5-8e9e-dce8a2a2a679_story.html?utm_term=.dad7cec3f311.

65. William Cheng, "The Long, Sexist History of 'Shrill' Women," *Time*, March 23, 2016, accessed July 12, 2017, http://time.com/4268325/history-calling-women-shrill/.

66. Erik Ortiz, "Trump Defends Attacking Hillary Clinton: 'I Know Men That Are Shrill,'" NBC News, September 24, 2015, accessed July 12, 2017, http://www.nbcnews.com/politics/2016-election/trump-defends-calling-hillary-clinton-shrill-i-know-men-are-n432806.

67. Jennifer Agiesta, "Hillary Clinton Wins Third Presidential Debate, According to CNN/ORC Poll," CNN, October 16, 2016, accessed July 19, 2017, http://www.cnn.com/2016/10/19/politics/hillary-clinton-wins-third-presidential-debate-according-to-cnn-orc-poll/index.html.

68. Emily Crockett and Sarah Frostenson, "Trump Interrupted Clinton 51 Times at the Debate. She Interrupted Him Just 17 Times," *Vox*, September 27, 2016, accessed July 19, 2017, https://www.vox.com/policy-and-politics/2016/9/27/13017666/presidential-debate-trump-clinton-sexism-interruptions.

69. Natasha Geiling, "The Third Debate Was a Sexist Mess," Think Progress, October 20, 2016, accessed July 20, 2017, https://thinkprogress.org/the-sexist-mess-of-the-third-presidential-debate-f9f7429c6a24.

70. For example, see Julie Pace, "Donald Trump Makes Some Voters Cringe," *U.S. News and World Report*, September 27, 2016, accessed July 20, 2017, https://www.usnews.com/news/politics/articles/2016-09-27/reason-to-cringe-female-voters-react-to-trump.

71. Quoted in ibid.

72. Sarah Frostenson, "Trump Interrupted Clinton 18 Times. She Interrupted Him Once," Vox, October 9, 2016, accessed July 20, 2017, https://www.vox.com/2016/10/9/13223000/trump-interrupted-clinton-18-times-she-interrupted-him-once.

73. Quoted in David Graham, "Donald Trump's Disastrous Debate," *Atlantic*, October 9, 2016, accessed July 6, 2017, https://www.theatlantic.com/liveblogs/2016/10/second-presidential-debate-clinton-trump/503495/.

74. Lyz Lenz, "America's Sexist History of Holding Women Accountable for Their Husbands," Fusion, October 9, 2016, accessed July 20, 2017, http://fusion.kinja.com/america-s-sexist-history-of-holding-women-accountable-f-1793862628.

75. Ibid.

76. "Donald Trump Lurking over Hillary Clinton Disturbs Some Viewers during US Presidential Debate," *Telegraph*, October 10, 2016, accessed July 20, 2017, http://www.telegraph.co.uk/news/2016/10/10/donald-trump-lurking-over-hillary -clinton-disturbs-viewers-durin/.

77. Sarah Frostenson, "Trump Interrupted Clinton 37 Times. Clinton Interrupted Trump 9 Times," Vox, October 20, 2016, accessed July 20, 2017, https:// www.vox.com/policy-and-politics/2016/10/20/13341754/trump-clinton -interrupted-third-debate.

78. Geiling, "The Third Debate Was a Sexist Mess."

79. Nicky Woolf, "'Nasty Woman': Trump Attacks Clinton during Final Debate," *Guardian*, October 20, 2016, accessed July 11, 2017, https://www .theguardian.com/us-news/2016/oct/20/nasty-woman-donald-trump-hillary-clinton.

80. German Lopez, "Trump Calls Clinton 'Such a Nasty Woman' on the Debate Stage," Vox, October 19, 2016, accessed July 20, 2017, https://www.vox.com /policy-and-politics/2016/10/19/13342054/debate-trump-clinton-nasty-woman.

81. Frostenson, "Trump Interrupted Clinton 37 Times."

82. Tierney McAfee, "Inside a Trump Rally: The Nasty, Sexist, Racist Chants by His Supporters," *People*, August 4, 2016, accessed July 23, 2017, http:// people.com/celebrity/trump-supporters-hurl-racist-and-sexist-slurs-at-rallies -nyt-video-shows/.

83. Claire Landsbaum, "The Most Misogynistic Gear Spotted at Trump Rallies," The Cut, October 12, 2016, https://www.thecut.com/2016/10/the-most -misogynistic-things-people-wore-to-trump-rallies.html.

84. Sarah McCammon, "Trump Campaign Says 'Dishonest Media' Misinterpreted His Second Amendment Comment," NPR, August 9, 2016, July 23, 2017, http://www.npr.org/2016/08/09/489364948/trump-appears-to-suggest-second -amendment-could-stop-clinton.

85. Jessica Taylor, "Trump's Second Amendment Rhetoric Again Veers into Threatening Territory," NPR, September 16, 2016, accessed July 23, 2017, http://www.npr.org/2016/09/16/494328717/trumps-second-amendment-rhetoric -again-veers-into-threatening-territory.

CHAPTER 6

1. For example, Nathan Heller, "The First Debate of the Twitter Election," *New Yorker*, September 27, 2016, http://www.newyorker.com/culture/cultural -comment/the-first-debate-of-the-twitter-election.

2. Bridget Coyne, "How #Election2016 Was Tweeted So Far, November 7, 2016, accessed May 8, 2018, https://blog.twitter.com/official/en_us/a/2016/how -election2016-was-tweeted-so-far.html.

3. Retweeting refers to the process of posting someone else's tweet on your Twitter timeline. Retweets can be reposted as the original author wrote them or with commentary above the original post.

4. Daniel Victor, "Clinton to Trump on Twitter, 'Delete Your Account.'" *New York Times*, June 9, 2016, https://www.nytimes.com/2016/06/10/us/politics /hillary-clinton-to-donald-trump-delete-your-account.html?mcubz=0.

5. Emily Stephenson, "Trump Charges U.S. Election Results Being Rigged 'at Many Polling Places,'" Reuters.com, October 16, 2016, http://www.reuters.com /article/us-usa-election-trump-rigged-idUSKBN12G0SU.

6. Sophie Tatum, "Pictured with Taco Bowl, Trump Proclaims, 'I Love Hispanics!'" CNN.com, May 6, 2016, http://www.cnn.com/2016/05/05/politics /donald-trump-taco-bowl-cinco-de-mayo/index.html.

7. An emoji is a small digital image meant to express an idea or emotion—for example, a smiley face to express happiness or approval.

8. Brian Walsh, "Hillary Clinton's Attempt to Use Emoji Backfires," MSNBC.com, August 13, 2015, http://www.msnbc.com/msnbc/hillary-clintons -attempt-use-emoji-backfires.

9. Regina G. Lawrence and Melody Rose, *Hillary Clinton's Race for the White House: Gender Politics and Media on the Campaign Trail* (Boulder, CO: Lynne Rienner, 2009).

10. Meredith Conroy et al., "From Ferraro to Palin: Sexism in Media Coverage of Vice Presidential Candidates," *Politics, Groups and Identities* 3, no. 4 (2015): 573–591.

11. Ibid., 15.

12. Hunt Allcott and Matthew Gentzkow, "Social Media and Fake News in the 2016 Election," *Journal of Economic Perspectives* 31, no. 2 (2017): 211–236, 211.

13. Victor Pickard, *America's Battle for Media Democracy* (New York: Cambridge University Press, 2015).

14. Joseph D. Straubhaar, Robert LaRose, and Lucinda Davenport, *Media Now: Understanding Media, Culture, and Technology* (Boston: Wadsworth Cengage Learning, 2010).

15. Allcott and Gentzcow, "Social Media and Fake News."

16. C. Eugene Emory Jr., "Evidence Ridiculously Thin for Sensational Claim of Huge Underground Sex Network," PolitiFact, November 4, 2016, accessed August 25, 2017, http://www.politifact.com/truth-o-meter/statements/2016/nov/04 /conservative-daily-post/evidence-ridiculously-thin-sensational-claim-huge-/.

17. Adam K. Raymond, "A Surprising Number of Democrats Think Pizzagate Is True," *New York*, December 28, 2016, accessed August 25, 2017, http://nymag .com/daily/intelligencer/2016/12/a-surprising-number-of-democrats-think-pizza- gate-is-true.html.

18. Aria Bendix, "'Pizzagate' Shooter to Serve Four Years in Jail," *Atlantic*, June 22, 2017, accessed August 23, 2017, https://www.theatlantic.com/news /archive/2017/06/dcs-pizzagate-shooter-sentenced-to-4-years-in-jail/531381/.

19. Pew Research Center, "Digital News Fact Sheet," August 7, 2017, accessed August 25, 2017, http://www.journalism.org/fact-sheet/digital-news/.

20. Eytan Bakshy, Solomon Messing, and Lada A. Adamic, "Exposure to Ideologically Diverse News and Opinion on Facebook," *Science* 348, no. 6239 (2015): 1130–1132.

21. Amy Mitchell et al., "Party Polarization & Media Habits," Pew Research Center, October 21, 2014, http://www.journalism.org/2014/10/21/political-polarization-media-habits/#social-media-conservatives-more-likely-to-have-like-minded-friends.

22. See Shelley Boulianne, "Social Media Use and Participation: A Meta-Analysis of Current Research," *Information, Communication, and Society* 18, no. 5 (2015): 524–538 for a meta-analysis of current research.

23. Magdalena E. Wojcieszak and Diana C. Mutz, "Online Groups and Political Discourse: Do Online Discussion Spaces Facilitate Exposure to Political Disagreement?" *Journal of Communication* 59, no. 1 (2009): 40–56.; M. D. Conover et al., "Political Polarization on Twitter," Association for the Advancement of Artificial Intelligence, 2011; and Bakshy et al., "Exposure to Ideologically Diverse News"; for evidence suggesting that online and offline audiences are no more or less fragmented, see Richard Fletcher and Rasmus Kleis Nielson, "Are News Audiences Increasingly Fragmented? A Cross-National Comparative Analysis of Cross-Platform Audience Fragmentation and Duplication," *Journal of Communication* 67, no. 4 (2017).

24. Elanor Colleoni, Alessandro Rozza, and Adam Arvidsson, "Echo Chamber or Public Sphere? Predicting Orientation and Measuring Political Homophily in Twitter Using Big Data," *Journal of Communication* 64 (2014): 317–332; and Itai Himelboim, Stephen McCreery, and Marc Smith, "Birds of a Feather Tweets Together: Integrating Network and Content Analysis to Examine Cross-Ideology Exposure on Twitter," *Journal of Computer Mediated Communication* 18 (2013): 154–174.

25. Conover et al., "Political Polarization on Twitter."

26. Ibid., 95.

27. Eytan Bakshy et al., "Exposure to Ideologically Diverse News."

28. Jieun Shin et al., "Political Rumoring on Twitter during the 2012 US Presidential Election: Rumor Diffusion and Correction," *New Media & Society* (2016), DOI: https://doi.org/10.1177/1461444816634054.

29. Jieun Shin and Kjerstin Thorson, "Partisan Selective Sharing: The Biased Diffusion of Fact-Checking Messages on Social Media," *Journal of Communication* 67, no. 2 (2017): 233–255.

30. See Merlyna Lim, "Clicks, Cabs, and Coffee Houses: Social Media and Oppositional Movements in Egypt, 2001–2011," *Journal of Communication*, 62 (2012): 231–248.

31. Benjamin Barber, *Jihad vs. McWorld: How Globalism and Tribalism Are Reshaping the World* (New York: Ballantine Books, 1996).

32. Evgeny Morozov, *The Net Delusion: The Dark Side of Internet Freedom* (New York: PublicAffairs, 2011).

33. See Brian Hague and Brian Loader, *Digital Democracy: Discourse and Decision Making in the Information Age* (London: Routledge, 1999); Elaine Kamarck and Joseph Nye, *Democracy.com? Governance in a Networked World* (Hollis, NH: Hollis Publishing, 1999).

34. See Clay Shirky, "The Political Power of Social Media: Technology, the Public Sphere, and Political Change," *Foreign Affairs* 90, no. 1 (2011): 28–41.

35. See also Meredith Conroy, Jessica T. Feezell, and Mario Guerrero, "Facebook and Political Engagement: A Study of Online Group Membership and Offline Political Engagement," *Computers and Human Behavior* 28, no. 5 (2012): 1535–1546.

36. See Kathleen Dolan, "Do Women Candidates Play to Gender Stereotypes? Do Men Play to Women? Candidate Sex and Issue Priorities on Campaign Websites," *Political Research Quarterly* 58, no. 1 (2005): 31–44.; and David Niven and Jeremy Zilber, "Do Women and Men in Congress Cultivate Different Images? Evidence from Congressional Web Sites," *Political Communication* 18, no. 4 (2001): 395–405.

37. Heather Evans, "Do Women Only Talk about 'Female Issues'? Gender and Issue Discussion on Twitter," *Online Information Review* 40, no. 5 (2016): 660–672.

38. Heather Evans and Jennifer Hayes Clark, "'You Tweet Like a Girl': How Female Candidates Campaign on Twitter," *American Politics Research* 44, no. 2 (2016): 326–352.

39. Shannon C. McGregor, Regina G. Lawrence, and Arielle Cardona, "Personalization, Gender, and Social Media: Gubernatorial Candidates' Social Media Strategies," *Information, Communication, and Society* 20, no. 2 (2016): 264–283; for effects of personalization strategies by candidate sex, see Lindsey Meeks, "Getting Personal: Effects of Twitter Personalization on Candidate Evaluations," *Politics & Gender* 13, no. 1 (2017): 1–25.

40. For example, Kathleen Dolan, "The Impact of Gender Stereotyped Evaluations on Support for Women Candidates," *Political Behavior* 32, no. 1 (2010): 69–88; and Kira Sanbonmatsu, "Gender Stereotypes and Vote Choice," *American Journal of Political Science* 46, no. 1 (2002): 20–34.

41. For example, Johanna Dunaway et al., "Traits versus Issues: How Female Candidates Shape Coverage of Senate and Gubernatorial Races," *Political Research Quarterly* 66, no. 3 (2013): 715–26; and Caroline Heldman, Susan J. Carroll, and Stephanie Olson, "'She Brought Only a Skirt': Print Media Coverage of Elizabeth Dole's Bid for the Republican Presidential Nomination," *Political Communication* 22, no. 3 (2005): 315–35.

42. Shannon McGregor and Rachel R. Mourão, "Talking Politics on Twitter: Gender, Elections, and Social Networks," *Social Media and Society* (2016).

43. Christina Newberry, "A Long List of Twitter Statistics All Social Media Marketers Should Know," Hootsuite, December 5, 2016, https://blog.hootsuite.com/twitter-statistics/.

44. Ibid.

45. See Social Media Research Foundation, http://www.smrfoundation.org.

46. The only way to avoid Twitter's black box of "statistically relevant samples" is to pay for access to the Twitter "firehose." While such an option ensures data that is far more consistent and representative, it is also an option that is often prohibitively expensive.

47. Lexicoder was developed by Mark Daku, Stuart Soroka, and Lori Young at McGill University. For more information about its development and uses, see http://www.lexicoder.com.

48. Thomas E. Patterson, "Pre-Primary News Coverage of the 2016 Presidential Race: Trump's Rise, Sanders' Emergence, Clinton's Struggle," The Shorenstein Center on Media, Politics and Public Policy, June 13, 2016, https://shorensteincenter .org/pre-primary-news-coverage-2016-trump-clinton-sanders/.

49. Conover et al., "Political Polarization on Twitter," p. 94.

50. Jennifer Agiesta, "Hillary Clinton Wins the Third Presidential Debate, According to CNN/ORC Poll," CNN Politics, October 20, 2016, accessed August 28, 2017, http://www.cnn.com/2016/10/19/politics/hillary-clinton-wins -third-presidential-debate-according-to-cnn-orc-poll/index.html.

51. Lydia Saad, "Trump Leads Clinton in Historically Bad Image Ratings," Gallup Poll, July 1, 2016, accessed August 28, 2017, http://www.gallup.com /poll/193376/trump-leads-clinton-historically-bad-image-ratings.aspx.

52. Alina Selyukh, "Postelection, Overwhelmed Facebook Users Unfriend, Cut Back," National Public Radio, November 20, 2016, accessed August 28, 2017, http://www.npr.org/sections/alltechconsidered/2016/11/20/502567858/post -election-overwhelmed-facebook-users-unfriend-cut-back.

53. David A. Fahrenthold, "Trump Recorded Having Extremely Lewd Conversation about Women in 2005," *Washington Post*, October 8, 2016, https:// www.washingtonpost.com/politics/trump-recorded-having-extremely-lewd -conversation-about-women-in-2005/2016/10/07/3b9ce776-8cb4-11e6-bf8a -3d26847eeed4_story.html?utm_term=.9629bcd5ec36.

54. Internet bots are software applications that perform basic, repetitive tasks, such as fake Twitter accounts retweeting false news stories or using specific hashtags.

55. Ben Schreckinger, "Inside Trump's 'Cyborg' Twitter Army," Politico.com, September 30, 2016, http://www.politico.com/story/2016/09/donald-trump -twitter-army-228923.

56. Lee Rainie, Janna Anderson, and Jonathan Albright, "The Future of Free Speech, Trolls, Anonymity and Fake News Online," PewInternet.org, March 29, 2017, accessed August 28, 2017, http://www.pewinternet.org/2017/03/29/the -future-of-free-speech-trolls-anonymity-and-fake-news-online/.

CHAPTER 7

1. Susan Bordo, *The Destruction of Hillary Clinton* (Brooklyn, NY: Melville House, 2017).

2. Jackson Katz, *Man Enough? Donald Trump, Hillary Clinton, and the Politics of Presidential Masculinity* (New York: Interlink Publishing Group, 2016).

3. NBC News exit poll desk, "Honesty vs. Temperament," November 8, 2016, https://www.cnbc.com/2016/11/08/nbc-news-exit-poll-honesty-vs-temperament .html.

4. Kim Nalder, Meredith Conroy, and Danielle Joesten Martin, "The Two Hillary Clintons: How Supporters and Detractors Describe the Democratic

Nominee," London School of Economics American Politics and Policy blog, July 22, 2016, http://blogs.lse.ac.uk/usappblog/2016/07/22/the-two-hillary-clintons -how-supporters-and-detractors-describe-the-democratic-nominee/.

5. David B. Holian and Charles Prysby, "Candidate Character Traits in the 2012 Presidential Election," *Presidential Studies Quarterly* 44, no. 3 (2014): 484–505.

6. Lynn Vavreck, *The Message Matters: The Economy and Presidential Campaigns* (Princeton, NJ: Princeton University Press, 2009).

7. William H. Flanigan and Nancy H. Zingale, *Political Behavior of the American Electorate*, 12th ed. (Washington: CQ Press, 2012).

8. Aaron Blake, "A Record Number of Americans Now Dislike Hillary Clinton," *Washington Post*, August 31, 2016, accessed July 11, 2017, https:// www.washingtonpost.com/news/the-fix/wp/2016/08/31/a-record-number-of -americans-now-dislike-hillary-clinton/?utm_term=.3aa666b4adae.

9. Quoted in Marc Duvoisin, "Here's What James Comey Said about Hillary Clinton's Emails Back in July," *Los Angeles Times*, May 9, 2017, accessed June 26, 2017, http://www.latimes.com/politics/washington/la-na-essential-washington -updates-comey-emails-1494374889-htmlstory.html.

10. Nate Silver, "How Much Did Comey Hurt Clinton's Chances?" FiveThirty Eight, November 6, 2016, accessed June 26, 2017, https://fivethirtyeight.com /features/how-much-did-comey-hurt-clintons-chances/.

11. David Wasserman, "2016 Popular Vote Tracker," Cook Political Report, January 3, 2017, accessed July 25, 2017, http://cookpolitical.com/story/10174.

12. Danielle Paquette, "The Unexpected Voters Behind the Widest Gender Gap in History," *Washington Post*, November 9, 2016, accessed July 26, 2017, https://www.washingtonpost.com/news/wonk/wp/2016/11/09/men-handed -trump-the-election/?utm_term=.f6c6340e1655.

13. Ibid.

14. Ilyana Kuziemko and Ebonya Washington, "Why Did the Democrats Lose the South? Bringing New Data to an Old Debate," National Bureau of Economic Research, November 2015, accessed July 26, 2017, http://www.nber.org/papers /w21703.

15. Chris Bonneau and Damon M. Cann, "Party Identification and Vote Choice in Partisan and Non-Partisan Elections," May 2, 2012, accessed July 26, 2017, http://www.polisci.pitt.edu/sites/default/files/pubs/BonneauCann.2012 .PartyID.pdf.

16. Ibid.

17. Angie Maxwell and Todd Shields, "The Impact of 'Modern Sexism' on the 2016 Presidential Election," Diane D. Blair Center of Southern Politics & Society, June 2017, accessed July 26, 2017, https://blaircenter.uark.edu/the -impact-of-modern-sexism/.

18. CNN Politics, "Exit Polls: Obama Wins Big among Young, Minority Voters," November 4, 2008, accessed on July 26, 2017, http://www.cnn.com/2008 /POLITICS/11/04/exit.polls/.

19. Maxwell and Shields, "The Impact of 'Modern Sexism.'"

20. Ibid.

21. Brian F. Schaffner, Matthew MacWilliams, and Tatishe Nteta, "Explaining White Polarization in the 2016 Vote for President: The Sobering Role of Racism and Sexism," paper prepared for presentation at the Conference on the U.S. Elections of 2016: Domestic and International Aspects, January 8–9, 2017, IDC Herzliya campus.

22. Ibid.

23. Ibid., 2.

24. Quoted in Medhi Hasan, "Top Democrats Are Wrong: Trump Supporters Were More Motivated by Racism Than Economic Issues," The Intercept, April 6, 2017, accessed July 26, 2017, https://theintercept.com/2017/04/06/top-democrats-are-wrong-trump-supporters-were-more-motivated-by-racism-than-economic-issues/.

25. Quoted in ibid.

26. Nicholas A. Valentino, Fabian G. Neuner, and L. Matthew Vandenbroek, "The Changing Norms of Racial Political Rhetoric and the End of Racial Priming," working paper, November 2016, accessed July 26, 2017, https://www.researchgate.net/publication/310230276_The_Changing_Norms_of_Racial_Political_Rhetoric_and_the_End_of_Racial_Priming," 28.

27. Daniel Cox, Rachel Lienesch, and Robert Jones, "Beyond Economics: Fears of Cultural Displacement Pushed the White Working Class to Trump," Public Religion Research Institute, May 9, 2017, accessed July 26, 2017, https://www.prri.org/research/white-working-class-attitudes-economy-trade-immigration-election-donald-trump/.

28. Ibid.

29. Sean McElwee and Jason McDaniel, "Fear of Diversity Made People More Likely to Vote Trump," The Nation, March 14, 2017, accessed July 26, 2017, https://www.thenation.com/article/fear-of-diversity-made-people-more-likely-to-vote-trump/.

30. Michael Tesler, "Views About Race Mattered More in Electing Trump Than in Electing Obama," Washington Post, November 22, 2016, accessed May 8, 2018, https://www.washingtonpost.com/news/monkey-cage/wp/2016/11/22/peoples-views-about-race-mattered-more-in-electing-trump-than-in-electing-obama/?utm_term=.06483c2a4292.

31. Philip Klinkner, "The Easiest Way to Guess If Someone Supports Trump? Ask If Obama Is a Muslim," Vox, June 2, 2016, accessed July 26, 2017, https://www.vox.com/2016/6/2/11833548/donald-trump-support-race-religion-economy.

32. Emily Flitter and Chris Kahn, "Exclusive: Trump Voters More Likely to View Blacks Negatively—Reuters/Ipsos Poll," June 28, 2016, accessed July 26, 2017, http://www.reuters.com/article/us-usa-election-race-idUSKCN0ZE2SW.

33. Ibid.

34. Maxwell and Shields, "The Impact of 'Modern Sexism.'"

35. Ibid.

36. Ibid. They measured sexism with a standard social science index that asks respondents about their level of agreement with a series of statements, such as

"Most women interpret innocent remarks or acts as being sexist" and "Many women are actually seeking special favors, such as hiring policies that favor them over men, under the guise of asking for equality." Authoritarianism was measured using a standard scale that asked respondents questions about their preference for children who are well-behaved, obedient, well mannered, and respectful of their elders. Ethnocentrism is measured with questions about attitudes toward one's culture versus other cultures.

37. Rebecca Traister, *Big Girls Don't Cry: The Election That Changed Everything for American Women* (New York: Free Press, 2010), 4.

38. Anne Kornblut, *Notes from the Cracked Ceiling: Hillary Clinton, Sarah Palin, and What It Will Take for a Woman to Win* (New York: Broadway Books, 2011), 1.

39. Caroline Heldman, "Piling on Palin, Hating on Clinton," Daily Beast, November 30, 2008, accessed August 12, 2017, http://www.thedailybeast.com /piling-on-palin-hating-on-hillary.

40. Katie Orr, "Trump's Election Drives More Women to Consider Running for Office," National Public Radio, February 23, 2017, accessed August 13, 2017, http://www.npr.org/2017/02/23/515438978/trumps-election-drives-more-women -to-consider-running-for-office.

41. Ashley Edwards Walker, "EMILY's List: More Than 11,000 Democratic Women Are Interested in Running for Office So Far This Year," *Glamour*, April 23, 2017, accessed August 13, 2017, https://www.glamour.com/story/emilys-list -more-than-11000-democratic-women-are-interested-in-running-for-office.

42. Quoted in ibid.

43. Christina Cauterucci, "How Do You Inspire Women to Run for Public Office? Elect Trump," Slate, January 16, 2017, accessed August 13, 2017, http:// www.slate.com/articles/news_and_politics/cover_story/2017/01/when_women_ run_they_win_and_trump_s_election_is_inspiring_a_surge_of_new.html.

44. Caroline Heldman, Susan J. Carroll, and Stephanie Olson, "'She Brought Only a Skirt': Print Media Coverage of Elizabeth Dole's Bid for the Republican Nomination," *Political Communication* 22, no. 3 (2005): 315–335.

45. Regina G. Lawrence and Melody Rose, *Hillary Clinton's Race for the White House: Gender Politics and Media on the Campaign Trail* (Boulder, CO: Lynne Rienner, 2009); Heldman et al., 2005; Kahn, 1992.

Index

ABC News, 77, 89, 154–155
Abramson, Jill, 90, 116
Access Hollywood tape, 112–115, 123–124, 150–151
Adam and Eve, 125
Adams, Abigail, 14
Adams, John, 14
Air Force One, 38
Alexander, Lamar, 79
Allcott, Hunt, 133
Allen, Mike, 81
Almond, Carrie, 166
Alternet, 134
Ambition gap, 9, 15–17, 29–30
Ambition shaming, 11, 16, 50–51, 64, 71, 77, 98
American National Election Study (ANES), 155–156
Amis, Martin, 75
Anderson, Karen Vasby, 3, 65
Anderson, Kristin, 114
The Apprentice, 7, 103, 114
Armed Services Committee, 155
Atlanta Constitution, 55
The Atlantic, 42

Babcock, Linda C., 15
Bachmann, Michele, 9, 52–53, 66–68, 96

Bakshy, Eytan, 136
Bannon, Steve, 87, 108, 117, 121
Baraka, Ajamu, 68
Barbara Lee Foundation, 91
Barbaro, Michael, 43
Barnicle, Mike, 65
Beck, Glenn, 65, 82
Bedard, Paul, 70
Bekiempis, Victoria, 38
Benghazi, 86–88, 108–109, 142–143
Bhutto, Benazir, 82
Biden, Joe, 89, 135
Bin Laden, Osama, 41
Birther movement, 7–8, 27, 66, 103, 119
"Bitch" frame, 53, 65, 74–75, 79, 81–82, 98, 127, 129
Blogs, 25, 52, 74, 108, 134, 149. *See also* New media
Blow, Charles, 92, 98
Bordo, Susan, 94–95, 153
Bornstein, Harold, 116
Bos, Angela, 19
Boston Globe, 55
Boxer, Barbara, 23, 69, 99
Bradley, James, 36–37
Breitbart, 87, 108, 117, 121, 134
Brescoll, Victoria, 23, 77
Broaddrick, Juanita, 124

Brooks, David, 90
Brown, Jerry, 61
Buchanan, Pat, 8, 65, 81
Buffalo Bill's Wild West show, 37
Burns, Dasha, 92–93
Bush, Billy, 112–13
Bush, George H. W., 39–40, 61
Bush, George W., 25, 34–35,
    40–41, 46, 61
Bush, Jeb, 43, 85
Butler, Judith, 2

Cain, Herman, 67
Cameron, Carl, 80
Caraway, Hattie Wyatt, 14
Carli, Linda, 13
Carlin, Diana, 79
Carlson, Tucker, 65, 81
Carroll, Susan J., 29
Carter, Graydon, 44
Carter, Jimmy, 66
Castellanos, Alex, 65
Cavuto, Neil, 65, 81
CBS News, 83, 89
Center for American Women and
    Politics, 165–166
Central Intelligence Agency, 39
Cher, 112
Cherokee Nation, 55
Chicago Tribune, 62–64
Chisholm, Shirley, 9, 15, 53,
    57–59, 63
Christian Science Monitor, 70
Christie, Chris, 70
Citizens United Not Timid, 65, 81
Citizenship as prototype, 26–30, 164
Civil Rights Act, 159
Civil rights movements, 7, 14–15,
    36–37, 159
Claflin, Tennessee, 53
Clark, Jennifer Hayes, 137
Clinton, Bill, 3, 7, 25, 34, 61,
    74–75, 80, 98, 104, 114,
    122–125

Clinton, Hillary: "another woman"
    frame, 96–97; Benghazi, impact of,
    86–88, 108–109, 142–143; "bitch"
    frame, 65, 74–75, 79, 81–82, 98,
    127, 129; "cool factor," 2, 73, 76,
    92–93, 101–102; "crooked Hillary"
    frame, 86–87, 107–116, 127–128,
    131, 138, 156; descriptive politics,
    role of, 95–96, 120; double-bind
    bias, 64–65, 74, 79–81, 91–92,
    101, 128; editorial cartoons, 78,
    116; e-mail server issue, 86–88,
    108–110, 113, 141, 145, 150,
    156–158; "establishment" frame,
    8, 74, 93–95, 101–102; exit talk,
    51, 64, 79, 102; first lady service, 7,
    74–75, 94; "first woman" frame, 49,
    63, 77, 101; "frail" frame, 52, 55,
    93, 106–107, 116–120, 128, 153;
    gender stereotypes, role of, 64–66,
    75–76, 78–80, 101–102, 154–156;
    issue-based media coverage, 64,
    84–85, 94, 102; Lady Macbeth
    frame, 3, 90, 109, 128; likeability
    measures, 2, 11, 73, 76–77, 80–81,
    90–92, 100–102, 107–108, 128;
    male vote, impact of, 158–63;
    media coverage volume, 63–64, 78,
    85, 100, 104–105, 128; new media
    coverage, 64–66; overt sexism,
    impact of, 11, 81–82, 97–102,
    111–112, 121–129, 153–154, 161–
    166; personal life focus, 65, 79–80;
    physical appearance focus, 11, 52,
    64, 80–82, 93–95, 98, 102, 108,
    121–123, 127, 129; popular vote
    totals, 3, 63, 73, 83, 157–158, 161;
    presidential debates, 123–26, 146;
    professional title usage, 63–64,
    78–79, 102, 124; public opinion,
    2, 74–77, 100–101, 119, 154–157;
    public service experience, 1–2,
    6–7, 73, 85, 94, 102, 104, 106,
    155, 164; scandals, impact of, 2, 4,

11, 73, 86–90, 100–102, 108–111, 113–115, 128, 143, 147, 150–151, 156–158; secretary of state service, 7, 75–76, 78, 85, 87, 116, 155; sexual objectification, 11, 64–66, 121, 129; Twitter coverage, 6, 98, 132, 138–151; Twitter usage, 131–132; viability questioning, 63, 80, 101; voice quality, 90–92, 96, 121, 123, 129; white vote, impact of, 159–162; "woman card" frame, 83, 95–96, 119–120, 128

Clinton Cash (Schweizer), 88

Clinton Foundation, 87–88, 90, 108

Close, Glenn, 79

Clovis, Sam, 117

CNN, 65, 82, 117

Cody, William, 37

Colleoni, Elanor, 136

Collins, Gail, 112

Columbia Journalism Review, 108, 121

Comey, James, 87, 110–111, 113, 145, 157–158

Commission on Freedom of the Press, 133

Congress of Racial Equality, 7

Congressional Black Caucus, 57–58

Conover, Michael, 136, 143

Conroy, Meredith, 26, 33–35, 39

Conservative Daily Post, 134

Conservative Treehouse, 108

Constitution, 14, 29, 33, 53, 58

Conway, Kellyanne, 166

Cooper, Frank, 42

Crockett, Emily, 124

Crooks, Rachel, 114

Crowther, Ashleigh, 80

Cruz, Ted, 43–44, 85

Daily Beast, 134

Daily Caller, 67, 108

Daily Kos, 74

Daily Mail, 121

Daily Wire, 121

Dakota Access Pipeline, 68

Deace, Steve, 70

Debold, Elizabeth, 46

Declaration of Sentiments, 14

Democracy Now, 68

Democratic National Convention, 57–58, 104, 109

Democratic Socialists, 7, 94

Diane C. Blair Center of Southern Politics & Society, 161, 163

Dixon, Alan, 62

Dolan, Kathleen, 20–21

Dole, Bob, 34, 61

Dole, Elizabeth, 9, 50, 53, 61–62, 71, 96, 166

Doonesbury, 39–40

Double-bind bias, 11, 23, 29–30, 50, 52–54, 57–59, 62, 64–65, 67, 71–74, 78–81, 91–92, 101, 128

Douglass, Frederick, 54

Doyle, Sady, 76–77

The Drudge Report, 74, 117, 119

Duck Dynasty, 44

Duerst-Lahti, Georgia, 33

Dukakis, Kitty, 40

Dukakis, Michael, 39–41

Eagly, Alice, 13

Ebony, 99

Eckhart, Aaron, 38

Edwards, John, 96

Electoral College, 3, 8, 54, 101, 109, 111, 120, 158

Emerge America, 165

EMILY's List, 165

Enten, Harry, 113

Epstein, Jeffrey, 114–115

Equal Rights Amendment, 58, 61

Equal Rights Party, 54

Evangelicalism, 52, 62, 67

Evans, Heather, 137

Exit talk, 51, 64, 71, 79

Facebook, 6, 26, 53, 65, 74, 81, 99, 108, 132, 135–136, 149. *See also* Social media

Falk, Erika, 49–51, 54, 56, 65

Family and Medical Leave Act, 59

Fatal Attraction, 79

FBI, 87, 110, 113, 134

Fels, Anna, 16–17

Ferraro, Geraldine, 65

Fifteenth Amendment, 53

Filter bubbles, 135–136, 149. *See also* Social media

Fiorina, Carly, 9, 53, 69–71, 111

Fisher, Marc, 90

FiveThirtyEight, 113

Fleischer, Ari, 61

Ford, Harrison, 38

Fortune, 69

Foster, Vincent, 75, 88

Fourteenth Amendment, 53

Fox & Friends, 63, 70

Fox News, 41, 64–65, 67, 70, 80–81, 88, 90–91, 97–98, 108, 111, 121

Fox News Sunday, 67

Foxx, Jamie, 38

French, David, 120

Frostenson, Sarah, 124

Frum, David, 45, 108

Fulani, Lenora, 9, 53, 60–61

Gacy, John Wayne, 66

Gallup polls, 20–21, 76

Gannon, Jeff, 41

Garland, Eric, 36

Gates, Henry Louis, 75

Gateway Pundit, 108

Geiling, Natasha, 126

Gender stereotypes: "another woman" frame, 96–97; "bitch" frame, 53, 65, 74–75, 79, 81–82, 98, 127, 129; Clinton, Hillary, impact on, 64–66, 75–76, 79–80, 101–102, 154–156; communal characteristics, 18–19, 25, 33;

double-bind bias, 11, 23, 50, 52, 57–58, 60, 62, 64–65, 67, 78–79, 91–92, 101, 128; emotional terms, 11, 19, 25, 50–51, 54–55, 57–58, 71, 77, 79, 126; "frail" frame, 52, 55, 93, 106–107, 116–120, 128, 153; gender marking, 50, 52, 77; issue expertise, 19–22, 25, 28, 50–51, 84, 137, 154–156; leadership evaluation, 22–23, 29–30, 79, 155–156; national security emphasis, 19–23, 28, 154–155; new media, role of, 25–26, 52; personal lives focus, 25, 50–51, 54, 59–60, 62, 65, 71, 77, 79–80, 155; physical appearance focus, 17, 32, 43, 50–52, 54–55, 57, 60, 62–64, 67, 70–71, 80–82, 98, 102, 108, 121–123, 127, 129; vice presidential frame, 11, 50, 57, 60, 62, 69–71, 98; voice quality, 90–92, 96, 121, 123, 129; "woman card" frame, 83, 95–96, 119–120, 128. *See also* Media bias

Gentzkow, Matthew, 133

Gingrich, Newt, 67, 74–75

Giuliani, Rudy, 79, 117, 122

Giustra, Frank, 88

Givhan, Robin, 80

Glick, Peter, 24

Goldberg, Michelle, 67

Goldenberg, Jamie L., 24

Goldwater, Barry, 56

Goleman, Daniel, 46

Good Morning America, 69

Goodman, Amy, 68

Gore, Al, 34

Goren, Lilly, 78

Government Accountability Institute (GAI), 87–88

Graham, David A., 119

Grant, Ulysses S., 54–55, 67

Green Party, 68, 97

Greenwald, Glenn, 99

Guckert, James Dale, 41

Hamblin, James, 118
Hannity, Sean, 90, 97–98
Hannity & Colmes, 79
Hart, Gary, 59
Harth, Jill, 114
Hashtags. *See* Twitter
Head Start, 7
Heflick, Nathan A., 24
Heller, Cathy, 114
Hess, Amanda, 99, 119
Hewlett-Packard, 69
Hill, Anita, 62, 165
Hitchens, Christopher, 82
Honkala, Cheri, 68
Huffington, Arianna, 112
The Huffington Post, 134
Humans of New York, 91
Hume, Brit, 91, 121
Hurt, Harry, 114
Hutchins Commission, 133

Identity incongruity, 27, 29–30, 33, 67, 74, 120, 122
Incumbency advantage, 9, 17, 24, 29, 74, 156
Indecline, 31–32, 36, 47
Independence Day, 38
Independent Journal-Review, 121
Infowars, 108–109, 134
Instagram, 26, 53
Iraq War, 40–41, 47, 86, 93

Jefferson, Thomas, 67
Jindal, Bobby, 116
Joan of Arc, 13, 30
Johnson, Gary, 68–69, 163
Johnson, Lyndon B., 159
Jones, Alex, 117
Jones, Paula, 124

Kahn, Kim Fridkin, 25
Kaine, Tim, 118

Katz, Jackson, 32, 37–38, 42
Kelly, Megyn, 111
Kennedy, Carole, 62
Kennedy, John F., 58, 119
Kerry, John, 25, 34–35, 40–42, 87, 118
Killer Mike, 96
Kilmeade, Brian, 121
King, Cheryl, 33
King, Steve, 66
Klinkner, Philip, 162
Klum, Heidi, 111–112
Koenig, Anne, 18–19
Kornblut, Anne, 165
Kremer, Amy, 117
Kuhnke, Elizabeth, 108

Laaksonen, Ninni, 114
Labyrinth of women's leadership, 13–15, 22–23, 30
Lady Macbeth frame, 3, 90, 109, 128
Lange, Roberta, 99–100
Lawless, Jennifer, 20
Lawrence, Regina, 78–79, 132
Leeds, Jessica, 114
Legal Services Corporation, 7
Legum, Gary, 45
Lewinsky, Monica, 122, 127
Lexicoder, 139
LGBT (lesbian, gay, bisexual, and transgender) rights, 37–39, 45, 60, 66, 95
Limbaugh, Rush, 75, 80, 98, 116
Locke, John, 28
Lockwood, Belva, 9, 53–55
Lynch, Loretta, 141
Lynch, Timothy, 20–21

Machado, Alicia, 112
MacWilliams, Matthew, 161–162
Mair, Liz, 70
Malkin, Michelle, 64, 80
Mansfield, Harvey, 37
Maples, Marla, 123

Mar-a-Lago, 114
Marcotte, Amanda, 38
Marist Institute for Public Opinion, 119
Matthews, Chris, 65, 82
Maxwell, Angie, 161–163
McCain, John, 24, 27, 34–35, 65, 69, 81
McCarthy, Kevin, 86
McCarthyism, 56
McConnell, Mitch, 116
McDaniel, Jason, 162
McDowell, Temple Taggart, 114
McElwee, Sean, 162
McGillivray, Mindy, 114
McGregor, Shannon, 137
Media bias: ambition shaming, 11, 16, 50–51, 64, 71, 77, 98; Bachmann, Michele, campaign, 9, 52, 66–68, 96; "bitch" frame, 53, 65, 74–75, 79, 81–82, 98, 127; Chisholm, Shirley, campaign, 9, 58; Dole, Elizabeth, campaign, 9, 50, 61–62, 96, 166; double-bind expectations, 11, 52, 57–58, 60, 62, 64–65, 67, 78–81, 91–92, 101; emotional terms, 11, 19, 25, 50–51, 54–55, 57–58, 71, 77, 79, 126; entertainment media, role of, 38, 79; "establishment" frame, 8, 74, 93–95, 101–102; exit talk, 51, 64, 71, 79, 102; Fiorina, Carly, campaign, 9, 69–71; "first woman" frame, 49, 63, 77; "frail" frame, 52, 55, 67, 93, 107, 116–120, 128; Fulani, Lenora, campaign, 9, 61; issue-related coverage, 11, 25, 50–51, 57–58, 60, 62, 64, 71, 77, 84–85, 100, 102, 137; Lockwood, Belva, campaign, 9, 55; Moseley Braun, Carol, campaign, 9, 62–63; new media, role of, 25–26, 52, 64–66, 134, 149; overt sexism, 11, 26, 70, 81–82, 97–102, 121–122,

129; personal lives focus, 25, 50–51, 54, 59–60, 62, 65, 71, 77, 79–80, 155; physical appearance focus, 11, 50–52, 54–55, 57–58, 60, 62–64, 67, 70–71, 77, 80–82, 93–95, 98, 102, 108, 121; professional title usage, 11, 50–51, 58, 63–64, 70–71, 77–79, 102; Schroeder, Patricia, campaign, 9, 59–60; sexual objectification, 11, 24, 50–52, 71, 78, 121; Smith, Margaret Chase, campaign, 9, 56–57; Stein, Jill, campaign, 9, 69; viability questioning, 9, 11, 25, 50, 54, 56, 58–63, 71, 77, 80; vice presidential frame, 11, 50, 56–57, 60, 62, 69–71, 98; "woman card" frame, 83, 95–96, 119–20, 128; Woodhull, Victoria, campaign, 9, 54. See also Clinton, Hillary
Mercer, Robert, 87
Meyer, Robinson, 98–99
Military Family Act, 59
Miller, Matthew, 87
Mink, Patsy Takemoto, 15
Misogyny. See Overt sexism
Morning Joe, 123
Morris, Dick, 121
Moseley Braun, Carol, 9, 53, 62–63
Mourão, Rachel, 137
MSNBC, 64–65, 81–82, 90, 123
Muñoz, Maria Elizabeth, 61

Nader, Ralph, 8
National Enquirer, 121
National Federation of Republican Women, 166
National Organization for Women, 63
National Women's Political Caucus, 58
Nazarenes, 52
NBC News, 89, 112–113, 118
Neely, Brad, 36

New Alliance Party, 60
New Deal, 56
New media, 25–26, 52–53, 64–66, 72, 132–135, 138, 149. *See also* Social media
New York Daily News, 56–57
New York Herald, 54
New York Magazine, 112
New York Post, 121
New York Times, 35, 43, 54–55, 63, 74–75, 88, 90, 116, 134, 161
Newsweek, 39, 42, 67
Newton-Small, Jay, 91
Nineteenth Amendment, 14, 29
Nixon, Richard, 61
NodeXL, 139
Norris, Pippa, 33
North American Free Trade Agreement (NAFTA), 125
Norton, Philip, 33
Nteta, Tatishe, 161–162
Nugent, Ted, 65

Obama, Barack: birther movement claims, 7–8, 27, 66, 103; candidate of change frame, 25, 93; Clinton, Hillary, appointment, 7, 75; Democratic National Convention speech, 104; descriptive politics, role of, 96; editorial cartoons, 78; gendered descriptions, 34, 42; identity incongruity, 27, 42, 164–165; male vote, impact of, 158; media coverage volume, 78; Muslim identity rumors, 162; negative media coverage rate, 78; political spectrum position, 93; popular vote totals, 42, 161; professional title usage, 78; public opinion, 82–83
Oceno, Marzia, 163
O'Dell, Nancy, 112
O'Donnell, Rosie, 112
Okimoto, Tyler G., 77

Olympus Has Fallen, 38
O'Reilly, Bill, 41, 81–82, 97
Ornstein, Norm, 8
Overt sexism, 11, 26, 70, 81–83, 97–103, 111–112, 118, 121–129, 153–154, 161–163

Palin, Sarah, 24, 67, 77, 132, 165
Party recruitment bias, 9, 15, 17–18, 28
Patterson, Thomas, 104–105, 110, 140
Penis size, 31–32, 36, 43–45, 47, 122
Perot, Ross, 60
Perry, Rick, 43–44, 66–67
Pew Research Center, 135
Pickard, Victor, 133
Pizzagate, 134
Planned Parenthood, 59, 94
Plante, Chris, 90
Podesta, John, 134, 147, 150
Politico, 81, 134
PolitiFact, 88, 90, 99, 111, 156
Pregnancy Discrimination Act, 59
Priebus, Reince, 108
Public Policy Research Institute, 162
Pullman, Bill, 38

Rainie, Lee, 151
Rankin, Jeannette, 14
Reagan, Ronald, 9, 35, 37–42, 45, 61, 66
Reddit, 99
Reitman, Janet, 88
Republican National Convention, 56, 61, 127
Rhodes, Randi, 82
Rivera, Geraldo, 90
Robertson, Phil, 44
Rogers, Lee, 80
Role congruity theory (RCT), 22–23, 106–107
Rolling Stone, 88
Romney, Mitt, 34–35, 42, 158

Roosevelt, Franklin D., 56, 67, 119
Roosevelt, Theodore, 9, 35–38, 45
Rose, Melody, 78–79, 132
Ross, Nellie Tayloe, 14
Rose Law Firm, 7
Rousseau, Jean-Jacques, 28
Rubio, Marco, 43–44, 85
Rudov, Marc, 65, 81

Safire, William, 75
Sanders, Bernie: "Bernie Bros,"
    98–99; campaign concession,
    100–101; "cool factor," 92–93;
    Democratic Socialist identification,
    7, 94; descriptive politics, role
    of, 96; economic populism, 8;
    establishment frame usage, 93–94;
    fundraising accomplishments, 7;
    media coverage, 83–85, 89–91;
    "outsider" label, 73–74, 93–94;
    overt sexism usage, 98–100, 102;
    political spectrum position, 93–94;
    popular vote totals, 73, 83, 161;
    public service experience, 7, 74,
    94; scandal history, 89; supporters'
    sexist behaviors, 98–100; Twitter
    coverage, 6, 132, 138–144, 148–
    151; youth-powered campaign,
    93–94, 99–100
Santorum, Rick, 42, 66–67
Sarandon, Susan, 96
Saudi Arabia, 109
Scarborough, Joe, 90
Schaffner, Brian, 161–62
Schneider, Monica, 19
Schreckinger, Ben, 150–51
Schroeder, Patricia, 9, 53, 59, 71
Schweizer, Peter, 87–88
Searles, Cassandra, 114
Seneca Falls Convention, 14
September 11, 2001, terrorist attacks,
    20, 23, 28, 40, 86, 118
Sexual objectification, 9, 11, 17, 24,
    29, 50–52, 64–67, 71, 78, 121, 129

Shareblue, 87
Sharpton, Al, 63
Sheeler, Kristina Horn, 3
Shelton, Kathy, 124
Shields, Todd, 161–163
Shin, Jieun, 136
Shorenstein Center on Media,
    Politics, and Public Policy, 78,
    83–85, 104–107, 110
Silver, Nate, 73, 76–77, 110–111
Sinzdak, Jean, 165–166
Smith, Clyde, 56
Smith, Margaret Chase, 9, 53, 55–57,
    59, 62
Snyder, Peter, 79
Social media: "bitch" frame, 53,
    65; citizen participation volume,
    10, 26, 53, 131–132, 135; debate
    mash-ups, 125; Facebook, 6,
    26, 53, 65, 74, 81, 99, 108, 132,
    135–136, 149; filter bubbles, 135–
    136, 149; hostile environments,
    10–11, 26, 52–53, 65, 98, 132,
    137, 149–151; Instagram, 26,
    53; misinformation facilitation,
    135–38, 149; negative sentiment,
    11, 26, 53, 65, 132, 139–141,
    143–145, 148–151; origins, 26, 53,
    133, 136; partisanship, 135–138,
    149; positive sentiment, 139, 141–
    151; Reddit, 99; sexist content,
    10, 25–26, 52–53, 64–65, 98–99,
    126–127, 132, 138, 140; trolls, 11,
    142–143, 150; user demographics,
    53, 138; YouTube, 64. See also
    Twitter
Society of Professional Journalists,
    133–134
Southern Baptists, 52
Steele, Andrea Dew, 165
Stein, Jill, 9, 53, 61, 68–69, 96–97,
    163
Stevens, J. Christopher, 86
Stone, Judy, 118

Stone, Roger, 81
"Stop Running for President and
  Make Me a Sandwich," 81
Stoynoff, Natasha, 114–115
Suffrage, 14, 26–27, 29, 53–54, 159
Sununu, John, 122
Sutton, Bob, 122
Swers, Michael, 20

Tantaros, Andrea, 98, 121
Tea Party, 8, 66
Tesler, Michael, 162
Thomas, Clarence, 62, 165
Time, 75–76
Traister, Rebecca, 164
Trudeau, Garry, 39
Truman, Harry S., 2
Trump, Donald: *Access Hollywood*
  tape, 112–115, 123–124, 150–151;
  Apprentice production, 7, 103, 114;
  birther movement support, 7–8,
  103; fitness accounts, 116–117;
  hypermasculinity, 2, 4, 35, 38–39,
  43–45, 103–104, 126–127,
  153–155, 164; Indecline statue,
  31–32, 36, 47; issue-based media
  coverage, 85–86, 90, 108, 110;
  male vote, impact of, 158–163;
  media coverage volume, 85–86,
  104–105, 128; negative media
  coverage rate, 105–107; overt
  sexism usage, 11, 111–116, 119,
  122–129, 153–154, 162–166;
  popular vote totals, 3, 8, 43,
  157–158; presidential debates, 117,
  123–126, 129, 146; professional
  background, 2, 6–8, 103, 114;
  public opinion, 154–157; public
  service experience, 2, 104, 106,
  155; rhetoric extremes, 8, 38–39,
  157; scandals, impact of, 89–90,
  108–116, 128–129, 150–151;
  sexual violence allegations, 114–
  115, 128–129; Twitter coverage,

6, 132, 138–139, 143–151; Twitter
  usage, 2, 131–132; white vote,
  impact of, 159–162
Trump, Ivana, 89, 114–115, 123
Trump, Ivanka, 112
Trump Tower, 112, 114
Trump University, 89
TruthFeed, 108
Tur, Katy, 112
Twitter: API functionality, 139;
  Clinton, Hillary, coverage, 6,
  98, 132, 138–151; Clinton,
  Hillary, usage, 131–132;
  citizen participation volume,
  10, 26, 131–132, 135; filter
  bubbles, 135–136, 149; hashtag
  applications, 6, 11, 96–97, 138,
  142–144, 146–151; hostility,
  expressions of, 132, 149–151;
  ideological tendencies, 135–136;
  misinformation facilitation,
  135–138; negative sentiment,
  11, 139–141, 143–145, 148–151;
  partisanship, 135–138; positive
  sentiment, 139, 141–151; Sanders,
  Bernie, coverage, 6, 132, 138–144,
  148–151; trolls, 11, 142–143,
  150; Trump, Donald, coverage, 6,
  132, 138–139, 143–151; Trump,
  Donald, usage, 2, 131–132; user
  demographics, 138

Uscinski, Joseph, 78

Valentino, Nicholas, 162–163
Vanity Fair, 82
Vietnam War, 37–38, 41, 58
The View, 71
Virginia, Karena, 114
Vorst, Eric, 131
Voting Rights Act, 159

Wakeman, Jessica, 67
Wallace, Chris, 67

Warren, Elizabeth, 161
Washington, 36
Washington, George, 9, 35–36
Washington Examiner, 70, 108
Washington Post, 42, 64, 74, 77, 80,
    88, 90, 98, 134, 154
Watergate scandal, 87
Watts, Sarah, 35–36
Wayne, Carl, 163
Wayne, John, 38, 66
Weaver, Jeff, 98–99
Welch, Edgar Maddison, 134
White House Down, 38
Whitewater, 88, 90
WikiLeaks, 113, 147
Willey, Kathleen, 124

Wilson, Woodrow, 2
Winfrey, Kelly, 79
*Women for President: Media
    Bias in Nine Campaigns*
    (Falk), 49
Women's Armed Service Integration
    Act, 56
Women's rights movements, 14–15,
    29, 37, 56, 61
Woodhull, Victoria, 5, 9, 53–54
Woodward, Bob, 90
World War II, 39–40, 56

YouTube, 64

Zervos, Summer, 114

About the Authors

Caroline Heldman, PhD, is an associate professor of politics at Occidental College in Los Angeles, California, and the research director for the Geena Davis Institute for Gender in Media. Her research specializes in media, the presidency, and systems of power (race, class, gender). Dr. Heldman coedited *Rethinking Madam President: Are We Ready for a Woman in the White House?* (2007). Her most recent books are *Consumer Activism in the U.S.: Some Democratic Implications* (2017) and *Women, Power, and Politics: The Fight for Gender Equality in the United States* (2017). Dr. Heldman has been active in "real world" politics as a professional pollster, campaign manager, and commentator for MSNBC, Fox News, Fox Business News, CNBC, and Al Jazeera America. She has also been featured in popular documentaries, including *Miss Representation*, *The Mask You Live In*, *The Hunting Ground*, and *Informant*. She splits her time between Los Angeles and New Orleans, where she cofounded the New Orleans Women's Shelter and the Lower Ninth Ward Living Museum. Dr. Heldman also cofounded End Rape on Campus (EROC) and Faculty Against Rape (FAR) and was one of the early architects of the new campus anti-rape movement.

Meredith Conroy, PhD, is an associate professor in the Department of Political Science at California State University, San Bernardino, California. She is also a senior researcher with the Geena Davis Institute on Gender in Media. She earned her PhD in political science from University of California, Santa Barbara. Conroy's research on the role of gender and media in politics has been published in academic journals like the *International Journal of Communication*, *American Politics Research*, and *Politics, Groups, and Identities*. She has also contributed chapters to multiple books, including *Controlling the Message: New Media in American Political Campaigns* (2015) and *Rethinking Madam President: Is America Ready for a Woman in the White House?* (2007). Her first book, *Masculinity, Media, and the American Presidency*, was published in September 2015. She has also contributed to the *Washington Post's* Monkey Cage blog, FiveThirtyEight.com, and the London School of Economics' American politics and policy blog.

Alissa R. Ackerman, PhD, is an associate professor in the Social Work and Criminal Justice Program at the University of Washington, Tacoma, Washington, and a criminal-justice policy researcher. Dr. Ackerman coedited *The Criminalization of Immigration: Contexts and Consequences* (2014) and *Sex Crimes: Transnational Problems and Global Solutions* (2015). Her most recent book, *Introduction to Criminal Justice: A Personal Narrative Approach* was published in August 2016. She is a founding member of the Sex Offense Policy and Research Working Group (SOPR), is an advisory board member for Stop Sexual Assault in Schools (SSAIS), and was a member of the Faculty Against Rape (FAR) leadership team.

www.ingramcontent.com/pod-product-compliance
Lightning Source LLC
Chambersburg PA
CBHW050706280326
41926CB00088B/2806